# Cultural
# Hegemony
# in the
# United States

# FOUNDATIONS OF POPULAR CULTURE

Series Editor: GARTH S. JOWETT
*University of Houston*

The study of popular culture has now become a widely accepted part of the modern academic curriculum. This increasing interest has spawned a great deal of important research in recent years, and the field of "cultural studies" in its many forms is now one of the most dynamic and exciting in modern academia. Each volume in the **Foundations of Popular Culture** series will introduce a specific issue fundamental to the study of popular culture, and the authors have been given the charge to write with clarity and precision and to examine the subject systematically. The editorial objective is to provide an important series of "building block" volumes that can stand by themselves or be used in combination to provide a thorough and accessible grounding in the field of cultural studies.

1. **The Production of Culture: Media and the Urban Arts**
   by **Diana Crane**

2. **Popular Culture Genres: Theories and Texts**
   by **Arthur Asa Berger**

3. **Rock Formation: Music, Technology, and Mass Communication**
   by **Steve Jones**

4. **Cultural Criticism: A Primer of Key Concepts**
   by **Arthur Asa Berger**

5. **Advertising and Popular Culture**
   by **Jib Fowles**

6. **Sexualities and Popular Culture**
   by **Carl B. Holmberg**

7. **Cultural Hegemony in the United States**
   by **Lee Artz and Bren Ortega Murphy**

# Cultural Hegemony in the United States

Lee Artz
Bren Ortega Murphy

Foundations of Popular Culture
7

Sage Publications, Inc.
*International Educational and Professional Publisher*
Thousand Oaks  London  New Delhi

*For information:*

 Sage Publications, Inc.
2455 Teller Road
Thousand Oaks, California 91320
E-mail: order@sagepub.com

Sage Publications Ltd.
6 Bonhill Street
London EC2A 4PU
United Kingdom

Sage Publications India Pvt. Ltd.
M-32 Market
Greater Kailash I
New Delhi 110 048 India

Printed in the United States of America

*Library of Congress Cataloging-in-Publication Data*

Artz, Lee.
  Cultural hegemony in the United States / by Lee Artz and Bren Ortega Murphy.
       p.   cm. — (Foundations of popular culture; vol. 7)
  Includes bibliographical references and index.
      ISBN 0-8039-4502-7 (cloth: alk. paper)
      ISBN 0-8039-4503-5 (pbk.: alk. paper)
    1. United States—Social conditions—20th century.   2. Popular culture—United States.   3. Dominance (Psychology)—United States.
  I. Murphy, Bren Ortega.   II. Title.   III. Series.
    HN57.A73   2000
    306'.0973—dc21                                                    00-008363

This book is printed on acid-free paper.

00   01   02   03   04   05   06   7   6   5   4   3   2   1

| | |
|---|---|
| *Acquisition Editor:* | Margaret H. Seawell |
| *Editorial Assistant:* | Sandra Krumholz |
| *Production Editor:* | Nevair Kabakian |
| *Copyeditor:* | Linda Gray |
| *Typesetter:* | Janelle LeMaster |
| *Indexer:* | Cristina Haley |
| *Cover Designer:* | Ravi Balasuriya |
| *Graphic Artist:* | Marques |

# Contents

# Introduction

In the popular children's book *The Runaway Bunny,* by Margaret Wise Brown (1972), a little bunny tells his mother that he is going to run away from home. He says he will become a fish in a trout stream. The mother bunny doesn't tell him not to run away nor does she punish him. Instead, she plays along, saying she will become a "fisherman" and come find him. The bunny then imagines he will become a rock, high in the mountains. The mother bunny says she will become a mountain climber and climb up to get him. The little bunny goes on to imagine becoming a flower in a garden, a sailboat, a bird, an acrobat, and even a little boy. The mother bunny joins each of these fantasies. Convinced his mother will always be there, the little bunny decides, "Aw shucks, I might as well stay home." And so he does. At the end, the mother bunny rewards her little bunny with a carrot.

In Brown's story, the little bunny doesn't want to run away because he is unhappy. Rather, like all children, he wants to test his limits, checking to see the consequences, if someone will be there for him. As a good parent, the mother bunny lets the little bunny explore the possibilities. By participating in the fantasy, she encourages his self-confidence and his trust in her. *The Runaway Bunny* teaches children about limits, trust, and healthy relationships in a very creative and entertaining fashion.

*The Runaway Bunny* also illustrates the complex concept addressed in this book: hegemony. In simple terms, hegemony is a relationship in which one consents to the leadership of another because it is beneficial. For example, youth in general benefit from the nurturance and guidance of adult "hegemony." In *The Runaway Bunny*, the mother bunny is in benevolent control, and the little bunny depends on her. The mother protects, teaches, and provides for the little bunny. Each time he changes the scenario for the relationship, she transforms herself into something important and dominant. She rewards the little bunny's good behavior with a carrot.

*The Runaway Bunny* depicts some of the important characteristics of hegemony: All hegemonic relations have leaderships that provide security, care, and rewards to subordinates; like the little bunny, all subordinates are continually developing new interests, desires, and needs that challenge existing conditions; like the mother bunny, all dominant leaders must provide material rewards and acceptable guidelines for behavior and repeatedly transform themselves if they are to meet the demands and expectations of their subordinates.

Of course, the complexities of the human condition and its attending issues of democracy, equality, and resource distribution cannot be reduced to stories about small animals. Consequently, illustrations of race, gender, and class cultural hegemony in the United States will not be as simple or direct as the runaway bunny story. Still, it is surprising the number of times that we find social groups struggling to improve their conditions of life deciding, "Aw shucks, we might just as well stay where we are."

To better understand why subordinate groups recognize and still consent to their social position, this book looks at instances of late 20th-century cultural practices in race, gender, and class relations. Chapter 1 presents a history of the concept of hegemony using some historical examples and considers a few scholarly reworkings of the concept. Chapters 2, 3, and 4 turn to cultural hegemony's effort to build race, gender, and class consensus for capitalist social relations. The closing chapter speculates on the staying power of capitalist cultural hegemony.

As exhibited in *The Runaway Bunny*, we argue that hegemony is not necessarily always undesirable, despite unequal dominant-subordinate relations. It depends largely on which social group is leading, for what purpose, and with what results. It also depends on the relative burden and benefit to each participant and on possible alternative social relations and practices. In short, each hegemony must be understood and judged in its own historic context. By looking at a variety of historic examples, including recent cultural and media practices, we hope to demonstrate that the concept of hegemony helps explain how and why U.S. society has been able to maintain contradictory, controversial, and continually unequal social relationships.

# 1

# Power Through Consent

When English translations of Antonio Gramsci's work (written for the most part in the 1920s and 1930s) became available in the 1970s, scholars enthusiastically received his concept of *hegemony* as an important tool for cultural analysis and social critique. The more familiar they became with the concept, the more they discovered its many possibilities. Before long, a wide variety of theorists, analysts, and researchers were reworking and applying their own variations of the concept. As an introduction to the discussion that follows, we define hegemony as *the process of moral, philosophical, and political leadership that a social group attains only with the active consent of other important social groups*. Whereas the traditional version of hegemony presented here still prevails, other creative readings have been developed since the rediscovery of the concept.

Gramsci's (1967, 1947/1971) translations came at an opportune time. Most traditional theoretical constructs had become inadequate for explaining the political crises, social changes, and cultural practices of the post-World War II era. American theories of democratic pluralism revealed their shallowness as the civil rights, student, and antiwar movements underscored the inequities of political and economic power in the United States. Before long, so-called administrative research in sociology and mass communication also came under attack for its tacit acceptance of corporate and

1

government power. Theories of economic determinism were mocked by the political conservatism of industrial workers in the West and embarrassed when striking French workers accepted mild capitalist reforms after flirting with revolution in 1968. Likewise, Stalinist claims to represent socialist "progress" were further discredited when Soviet troops invaded Czechoslovakia. Various structuralist theories neither anticipated nor comprehended worldwide movements for social change that appeared in the 1960s and 1970s. A political "new left" emerged that rejected liberal pluralism, classical Marxism, and structuralism.

This historic shift in political and social thought is largely a nonissue for most Americans, illustrating an important characteristic of cultural hegemony in the United States: We are routinely sheltered from trends in international political and social thought, especially those that include Marxist influences. We may consume the latest "postmodern" treat, such as an avant-garde movie, music video, or fashion trend, but we remain largely unaware of the resources, ingredients, and processes that made that production possible. Like urban preschoolers who think milk comes from the supermarket, we haven't yet seen the cow. Of course, academics and political activists have noted and incorporated alternative insights and new approaches into their work, but the critical edge is routinely toned down for the American palette (Budd, Entmann, & Steinman, 1990). The following discussion may seem foreign to many readers. We have done our best to "translate" the conversations. Some critics will applaud, others disparage our effort. In either case, there is no substitute for a thorough investigation of primary sources and repeated application of the concepts and theories presented.

We are surrounded by power: corporate power, media power, power of boss over worker, power of teacher over student. Whatever the relationship, power does not arise naturally. Power must be established through behavior. Power often relies on physical force, economic constraint, legal guidelines, or other coercive techniques. But coercion is expensive and dangerous. Subordinates can organize, revolt, and find other allies. Power is best secured if subordinates buy into the arrangement, agree to the terms, and make the relationship theirs. Hegemony is that system of power that has the support of the subordinate.

Hegemony addresses how social practices, relationships, and structures are negotiated among diverse social forces. Hegemony offers a template for understanding why women wear makeup, employees participate in actions to improve company profits, and homeowners and renters accept segregated housing patterns. In each case, subordinate groups (women, workers, or ethnic minorities) willingly participate in practices that are not necessarily in their best interests because they perceive some tangible benefit. The mass media, educational institutions, the family, government agencies, industry, religious groups, and other social institutions elicit support for such hegemonic relations through patterns of communication and material reward. Hegemony considers how the conditions of society take shape in our minds—philosophically, religiously, culturally, politically, and ideologically—and how humans are thus brought into various social relationships and their explanations.

Recognizing that social structures and practices exist largely due to their acceptance by important publics, social theorists and critics as diverse as Walter Lippmann, Noam Chomsky, Stuart Hall, Louis Althusser, Douglas Kellner, Göran Therborn, Maxwell McCombs, and Donald Shaw, among others, have argued that contemporary societies exist largely through the so-called manufacture of consent. However, hegemony does not arise primarily as a result of a dominant group performing some sleight of hand to deceive the "masses" nor by a dominant group conducting a clever propaganda campaign to mislead subordinate groups. Rather, hegemony exists only when dominant social forces represent and incorporate some very real material interests of subordinate groups into their social relationships. Without conscious choice, hegemony disappears, and the social order slips to various forms of domination, coercion, or co-optation. Put differently, dominant social groups may have leadership and power in a society, but without the active consent of the population, dominant groups do not have hegemony. Consequently, as we will see, the concept of consent also becomes a point of contention in any discussion of hegemony.

Hegemony as a process is neither good nor bad. Hegemony is about hierarchical relations and vested interest. The most important question is, Who is dominant and for what purpose, and who is subordinate and what do they gain or lose?

## Hegemony in Ancient Greece

Like other concepts used in the Western world, such as democracy, rhetoric, and ethics, hegemony has linguistic and social origins in early Greek civilization. In early Athens, one of the twin gods of Charity was Hegemony, who "conducted" plants to their bloom and directed or "led" them to bear fruit. Peasants offered tithes to Hegemony in hopes of securing "natural plenty and fertility" (Burns, 1957, p. 373). From having the power to direct and lead agriculture to fruition, hegemony soon came to mean a leading power in politics and foreign policy.

In the great colonizing age from the eighth to the sixth centuries, Greece dominated a vast territory in the Mediterranean and ruled over an extensive colonial network. Alexander's army totaled only 50,000 when he conquered Mesopotamia, Asia Minor, Palestine, Egypt, and Persia. The conquered population greatly outnumbered that of the smaller Greek city-states. Resorting to constant repression or intimidation of the new colonial partners would have been costly, dangerous, and essentially unworkable. Every state rules over its citizens through some combination of coercion and consent, but Greek leaders understood the importance of consent in government and in foreign policy. As an alternative to military action or other coercion, Greece offered a deal to its subordinate allies.

Well schooled in the art of rhetoric, Greek leaders first identified the concerns of their colonial allies and then incorporated those topics into the ensuing political and economic relationships. Greece offered to use its armies to protect the colonies from less "civilized" invaders; provide education, art, and other cultural resources to the colonies; and accept various forms of limited self-rule. In exchange, Greece asked its so-called allies to join in trade with Greece and consent to Greek authority in any dispute. Most of the subordinate nations decided that such a partnership with Greece would be beneficial.

Greece negotiated dominance with the consent of its colonies and allies. Greek authority soon directed the growth of the Hellenistic world. "The relationships thus established were uneasy and far from static"(Walbank, 1982, p. 15); Greece influenced the colonies, and the colonies influenced Greece. In this coming together of cultures, Greek dominance was paramount but consented to, because the colonies benefited from Greece's economic and political leadership.

The Greeks called this new relationship "hegemony," in honor of the God who directed growth. Conceptually, hegemony came to mean the directing authority in a confederacy. Politically, as the economic and military power in the region, Greece assumed the leadership of this hegemony.

## Hegemony Lost

The moment of hegemony for Greece did not last. As the economies and civilizations of Greece's subordinate allies developed, partly due to their favored status with Greece, they demanded more from the hegemonic relationship. Greece attempted to satisfy the increasing demands but resorted to coercion whenever requests challenged Greek dominance. Military incursions were increasingly required, and a vast bureaucracy was established. Nonetheless, an embattled Greek hegemony survived for several hundred years. With the advance of the Roman Republic in the second century, however, hegemony was displaced by direct domination. Although local customs and leaders were recruited and integrated into the colonial state, the Roman Empire relied more directly on its armies than had Greece.

Hegemony thus disappeared as a form of political rule; as a concept, it went into disuse. Although some might consider the British

Commonwealth an example of hegemonic rule, understood in "its sense of a political predominance of one state over another," hegemony does not reappear as a widely used term until the mid-19th century (Williams, 1976, p. 144).

## Hegemony Regained

Hegemony returns as a sociopolitical concept in the late 1800s in Europe, along with the dramatic growth of capitalism and its accompanying social contradictions. Before long, social theorists in the radical working-class movement were debating strategies for overcoming the dominance of the nation-state and promoting the interests of the working populations.

In *The German Ideology*, Karl Marx (1859/1970) argued that because social being determines social consciousness and because the leading ideology of any age is that of the ruling class, the capitalist class was the leading political force in Europe. He explained that capitalist hegemony over society would continue until representatives of the working class raised demands that challenged existing social relationships. Whereas the ingredients for a concept of domination with consent existed in the works of Marx and Frederich Engels (1932/1970), their concept of the state has often been reduced to one of "bodies of armed men." Others have since grappled with the complexities of power and consent in government, civil society, and cultural practices.

Perry Anderson (1977) noted that hegemony was one of the central political slogans in the anti-Czarist movement in Russia from 1890 to 1917. Plekhanov codified the concept in 1883 when he urged a political and ideological struggle against the Czar (see Anderson, 1977). This battle would be led by the working class, which would necessarily take up the demands of all the other sectors of society. In other words, the working class—which was numerically very small in Russia—would have hegemonic leadership in the fight against the Czar because the working class would champion and represent the interests of all the democratic forces: the underdeveloped Russian capitalist class and the growing middle class of entrepreneurs and small farmers, as well as the massive peasant populace.

Lenin, a central leader in the 1917 Russian Revolution, also stressed preference for hegemony instead of a narrow "self-interest" approach to politics. Given the divisions within any society, no one class or sector could expect to lead without resort to force unless public consensus was reached. If a democratic revolution was to occur, the leadership of any alliance must be based on hegemony (i.e., the interests of each social sector must be served by the political program of the leading social sector). Thus, Lenin wrote,

> In the struggle of the whole people for a fully democratic revolution, in the struggle of *all* the working and exploited people against the oppressors and exploiters, the [working class] is revolutionary only in so far as it is conscious of and gives effect to this idea of hegemony. (Anderson, 1977, p. 17)

As Buci-Glucksmann (1980) wrote, "Lenin gave new importance to the front of cultural struggle and constructed a doctrine of hegemony as a complement to the theory of state as force" (p. 390).

To promote hegemony, Russian socialists made strategic alliances in the democratic struggle against the Czar's dictatorship. In the early years of the Russian Revolution, before the rise of Stalin, the socialist state was based on hegemony: Negotiations among classes regulated social practices and relations. This conception of hegemony appeared at the World Congresses of the Third International organized by the Russians, where working-class parties were encouraged to "act in every manifestation and domain of social life as the *guide* [italics added] of the whole working and exploited population" (Anderson, 1977, p. 18). In 1922, theorists extended the concept of hegemony to include class relations under capitalism. At the Fourth World Congress, delegates discussed how the capitalist class maintains its so-called hegemony by convincing the working class to limit its activities to economic demands and consent to other existing social relations. They discussed how dominant classes in society maintain their position by winning the support of other important social forces.

## Antonio Gramsci

A young Italian radical closely followed the discussions on hegemony at the World Congresses. Drawing from his own rich experiences as a leader of the Turin, Italy, trade union battles in 1918 to 1920, this socialist thinker was to later contribute more to the conception of hegemony than anyone before him. An intellectual, a political activist, a trade union leader, and a working journalist, he embodied the unity of theory and practice in his everyday life. Today, no one is so universally identified with the concept of hegemony as that Italian intellectual: Antonio Gramsci (see Figure 1.1).

Born in Sardinia in 1891, Gramsci grew up experiencing the cultural and social prejudice against southern Italy, which historically had been underdeveloped in favor of northern urban centers. The 1870 unification of Italy had maintained these traditional inequalities, even as Sardinia was incorporated into the greater Italian state and culture.

Gramsci's older brother, a political activist, introduced him to magazines and newspapers of every persuasion, including the socialist press. Gramsci began contributing to a small country newspaper and later competed for and won a scholarship to the College of Turin. By the time he arrived in Turin, it had become the center of the radical working-class movement in Italy.

As Europe prepared for war, Italian production increased along with the size and power of the urban working class. Workers, politicians, and intellectuals fiercely debated Italy's neutrality in the widening war. Gramsci brought a unique perspective to the political debates, arguing that prejudice against southern peasants was hampering the efforts for equality, peace, and democracy in the north. He urged the Turin workers to join forces with southern peasants in a united campaign against police repression, Italian participation in the war, and the general social crisis in Italy. Few heeded his counsel, and in the absence of any united response by workers and peasants, the Italian government and the developing industrialist groups effectively played the demands of the northern workers off against the interests of the southern farmers. Gramsci continued his university studies, wrote for the working-

**Figure 1.1.** From Antonio Gramsci's Soviet passport, 1923.

class newspaper *Voice of the People,* and became ever more deeply involved in the discussions in the trade union and socialist movement of Turin.

In response to the high cost of living, the lack of bread, and the continuation of the war, Turin workers launched a general strike that led to an open insurrection in August 1917. An outspoken supporter of the strike, Gramsci became editor of *Voice of the People,* still advocating a unified worker-peasant campaign for peace and democracy. The magazine focused on the need for a new culture, a new education for the entire Italian people. Gramsci did not simply conduct a theoretical debate on the questions of culture and politics, however. In November 1917, he helped found a " 'club of moral life' with the purpose of asserting the need for culture in political and revolutionary activity" (Pozzolini, 1990, p. 29).

Despite national elections, repression, and concession, the Turin workers continued to organize, launching factory councils that sought to control production, working conditions, and distribution of goods to meet the population's needs. A group of intellectuals and activists, including Angelo Tasca, Palmero Togliatti, Umberto Terracini, and Gramsci launched a newspaper in November 1919 called *Ordine Nuovo, The New Order*. In keeping with Gramsci's broader perspective on politics, the weekly was published as a "review of socialist culture."

In March 1920, the Turin industrialists locked out the workers in an attempt to disperse the factory councils. The social crisis had reached the breaking point. Gramsci wrote that the crisis would end with "either the conquest of power on the part of the [workers] for the transition to new modes of production and distribution . . . or a tremendous reaction on the part of the propertied classes and the governing class" that will "shatter the organs of political struggle" (quoted in Pozzolini, 1990, p. 31) and incorporate the unions into a repressive state. Gramsci's words were prophetic. Capitalist hegemony fractured, and the dominant classes resorted to force. The factory councils that had championed popular democracy and culture were defeated. In 1922, Gramsci was elected to parliament, but the fascist movement of Benito Mussolini soon took power and proceeded to destroy all democratic institutions. Gramsci was arrested in 1926 for his opposition. Mussolini's courts sentenced Gramsci to 20 years in prison to "keep his brain from functioning" (Hoare, 1983, p. lxxxix). Gramsci spent the rest of his life behind bars, but his brain kept on functioning, and his writings are valuable for understanding culture and society today.

## Gramsci's Contributions

Gramsci has perhaps suffered more than any other Marxist writer from partial and partisan interpretation, both by opponents and supporters, especially in regard to his concept of hegemony. Some of these contributions are presented toward the end of this chapter. Unlike subsequent interpretations, Gramsci's hegemony is grounded in history and political activity. To appreciate the richness of his approach, one must begin with Gramsci's understanding of knowledge and its relation to social practice, his definition of intellectuals and their social function, and his conceptualization of *historic blocs*.

Gramsci's insights developed from his experience and reflection. The vibrant intellectual life of Italy in the early 1900s was both cosmopolitan and homegrown. Intellectuals and workers debated British political economy, French radical politics, and German philosophy. Works by Marx, Hegel, French syndicalist Georg Sorel, Antonio Labriola, Lenin, Plekhanov, and Machiavelli were read along with futurist works inspired by D'Annunzio and the Italian philosopher Benedetto Croce.

Gramsci believed that all social relations had an economic basis, but in economically backward Italy, he was also influenced by the idealist tradition. Gramsci was less concerned with socioeconomic relations per se and more interested in how those relations were understood and accepted by the general population. Gramsci recognized that power is a combination of force and consensus, accepting the importance of ideas in organizing consent for society. Yet in opposition to Croce, Gramsci argued that one's activities and beliefs are greatly influenced by existing social and cultural conditions. Italian peasants were Catholic and German peasants were Protestant, not because of the rigor of their particular ideas but because as subordinate groups, they largely adopted dominant religious ideologies. Gramsci advocated the active intervention of an intellectual and political leadership drawn from the working class that could influence the understanding and activity of the general population by providing an alternative power and ideology.

During his years in prison, Gramsci reconsidered the history of Italian intellectuals as he grappled with the triumph of fascism and the failure of an alternative ideology to capture the imagination of the Italian peasants and workers. Because much of Gramsci's work was written in prison, his writings appear disjointed: To avoid the prison censor, he often wrote obliquely and guardedly. Nonetheless, from his earlier journalism, through his political and cultural writings in Turin, and in his prison writings, Gramsci maintained a coherence and continuity of thought. Throughout, his social theory was less concerned with underlying structural conditions than with how these conditions were socially constructed through communication and practice. To appreciate the richness of Gramsci's approach, one must begin with his epistemology of politics (why we know what we know), which includes understanding knowledge as practice, a new definition of *intellectual*, and the discovery of what he called *historic blocs*.

### Knowledge as Practice

Perhaps Gramsci's most important contribution to contemporary social theory and communication is the recognition that "practice is a process of knowledge" (quoted in Buci-Glucksmann, 1980, p. 347). We do what we know. We also learn through doing. For Gramsci, the "unity of theory and practice is not a mechanical fact, but a historical becoming" (quoted in Buci-Glucksmann, 1980, p. 347). We have knowledge of the world and society, including its underlying socioeconomic structures, primarily because we experience this knowledge in practice. Our practices give rise to theories. Theories, in turn, have practical consequences to the extent that we act on our beliefs. For instance, so-called common sense is theoretical, in that it explains and predicts outcomes for our everyday activity. Based on our experiences, common sense tells us that fire is hot, the pavement is slippery when wet, boys don't wear dresses, and smiling faces sometimes tell lies. Little girls get picked up and cuddled when they fall; little boys are told, "That doesn't hurt; be a big boy." Little girls are encouraged to be "pretty," little boys to be "tough." In the process of living, doing, and making our world, we come to know it.

Gramsci implicitly rejected the reduction of knowledge to "scientific" fact. He also rejected a view of ideology as simply illusion. Gramsci did not argue that ideas make history, but he did give ideology an increased importance in the process of social change. He believed that ideologies have serious consequences because they organize human *practices*. Ideologies may be disputed as true or false, but more important, they are *legitimate* to the extent that they are active in everyday life. Because ideologies are known through practices, they cannot be counteracted by some appeal to "science" or "fact." Instead, ideologies thrive, change, or disappear as a result of human practices corresponding to social interests, social power, and political struggle. New practices and new knowledge arise with new social power.

Gramsci posited an objective and active reality for ideology: Ideologies change under the influence of practices corresponding to a different ideology. In short, thinking is not divorced from being. Ideas don't float around like leaves in a breeze. Ideas are always carried in and through human beings. Consequently, ideas don't make history. People make history—people *do* history. This inseparable connection between people and ideas underscores Gramsci's insistence that theory cannot be divorced from practice.

The unity of theory and practice in human activity is a material condition of our social existence. Ideology has a material existence because of social practices and institutions that depend on or give support to a given ideology. At the same time, ideology has a materiality in its language, symbols, and signs. We can hear speech. We can feel the vibrations of the loudspeaker. We can touch the written page. We can see the symbols on the billboard. Language, speech, and other social *practices* interact, providing meaning to our condition and organizing our ongoing activities. Everything we do passes through our minds, but Gramsci refused to give priority to thought and language over social and cultural practices and institutional relations. For Gramsci, knowledge needs thought and practice.

How do we understand politics? Economics? History? We use language, yes, but the language we use is not simply a tool for understanding. Language is also a product of the social relations that occur in the very process of communicating. *All of communication (as culture and language) is simultaneously a product, process, and tool.* Each dimension of communication and culture may be analytically distinct, yet each dimension remains tethered to the other. Society produces language and culture; it also uses the tools of language and culture in the process of creating meanings and cultural practices.

Language constructs all knowledge from the personal to the global in keeping with existing social relations. For example, recog-

### Ideas in Action

U.S. ideology has long been subservient to the need of dominant-class interests. From settlement to colony to independent nation to world power, American ideology has adjusted to reflect changed social relations.

Landing at Plymouth Rock, early settlers were dependent on the generosity and knowledge of Native Americans and the benevolence of "his Majesty" King George. Within a generation, the Pilgrims and other "Americans" found the king to be intrusive. They rebelled against the British, holding certain truths to be self-evident—but evidently not applicable to Native Americans. The new democratic ideology did not extend to so-called savages, who were considered inferior to European descendants. As the New World expanded, European connections were renegotiated, but Native Americans were exterminated. Politicians, newsmen, historians, and preachers provided needed political and "factual" justifications for each social adjustment.

The *idea* of democratic independence didn't make the revolution; the *idea* of white supremacy didn't kill the Indians. Ideas helped human actors organize and promote their social interests as they were already acting them out.

nizable ethnic differences do not have much significance unless social relations dictate. Consequently, ethnic slurs are plentiful against African Americans, Italians, Poles, Jews, and others who have been subordinate during different historical periods. The power of speech depends on the social power of the speaker. There are few derogatory words in English for the British because the British Empire once covered the globe, dominating most social relations with other nationalities and groups. Our language simply reflects that historic reality. In other words, we understand politics, economics, history, and the rest of our world through the language used by its actors.

As we act, we construct social relationships. The language we use has its material basis in those social relationships. We share experiences, negotiate meaning, and build vocabularies. According to Gramsci, language is where social distinctions are expressed and cultural inequalities ossified. In other words, language per se does not encode meaning, but historically constituted and contextually bound human practices encode meanings through language. Language is historically produced: The meanings of words and phrases depend on existing social relationships. Meaning depends on who has the power to name practices, persons, and conditions. We create realities out of conditions not of our own making, using languages and cultures developed by our ancestors. What meanings and what cultural practices will prevail? It depends in large part on the interaction between contending members of society, how they resolve their often disparate interests, and how they employ their unequal access to power and decision making.

Consider the prevalence of the words *Negro* or *colored* before the 1960s and the widespread acceptance of the words *black* or *African American* today. The change is not simply linguistic. The changing language reflects historically altered social relations. From Gramsci's perspective, obstacles to communication between social groups are not primarily linguistic but social. Gramsci believed that the grammar of social relations could be translated to ideological presuppositions, political platforms, philosophical positions, and even everyday language use.

*Intellectuals as Media*

If knowledge cannot be divorced from politics and practices, then what we know can be found in everyday behavior. If the production of ideology lies in identifiable life practices, including language use, then each society must have a means of creating and mediating its knowledge. Throughout history, knowledge has been mediated by so-called intellectuals—persons who explained and translated culture. Gramsci (1988) extended the traditional definition of intellectual to include all humans because everyone practices theories and creates theories from practices. There is no job that is so simple that some amount of intellectual labor is not required to perform it. Everyone is capable of mental labor. We all think; some just get paid to do more of it. For Gramsci, anyone who organizes, administers, explains, or leads the construction and operation of knowledge is an intellectual. Teachers, technicians, managers, civil servants, and journalists can be considered intellectuals who mediate social practices and construct explanations for the way we live.

Gramsci identified traditional intellectuals as scribes, priests, political advisers, and others who monopolize the translation of the world for the limited audiences of the social elite. Traditional intellectuals promote ideas that express the interests of dominant classes and defend social structures that reproduce the status quo. Gramsci noted that "organic" intellectuals, on the other hand, are members of subordinate classes who actively promote ideas that favor the interests of nondominant social classes. In Gramscian terms, organic intellectuals compose the political leadership of the rising social classes. In either case, traditional or organic, Gramsci understood that the function of intellectuals was to explain and defend social relationships preferred by the social classes they represented.

Gramsci (1988) rejected any definition of intellectuals according to "the intrinsic nature of intellectual activities, rather than in the ensemble of the system of relations in which these activities" are placed (p. 8). Gramsci's concept of intellectuals is radically demo-

cratic and humanist. His vision of organic intellectuals who promote the interests of a subordinate social class positions "practice
as knowledge" as the means for changing society.

Unfortunately, the so-called organic intellectuals of the Italian
working class—the political leaders of the labor movement in
Turin—were unable to construct a program of action capable of
preventing the triumph of fascism in 1922. Ironically, most radical
intellectuals accepted defeat as a consequence of the superior
physical force of the vigilante fascist "brown shirts." Only Gramsci
(1988) explained that Mussolini's physical force was built by recruiting the urban middle classes and southern peasantry to capitalist fascist ideas. The working class could not resist fascism alone,
and its ideological program did not speak to other subordinate
groups —peasants, shopkeepers, mid-level civil servants, and
other potential democratic allies.

Fundamental to Gramsci's (1988) critique of the triumph of fascism was a concrete expression of knowledge through practice. He
explained that without an organized political leadership that presented a program dedicated to the interests of all subordinate
classes, antifascist popular organizations could not assemble the
physical force necessary to defeat fascist forces. On the other hand,
the traditional intellectuals, led by Croce, built an ideology that
promoted the interests of an Italian "nation," understood as government leaders, industrialists, urban shopkeepers, managers, the
unemployed, peasants, and landlords. This reactionary united
front politically out-maneuvered, diffused, and physically isolated
the working class, which never got beyond its narrow, "corporate"
interests as trade unionists. In post-World War II Italy, knowledge
as practice was mediated by traditional intellectuals to form what
Gramsci termed a *historic bloc.*

*Historic Blocs*

Gramsci (1967, 1947/1971, 1988) used the term *historic bloc* to describe the complexities of relationships between social classes and
other social forces. Although the Marxist tenet that social struc-

tures and class antagonisms are determined by society's economic base is more nuanced than many critics have acknowledged, Gramsci's historic bloc expressed a more intricate and conscious connection between social, economic, political, and cultural spheres. *A historic bloc unites disparate social forces under a common political program.* Each group participates in the bloc for its own reasons, united in the commitment to organize institutions and practices according to a given ideology. Gramsci recognized that one faction of a dominant class can strike a deal with some subordinate classes in a campaign against a competing faction of the dominant class (as happened in Italy and elsewhere). The idea that two sections of industrialists could be in conflict and sections of the working class and peasantry would take sides in the conflict did not fit into the traditional Marxist paradigm of capitalist-worker conflict. Gramsci recognized a more interactive relationship between what had been seen exclusively as an antagonism between dominant and subordinate classes. In theoretical terms, the historic bloc conceptually overcame the reductive notion of two big classes, workers and capitalists, pitted against each other like two powerful dinosaurs, impervious to other social forces.

Gramsci also explained that any historic bloc was subject to influences by all of society's interactions: (a) socioeconomic conditions, such as production, employment, work practices, and distribution of goods; (b) cultural conditions of entertainment, education, and religion; and (c) political conditions of decision making, representation, and access to resources. Given the complex contradictions in mass society, a historic bloc has to be more than a temporary political alliance; it must be forged on many levels. To lead society, dominant groups have to speak for all social classes, demonstrate cultural and intellectual superiority, and provide political and social solutions to a multitude of problems. Because the leadership of any historic bloc depends on the support given by other social forces, Gramsci suggested that under certain conditions, a historic bloc may be subverted or overturned. For a dominant class to lead any historic bloc, it must have the consent of significant subordinate participants. Once the historic bloc, mediated by the intellectual and political leadership of the dominant

### Ninety-Five Theses

Historic blocs take many forms. In 1517, Martin Luther nailed
95 theses on the church door in Wittenberg, Germany, precipi-
tating "what became the greatest crisis in the history of the
Western church" (Jowett & O'Donnell, 1992, p. 47). In hegemonic terms, the Lutheran Reformation was the ideological
manifestation of a powerful historic bloc that sought to over-
throw the religious and political dominance of the Catholic
Church in Germany. Luther's appeal was successful because
it drew on popular folk customs communicated in everyday
idioms of Northern Germany. His religious challenge to the
rule of the Pope found its parallel in the political opposition to
Rome shared by the German nobility and capitalist merchants. Disseminated by the latest media technology, the
printing press, and popularized in cartoons by satirist
Cranach, Luther's religious appeal provided the social cement for a nationalist uprising in Germany. The historic bloc
espousing the ideals of church reform built a new political
and social order. Such is the dynamic nature of historic blocs
that grow in power as popular consent expands.

class, gains enough popular support to assume political power, the social relations may be called hegemony.

Conversely, given that the modern state extends the reach of the dominant social class into civil society (e.g., media, family, church, schools, corporations, community groups), a contesting social force cannot capture state power without first achieving leadership in other venues. Wide-ranging social organization in many spheres is required to overcome the hegemony of the existing historic bloc. A kind of trench warfare develops, with partisans of a new society challenging dominant ideology in culture, media, education, and other social practices.

Understanding knowledge as practice, identifying intellectuals through their social function, and recognizing the historic bloc as the alliance necessary for leading society gives us the background necessary to understand hegemony as conceived by Antonio Gramsci.

*Gramsci's Hegemony*

Although the term hegemony now appears in many contexts, understanding of the concept varies widely. The popular use of the term has wandered far from the original concept, equating hegemony with dominance. Gramsci's perspective is considerably more developed, however. In his writings, hegemony is not simply a process of indoctrination, nor merely another term for ideological and cultural activity. Rather, hegemony appears as a consensual culture and politics that meet the minimal needs of the majority while simultaneously advancing the interests of the dominant groups (Sassoon, 1987, p. 94).

Gramsci (1967, 1947/1971, 1988) used the term in two qualitatively different ways. In one sense, hegemony provides a means for a dominant class to effectively govern. Hegemony also provides a strategy for organizing a historical bloc of oppositional classes, which can challenge and replace existing social structures and relations. Here, we focus on the first sense and return to hegemony as a strategy for change in the final chapter. In both cases, however, hegemony appears as a possibility, a political preference, and a necessary goal for any leadership in the modern world.

Hegemony has not always been necessary, possible, or even desirable as a means of political leadership. Social relations in most previous historical periods had little need for the consent of the governed. Feudal society, for instance, was not hegemonic. Outside of their inner circles, dominant classes ruled largely through coercion. Landlords relied primarily on physical force and intimidation in governing serfs. Resistance periodically erupted in the face of the harsh conditions of life, but the plebeian masses were too isolated and geographically divided for any consistent political organization. Although governments were formed and laws and courts established, no national state apparatuses developed. It was not until the 1700s, when merchants, manufacturers, and local burghers in towns scattered across Europe found the need for a common currency and language, that states could become nations with widespread support.

In the mid-1700s, feudalism came under attack as capitalist merchants, traders, and their spokesmen politically and economically led an all-out assault on "divine right," royal privilege, and the feudal order that restricted trade, manufacture, and worship. Although they were a numerical minority in society, the new capitalist classes had superior economic and cultural resources. They gained leadership by articulating the interests of all the subordinate classes. As the industrial revolution increasingly urbanized the population, rising capitalist classes constructed historic blocs capable of challenging feudal relations.

In Europe and America, the majority of citizens who supported the social revolutions against the monarchy did so in large part because the social project of "Liberty, Equality, Fraternity" spoke to their interests. The majority identified with and supported (or at least accepted) the emerging national identities. The construction of national identities helped forge the nation-states necessary for trade and manufacture and corresponding social relations. Nation-states nurtured mass exchange, extensive social interaction, and shared cultural norms. Because the social and cultural vision in-

cluded freedom, opportunity, and security, many willingly participated in the battles for a new society. Their participation was massive and decisive. As Christopher Hill (1972) recounted, without
the consent of the mass population of workers, traders, farmers,
and service people, the social revolutions of the 17th and 18th centuries would have been impossible.

Hegemony in the modern nation-state has been preconditioned
on the growing social and economic importance of a massive urban
working class. Without the continued support of the majority of
working people, society would collapse, and alternative social relations could be proposed, as happened in France in 1968, Chile in
1970, Portugal in 1975, Nicaragua in 1979, Poland in 1980, and the
Soviet Union in the 1990s, to name a few examples. We may conclude that any successful leadership must truly champion the *national* interest, representing the aspirations of diverse classes and
social groups.

Dominant classes that are too self-serving in their political, social, and economic leadership will inevitably confront serious challenges by other social groups. As popular consent is withdrawn,
hegemony shrinks. As leading groups secure and consolidate support, hegemony expands. For example, to the extent that significant nondominant social forces create their own alternate identity
for politics (e.g., industrial workers, African Americans, Chicanos,
farm workers, women), the leadership of traditional groups will be
challenged. To the extent that the demands of these challengers are
incorporated back into the dominant discourse, the hegemony of
the dominant social group remains intact, albeit in a modified
form. All states undergo this political negotiation; challengers seldom fully achieve their demands within another's hegemony. In
subsequent chapters, we discuss examples of this process of negotiation as applied to race, gender, and class. For now, we suggest
that a leading class can maintain desired relations only if it enjoys
widespread popular support. For a social group to gain and hold
legitimacy, it must first secure hegemony economically, politically,
and culturally.

### Yankee Doodle

Although the American Revolution is often told as a tale of individual heroes, such as Paul Revere, Patrick Henry, and George Washington, from the Boston Massacre and the Boston Tea Party to Lexington and Concord and Bunker Hill, the majority of political activists, revolutionaries, and soldiers were farmers and workers, without whom the revolution would have been impossible. In fact, popular support for the fight against the British was lukewarm, at first. However, once the call for freedom was extended to the common citizen by Thomas Paine, Sam Adams, and others, the social forces necessary were recruited to the revolution for independence.

The popularity of the revolution among the working poor was soon reflected in popular culture. Songs such as the ballad "Liberty Song" and the unofficial national anthem, "Yankee Doodle," which exuded pride in American simplicity and lack of class affectation, "were wildly popular in the colonies . . . sung virtually everywhere—on public occasions and often just to annoy the British and their American friends" (Ravitch, 1990, p. 14). After the revolution, the elite "founding fathers" were forced to negotiate a revised hegemony with the American populace. Citizen representatives from the 13 colonies refused to ratify the Constitution until the Bill of Rights was added—10 amendments that still speak to democratic rights.

## Conditions for Hegemony

Capitalist classes successfully built hegemony in the popular democratic revolutions of the 17th and 18th centuries because they provided tangible material benefits, a coherent political leadership, and meaningful cultural practices. Without a doubt, these conditions are completely interrelated, underscoring Gramsci's (1967, 1947/1971, 1988) insistence on the unity of theory and practice. Nonetheless, these conditions are analytically distinct. We may envision these three conditions as supports or legs that hold up the hegemonic table. If one of the legs breaks or splinters, society teeters precariously until it is reinforced or reconstructed. A stable hegemony needs each of its supports.

*Material Conditions*

Common sense tells us that any leadership is chosen because its supporters expect some appreciable benefits in return. Real, material benefits must be forthcoming to maintain continued support. Any leadership needs to have sufficient resources to realize its program, reward its supporters, and re-create its preferred relations. In the United States, for instance, most adults have jobs, relative security, and a decent standard of living that provides a sense of well-being. Under such conditions, it's not hard to understand the relative social peace in the United States. Nor is it hard to understand the social crises that arise when material conditions deteriorate.

During the Great Depression in the 1930s, millions lost their jobs as manufacturers cut back production. Farmers were evicted from their land as banks foreclosed. Suddenly, millions of Americans no longer consented to traditional business practices because the depression disrupted business as usual. Under such conditions, millions joined unions, farm organizations, and radical parties (Preis, 1964). As the dominant capitalist hegemony fractured, alternative ideas appeared, from fascism, to populism, to socialism. Without jobs, security, or opportunity, the so-called American way of life was not very appealing. In response, Democratic president Franklin D. Roosevelt (FDR) constructed a new hegemonic relationship. His New Deal program rescued U.S. capitalism. By providing Social Security, unemployment compensation, federal jobs programs, and farm subsidies, the New Deal laid the material basis for renewed popular consent. Any hegemony that can deliver the goods will survive. As the gap widens between rich and poor, the future of capitalist hegemony will be threatened.

A note of caution: Material benefits need not be abundant nor strictly economic. Lacking options, subordinate groups may be satisfied with minimal rewards. Although consent may be reluctant, groups often consent to hegemony because the limited benefits are immediate and easily attainable. More substantial benefits may be possible, but if they can be attained only through actions that jeopardize current benefits, the risk may be too great. In simple terms, a bird in the hand is worth two in the bush. In personal relationships, for example, couples frequently continue unsatisfying partnerships because the prospect of being alone is more frightening. For social groups, material conditions often go beyond an accountant's balance sheet: An unsatisfactory but known present may be more acceptable than an appealing but unknown future. Limited material conditions may be sufficient, then, if alternative relations appear unattainable or unrealistic. Hence, material conditions interact with political conditions.

## Political Conditions

In the process of controlling material resources, a hegemonic leadership must transcend its own narrow interests and politically carry forward the whole of society. On a societal scale, rewards and punishments, laws and privileges, courts, police, prisons, and so forth must be organized according to a political plan that represents (or secures) the interests of the majority. Hegemony, which requires the consent of the majority, can be secured politically only through alliances, agreements, and consensual national policies. As labor unionized industry and threatened employer privileges in the 1930s, FDR accepted labor's right to organize—on his terms. Even though FDR's political program displeased some corporate leaders, he was recruiting lower-class and middle-class supporters to the American political system and the continued hegemony of the dominant classes. Appearing as an ally of labor, FDR was the best friend of business, because hegemony depends on the leading group's ability to organize others to support its decision-making practices.

Political conditions are important for hegemony in any sphere because social institutions, groups, or movements that depend on voluntary participation must organize available resources according to some consensual criteria. Leaderships need group support to avoid conflicts over resources and behaviors. Even parsons and priests must organize their congregations according to shared interests, responsibilities, and rewards. In the political realm, leaderships must capture the popular attention and the popular vote. The labor movement grew in the 1930s and 1940s because it was a popular cross-class social movement that championed the interests of immigrants, the unemployed, and urban communities (including small shopkeepers who were dependent on working-class customers).

Popular support is so essential for hegemony that in the United States, dominant social forces have resorted to what seems like one perpetual election campaign. Presidential elections do not function primarily as decision-making processes but rather as rituals that "make us feel generally content with the process" while producing "both acquiescence and quiescence" (Gronbeck, 1984, p. 493). Dominant social forces use mass media, education, propaganda, and political agitation in an unending public discourse to maintain consent within the agenda set by the dominant social groups. If alternative views were to gain any significant adherence, demands might be raised, political challenges issued, and hegemony eroded. Given the high stakes in contemporary society, the construction and reconstruction of political hegemony has invaded cultural practices that interact with political and material conditions.

## Cultural Conditions

Within a stable hegemony, how we live our lives and how we understand our lives generally correspond to the political and material conditions for that hegemony. Major social groups that benefit from the hegemonic arrangement support the political institutions that administer the allocation of resources. They also participate in the production and consumption of popular culture and those rituals and practices that underwrite the hegemonic relationship. Remember: Practice is a way of knowing, and how we live our lives is how we know our lives. We understand the world through our participation in economic, political, and cultural practices. Hegemony is thus forged in the very relationships that groups and individuals consent to and benefit from. Cultural conditions for hegemony constitute a whole philosophy of life.

This philosophy of life appears as consensual and mutually beneficial because we see the world primarily from our position within the hegemonic relationship. Dominant meanings tend to privilege the interests of the dominant social groups because they are based on the very hegemonic relationships that reinforce their political and economic dominance. Journalistic norms that accept institutional authority as the most legitimate sources for verifiable facts reinforce dominant values and readings of political and social events, for example (Sigal, 1986). A more horizontal or partisan style of journalism would not be less accurate but would recognize the average citizen and working participant as a legitimate news source as well, significantly changing interpretations of events and activities (Mattelart, 1986). Most media practices in the United States illustrate how culture relates to political and material conditions. For example, antiracist *and* antifemale lyrics in some rap music reflect the contradictory, yet subordinate, political and social conditions of Black America. Likewise, the evolution of rap from live deejay, audience response performances to mass marketing by major record labels underlines the subordinate economic position of black artistry. Other media practices have different political, economic, and cultural histories, but all have similar hegemonic interrelationships.

The mass media, including movies, television, magazines, and books, tend to use accepted representations and standard professional practices drawn from cultural values, stereotypes, and social rituals that predominate in the United States today. Media language, symbols, and practices are the result of years of social interaction and meaning making. In the United States, meanings are based largely on the ideology of consumerism (Budd, Craig, & Steinman, 1999; Willis, 1991). Media processes occur through existing technologies, accepted professional practices, and the parameters determined by conditions of monopoly ownership and control (Mosco, 1998). Communication in the United States is directed largely by corporations that dominate public decision making and influence everyday life. Media products and processes occur in relation to other social practices and the material conditions of capitalist hegemony.

Given the dynamics of material, political, and cultural conditions, parallel yet distinct worldviews re-create the hegemonic relations that appear throughout culture: in art, law, philosophy, fashion, movies, entertainment, religion, family relations, and other cultural practices. Each of these cultural realms intimately intersects with corresponding economic and political conditions of any hegemony. Yet, specific cultural activities may become sites of contention whenever practices fail to satisfy the interests of a subordinate group. Thus, the Protestant Reformation challenged previously hegemonic religious doctrines even as it reinforced the hegemony of the German merchants. Women may reject the social philosophy of patriarchy but sign on to the essentially patriarchal political systems of the Democratic and Republican parties. Due to mass society's cultural diversity and complexity, hegemony must continually be stitched together at many seams and thus has many points where it may unravel.

Of the three conditions, the cultural basis for hegemony is perhaps the most consistently problematic, because here, hegemony depends on the leading group's ability to provide philosophical and ideological explanations for why we do the things we do. Material resources or political organizations may be difficult to control but are more susceptible to reward and punishment. Culture ultimately depends more on voluntary popular participation and hence is subject to recurring challenge.

## Culture and Ideology

Culture for humans is a lot like water for fish; we live in it without always noticing how much it determines our activity. We don't always notice our culture because it gets "naturalized" through popular belief, repetition, and familiarity. But culture is not natural in the sense of biology or genetics. Rather, culture is social. Culture is all of human life—life that is distinguished by the appropriation of nature with tools, social interaction, and the construction of meaning. Culture includes all that has been created, built, learned, conquered, and practiced in the course of human history (Trotsky, 1973). Culture comprises a whole way of life (Williams, 1976). In this respect, human history is distinct from natural history. Individuals, groups, and societies can choose to create, build, and practice a variety of ways of living—depending, of course, on available resources. All social relations are subject to adjustment. The point here is that human life involves conscious choice. We are not destined by nature to live in any predetermined fashion. Although we begin under conditions not of our own making, we can construct our lives in many different ways.

How we choose to live depends, in large part, on the meanings we give to actual and possible social relations and practices. In any lasting hegemonic relationship, common practices and familiar explanations are readily available. Without much work, existing cultural practices appear preferable, even natural, whereas other less common practices or critiques are perceived as "deviant" (Hall, 1982). Consequently, meanings are generally constructed based on existing social relationships, and hegemony negotiates practices based largely on verbal and nonverbal understandings that reinforce dominant-subordinate relations. Ritual practices and symbolic meanings combine to communicate a philosophy of life or what is often called *ideology*.

In some descriptions, ideology refers to a distortion of thought that conceals or inverts actual social contradictions. Thus, anthropologists understand that humans created religion; the idea that God made humans is an inversion. In other descriptions, ideology is the means by which dominant groups consciously misrepresent or conceal social inequality. Radical sociologists explain how the ideals of equality and freedom often conceal inequality, poverty, and oppression. In either case, ideology appears as a negative and restricted concept referring primarily to ideas. However, ideology, understood as an explanation legitimizing a worldview, plays a much too important role in knowledge to be reduced to mistaken ideas or distorted thought.

For Gramsci (1967, 1947/1971, 1988), social relations depend on the particular mix of material, political, and cultural conditions of society, but any understanding of social relations depends on how actions, relations, and conflicts are explained, categorized, and rationalized. Ideology does not replace or transcend the world, but it helps us make sense of material, political, and cultural conditions. As Gramsci recognized, ideologies exist only in human thought because they also exist in human actions. Ideas cannot float freely, independent of human communicators. Ideas depend on people articulating thoughts in speech to human audiences that can act on these ideas.

In any hegemony, events, activities, and relationships have certain meanings depending on how prevailing ideologies are systematically incorporated and expressed. Ideologically speaking, we are conscious of our social relations because we live those relations and because we give meaning to the way we live. In short, knowledge is a product of social interaction among humans. This is crucial for any hegemony because the basis for consent is directly dependent on how the subordinates express, understand, and act out existing relations. In the course of negotiating and struggling over what will be accepted as knowledge, social groups adopt practices and meanings, collectively expressed as ideologies, that give a view of the world and its human relations.

Every ideology arises from cultural practices even as it organizes (or challenges) those practices. For instance, staffing soup kitchens and constructing temporary shelters for the homeless promote an ideology of charity, reinforcing (or at least tolerating) the continued dominance of the ideology of the American Dream (individual responsibility, hard work, home ownership, good fortune, etc.). Such charitable practices avoid challenges to the ideological explanations and hegemonic conditions of real estate development, rental policies, and private home construction.

Similarly, demands for equality of opportunity for women or gays in the armed forces challenge discriminatory practices while tacitly accepting assumptions about the legitimacy of U.S. military institutions and actions. Likewise, most demands for affirmative action accept practices that limit the number of doctors, college students, and even full-time employees as a natural fact of life. In these cases, challenges to existing cultural practices reinforce those practices. Consider these challenges: What if discrimination in the armed forces was resolved by abolishing the military? What if medical schools and associations did not limit the number of licensed doctors? What if anyone who wanted to work had a decent-paying job? We are not suggesting that these are unproblematic alternatives, but we do argue that some challenges more directly implicate the assumptions about dominant cultural practices. No ideology is natural or simply dominant or subordinate but occurs in a complex web of social relations. Ideologies of a stable hegemony are so ingrained that even challenges can reinforce relationships and re-create practices that favor dominant interests.

## Language

Ideology encompasses all those practices that explain our world, including the practice of communication. How we communicate about our world helps us organize our world (Cronen & Pearce, 1982). Language, in particular, helps us make sense of the world. We use language to name activities, define relationships, and express feelings. The label *housewife*, for instance, graphically inscribes an individual's role, responsibility, and personal relations.

Such language codes guide our interactions with others and our culture. Of course, like other cultural practices, language is hegemonically multidimensional. Language is an instrument in hegemony, a product of hegemony, and a battlefield where hegemony is negotiated. To build ideologies that permit and reinforce a given hegemony, a common language is needed. Words, symbols, and practices must carry shared meanings. But what meanings will be given to words, symbols, and practices? The meaning of housewife depends on the social power of those who occupy that position. To call Mrs. Smith, *Ms.* Smith, undermines engendered assumptions and uncovers the social character of such labels, but ultimately, those roles and assumptions will not be overturned by relabeling but only by changing relations that construct the labels. The answer to the question of meaning is not primarily linguistic but cultural, political, and social.

To challenge the meaning of any practice, to adjust the representation of a symbol, or to alter what a word signifies implicitly challenges the given ideological and cultural hegemony. If most people in a culture accept a given practice as legitimate, beneficial, or "natural," then the meaning of the practice is shared and continued. If the majority of society identifies itself as a unified nation under a legitimate government, the symbols of that government are respected and revered. However, for those who reject the legitimacy of a government, the symbols of national identity, such as a flag, a badge, or an accepted history, are ridiculed and opposed. If too many challenge a practice, hegemony dissipates (as when the majority of Americans rejected U.S. involvement in Vietnam, for example). Because consensual practices and meanings are essential for molding hegemony, language itself is a political and cultural issue.

Language is based on shared meanings created through common cultural and historical experiences. Different languages often create different meanings for a social reality. Language influences cultural identity, a primary condition for hegemony and a pressing reason for dominant forces to oppose cultural diversity and bilingual education. Thus, from the Spanish conquistadors in the 1500s to the State of California today, attempts are made to impose a

## Language as Culture:
## The Dandy Yankee Doodle

*Yankee Doodle went to town, a-riding on a pony. Stuck a feather in his hat and called it macaroni.* Familiar words from the song "Yankee Doodle," but what do they mean? The word *yankee* is from the Scottish *yankie*, which meant a dishonest person. The word *doodle* was English slang for fool. Literally, a "yankee doodle" was a dishonest fool—a British slur against the colonists (Egger-Bovet & Smith-Baranzini, 1994, p. 10).

In the context of American resistance to British colonialism, however, yankee doodles became rebels thumbing their noses and their language at British rule. In 1775, Edward Bang added the refrain about macaroni (a favorite food of the English elite), underscoring the colonist's disdain for British fashion and culture. In vocabulary, phrases, and idioms, the cultural norms and political trajectory of the American revolution were expressed and reinforced.

dominant language on the whole of society. Alternate languages, based on alternate cultural and historical experiences, contain elements of alternate ideologies. A stable hegemony, however, requires a compatible ideology with a corresponding linguistic and cultural grammar.

A similar dynamic can be noted in the malleability of "languages" in other fields. Liberation theology, for example, speaks a new language of the Gospel, which finds different meanings for social responsibility and religious practice. Drawing from the same texts as the church hierarchy has, liberation theology does not create a new linguistic structure but communicates with a grammar, as it were, that has been politically and socially reconceived. In opposition to the hegemony of archbishops, cardinals, and popes who articulate a strictly religious version of "God's kingdom," liberation theology presents a counterhegemonic language with "God's kingdom on earth" based on the "preferential option for the poor" (Berryman, 1987). Different languages coincide with different practices, implicating different worlds, different hegemonies. It is important that the plurality of languages and the malleability of each language indicate that humans continually negotiate and battle over meaning. Hegemony rests precariously on relations that are continually being redefined and rearticulated by subordinate social forces opposed to the status quo.

## Hegemony in the United States

The material, political, and cultural conditions necessary for hegemony are complexly interrelated. Recurrent social battles over meaning continually disrupt hegemony. Stability is so unlikely that Gramsci (1967, 1947/1971, 1988) even referred to hegemony as an elusive "moment" in social conflict. Of course, some moments last longer than others. The history of the United States can be considered a series of extended moments of capitalist-class hegemony.

Many contemporary political scientists dispute the existence of social class in the United States, although Erik Olin Wright (1985), Rick Fantasia (1988), G. William Domhoff (1986), and others have demonstrated that dominant-subordinate social divisions exist and generally adhere to identifiable social class outlines. (In passing, we note that the widespread disbelief in social class by U.S. academics ironically supports Gramsci's contention that the social function of intellectuals is to create an ideology compatible with dominant interests.) Substantial evidence exists for positing the division between dominant and subordinate social groups according to corporate ownership, personal resources, and occupation: Statistically, whites have greater socioeconomic assets and political power than African Americans, Mexican Americans, Puerto Ricans, Asian Americans, and other non-Anglo-Saxon national minorities. Likewise, most of the racial, ethnic, and gender divisions in the United States have a similar dominant-subordinate division that can be empirically supported: Men generally have superior resources and power compared with women, for example. If white males have historically held positions of power and continue to secure these positions despite existing "democratic" institutions and "affirmative action," then democratic pluralist theory cannot adequately explain the inequities in power in the United States without implicitly accepting racial and gender inferiority. On the other hand, hegemonic theory also must explain why millions of working people, national minorities, and women have supported and continue to support (actively or tacitly) the unequal distribution of resources and opportunities.

If hegemony depends on consent attained through tangible material benefits, political organization, and cultural practices, then to posit an American hegemony is to argue that subordinate social groups have significantly benefited from and supported social relations that primarily serve dominant interests. Historically, the hegemonic arrangements between corporations, the government, and the working population have had widespread support because popular belief has held that anyone could become rich and successful. The American Dream is not just for those with power. In fact, it's primarily for those without. Significantly, the American Dream has solid material, political, and cultural manifestations that underwrite the consent of the majority to the hegemony of the dominant capitalist classes.

In 1776, dominant forces (large mercantile and plantation interests) won support for the Constitution from subordinate social forces (small farmers, traders, artisans) by adding the Bill of Rights—an example of a negotiated arrangement that tolerated the dominant leadership on subordinate terms. Dominant classes in the early United States could materially afford this political settlement because resources were bountiful. Even before available resources were tapped, colonists were pushing back the frontiers. During the United States' first 100 years, federal policies materially ensured opportunities for hard work and individual freedom by providing an abundance of land taken by military force from Native Americans, an exceedingly nonhegemonic operation.

The ideology of the American Dream and Manifest Destiny has been secured because Uncle Sam has delivered. The westward expansion included the California gold rush in 1849, the Homestead Act (which distributed public land without cost to farmers in the 1860s), a Civil War that freed African Americans in 1865, and a late-19th-century industrial revolution that extended manufacture, trade, and communication coast to coast. Until 1912, when Arizona and New Mexico became the last continental states, anyone who didn't like the rules and regulations could always go west and settle new lands. Overall, American history is a record of recurring race and class conflicts surmounted by an increase in the standard of living for the subordinate majority of workers and farmers.

Material advances were nonetheless always partial and contradictory. Blacks never received their "40 acres and a mule," but during the post-Civil-War Reconstruction, they could raise families, own property and businesses, and (for a short while) exercise their political rights, including holding office. Conditions for other American workers were often brutal, as well. Land expansion benefited railroads, oil companies, and speculators, as well as individual farmers. In the 19th-century "land of opportunity," enough Americans carved out a comfortable life to politically and socially fund the Manifest Destiny of the dominant classes' rise to power. Likewise, women won the right to vote but remained largely outside the decision-making processes of government and civil society.

Herbert Hoover didn't put a chicken in every pot and Henry Ford didn't put a car in every garage in the early 1900s, but given the rising standard of living, most Americans thought it was possible. It wasn't until the crash of 1929 that the material conditions necessary for America's popular consensus were momentarily displaced. By the late 1930s, the international economic collapse had ushered in major social and political conflict in the United States and elsewhere. Only World War II stopped the hemorrhage. By the end of the war, the United States was the undisputed world economic leader. Two decades of North American prosperity followed. Millions of Americans had secure jobs with rising incomes. Many owned their own homes and had increased leisure time. Life was getting better. U.S. workers were the most well-off subordinate group in the world: For at least two centuries, the U.S. capitalist class has had the material resources necessary for purchasing support for its hegemony at home.

Equally important, dominant social forces have been able to organize the political conditions necessary for continued dominance. The Civil War resolved the most serious challenge to capitalist hegemony by militarily crushing the semifeudal plantation system of the South. Yet the social revolution was stunted. Once capitalist economic relations were in place, the scaffolding of reconstruction was dismantled. African Americans were cast aside by the federal government, and a power-sharing deal was struck with southern landowners. The post-Civil War Industrial Revolution led to "a dangerously uneven distribution of new wealth [that] provoked ugly resentment among the farmers" (Oliver & White, 1966, p. 207). In the South and Midwest, workers and farmers organized against the economic power of banks, railroads, and financial institutions. In 1896, the populist Democratic candidate for president, William Jennings Bryan, thundered his anti-big-business "Cross of Gold" speech to millions of people but lost to a heavily financed Republican campaign. Afterward, America's rulers inserted populist concerns into dominant ideology—a process repeated by Democratic and Republican politicians as recently as the 1996 national elections.

In 1904, Theodore Roosevelt appropriated much of the platform of Bryan and the populists, campaigning as a so-called trust buster who would regulate big business, conserve natural resources, and establish social justice (Oliver & White, 1966, p. 218). Throughout the 20th century, leading political organizations and government agencies have responded to challenges in a similarly successful manner: FDR's New Deal politically undercut both radical and fascist challenges to the so-called liberal capitalist system; in the late 1960s, the Democratic Party recruited blacks from the civil rights movement into established decision-making structures; Lyndon B. Johnson organized the Great Society by diverting underclass political protest into federal social welfare programs; Richard Nixon gave 18-year-olds the vote at the height of the anti-Vietnam War movement; and up until the past few years, colleges and universities opened the doors to opportunity for a number of minority and women students. In opposition to these hegemonic political campaigns, movements of labor, African Americans, and women never developed political programs with leaderships capable of forging alternative historic blocs.

All opposition that strayed beyond the borders of the status quo has been met with orchestrated coercion, that hegemonically necessary antidote for consent withheld. Federal agents persecuted radical labor militants with the (U.S. Attorney General) Palmer raids after World War I. McCarthy led the witch-hunt against labor unions, schools, and the entertainment industry after World War II. The FBI's COINTELPRO (counterintelligence program) organized systematic disruption against blacks, students, and socialists during the Vietnam War years; similar "red squads" still exist in major U.S. cities. Through the years, such systematic coercion against political resistance has been possible because challengers have been unable to break the widespread subordinate consent for dominant social relations and ideologies.

Existing socioeconomic relations and leading ideologies for capitalist hegemony have been complemented by cultural practices, increasingly disseminated through the media. During the turn of the century, Gay Nineties book and magazine publishers promoted middle-class ethics and etiquette, and concerts, lectures, and fairs sponsored by a growing urban elite publicly demonstrated the personal freedoms and pleasures offered by market capitalism (Kasson, 1990). The post-World War I economic upturn was expressed in the fashion, music, and lifestyles of the Roaring Twenties. As material conditions worsened in the 1930s, a growing mass media psychologically cushioned the worst of the economic depression: Fred Astaire romanced Ginger Rogers, "Battling" Joe Louis floored all opponents, and popular singer Ethel Merman assured radio listeners that "Life Is Just a Bowl of Cherries." The Second World War saved the American economy and influenced its cultural practices: Hollywood and the music industry happily turned out patriotic films and songs (Steele, 1985). Fred Astaire danced some more, Bing Crosby crooned, and Danny Kaye made funny faces. Today, popular music and cinema remain important social mediators, and television has become a major cultural back-drop for material and political conditions in the United States.

The foregoing narrative tells only part of the story. Although media practices are a primary site for the production of meaning and reinforce other cultural practices, they are not the only instances of cultural practice. Countercultural social movements (such as populist, labor, civil rights, antiwar, women's, Chicano, and gay and lesbian movements) have frequently challenged dominant cultural practices, but in most cases, existing institutions have turned challenges back into existing social structures. The telescoped version of American capitalist hegemony offered here is widened when we turn to examples of race, gender, and class in the next chapters.

## Hegemonic Apparatuses

The resilient durability of capitalist cultural hegemony in the United States illustrates that successful ruling classes make significant adjustments materially, politically, and culturally to maintain their leadership. Such adjustments have limits, however. The capitalist class cannot transform itself at will like Margaret Wise Brown's (1972) mother bunny does. Consensus cannot withstand chronic, severe material shortages. Nor will dominant classes simply relinquish power if they lose mass support. Serious challenges are always met with coercion even as modifications to hegemony are undertaken.

As the U.S. experience illustrates, to preempt or diffuse challenges, historic blocs work to reproduce social formations and practices that promote dominant-class leadership. Over the long term, hegemony tends to organizationally crystallize into supporting institutions. Practices create relations that constitute structures that legitimate dominant practices as the norm. Gramsci (1967, 1947/1971, 1988) called structures that organize such consent *hegemonic apparatuses*.

Gramsci highlighted the intimate connections between government and civil society that together characterized the modern capitalist state. He recognized that dominant social forces lead the government because their hegemony permeates civil society. Gramsci frequently referred to the state as "hegemony armed with coercion"—civil society protected by government force. In this sense, the state is not the same as the government because modern ruling classes (capitalists in Western Europe and workers in 1917 Russia) govern hegemonically through institutionally organized consent rather than government-enforced directives. Capitalist classes in the United States and Europe have led society by negotiating and collaborating with all other social groups through what Louis Althusser (1969) calls ideological state apparatuses (ISAs), such as schools, churches, the media, corporations, and so forth. According to Althusser, challenges to capitalist leadership that cannot be resolved in civil society are dealt with coercively by repressive state apparatuses, such as the police, courts, prisons, and so forth. The modern state comprises government politics *and* civil society, hegemonically encompassing all the theoretical, ideological, and practical activities of social organization and consent. However, if the dominant-class leadership loses the willing consent of subordinate groups, hegemony loses its legitimacy, and dominant powers resort to government enforcement.

Gramsci's discovery of hegemonic apparatuses reinforced his belief that ideas are embodied and theory unites with practice. Leadership in practice is inseparable from leadership in thought; hegemony and ideology are united like bricks and mortar. Hegemonic apparatuses build consent by establishing accepted practices through sheer repetition ("this is the way we do things here"), then legitimizing them as valuable and natural ("this must be the best way to do things").

Hegemonic apparatuses appear throughout society in political, cultural, educational, informational, religious, and other arenas of human activity. As fortifications of the ruling classes, hegemonic apparatuses have their roots in many indirect political functions that share a common national vision. Hegemonic apparatuses are actual organizations with decision-making powers designed to maintain, defend, and develop the theoretical and ideological fronts of hegemony. For example, participants in hegemonic apparatuses as diverse as *USA Today* (mass media), parish catechism classes (religion), MTV (entertainment), Democratic Party local campaign committees (elections), and Stanford University (education) generally share a common cultural language based on predominant social practices.

A pedagogy promoting market relations and two-party politics regularly occurs in public and private schools. Prep schools, vocational schools, community colleges, and universities are all neatly arranged to socially re-create and ideologically defend the various social, cultural, and productive needs of the existing capitalist hegemony. Universities have boards of trustees, mission statements, textbooks, curriculum, faculty councils, and professional and institutional practices. Like other hegemonic arrangements, individuals and groups support these structures and practices because of the rewards: employment, prestige, security.

Any doubts about the social function of such apparatuses disappear as soon as we observe how they function whenever hegemony ruptures because once social antagonisms invade a hegemonic apparatus, the apparatus is no longer useful to the dominant social group. Illusions about the independent status of the particular practice fade quickly. Consider how easily the U.S. State Department disregards or discounts the hegemonic apparatus of elections whenever the preferred candidate loses, as happened in Guatemala in 1954, the Dominican Republic in 1965, Chile in 1970, Nicaragua in 1984, or Haiti in 1991. Observe how easily the Catholic hierarchy dismisses the hegemonic apparatus of a local parish whenever the preferred interpretation of the Gospel gives way to liberation theology as happened with Camilo Torres in Peru, Ernesto Cardenal in Nicaragua, and Father Aristide in Haiti. Study how quickly the hegemonic apparatus of journalism discards its defining professional practices of "objectivity" and "impartiality" when they no longer efficiently promote the interests of dominant social forces, as happened in Chile in 1970 to 1973, in El Salvador for the last two decades of the 20th century, or in the United States during the invasions of Grenada, Panama, and Iraq. The United

States stopped contributing to the international hegemonic apparatuses of UNESCO (United Nations Educational, Scientific, and Cultural Organization) and UNICEF (now, United Nations Children's Fund) when the organizations stopped promoting U.S.-sponsored "free market" solutions. During the Chicago school crisis of 1993, the federal judge undermined the hegemonic apparatus of law as he repeatedly forced teachers to work and schools to open in direct violation of the state constitution. In general, whenever schools, arts foundations, charitable organizations, religious institutions, electoral processes, courts, laws, or other hegemonic apparatuses fail to reinforce or re-create desired practices and ideologies, the apparatuses are abandoned by dominant social groups.

Hegemonic apparatuses function only to the extent that ideologies "fit" hegemonic relationships. If the ideological cement crumbles, the apparatus breaks down. For example, the institution of marriage loses some of its social efficacy as women reject romantic constructions of courtship and marriage, challenge patriarchal constructions of gender roles, and issue demands for equal rights and opportunities. Universities have failed to indoctrinate the young if they become sites for organizing opposition to the existing order, as happened in France and Mexico in 1968, the United States in 1970, and throughout Latin America in the late 1970s. In each of these cases, authorities responded by closing the schools, weeding out faculty and students with unacceptable ideologies and political affiliations, and reorganizing student codes, campus security, and even the physical environment. Following student protests in California in the 1960s and 1970s, the new University of California at Santa Cruz was geographically engineered to be "protest proof" — buildings, departments, and open spaces were deliberately dispersed, leaving no campus center that could serve as a public gathering place for students and faculty.

Sometimes, rather than supporting it, an ideology weighs down a deteriorating social structure. For example, when the civil rights movement rejected the ideology of "separate, but equal," the political hegemony of the dominant power structure was threatened. A new ideology of "integration" was poured into the social cracks opened by antiracist demands. Suddenly, remodeled hegemonic apparatuses in education, politics, and the law followed and promoted a new ideology for race relations in the United States.

Ideologies, new or old, are promoted by public opinion leaders and intellectuals recruited by functioning hegemonic apparatuses. These spokespeople organize and articulate popular consent for practices in education, politics, culture, and other social spheres. Complementary apparatuses produce editorial opinions, high school textbooks, television comedies, and political party campaign materials that popularize support for American hegemony. As Walter Lippmann (1922) advocated in *Public Opinion* and Gramsci (1967) recognized in *The Modern Prince*, the task of intellectuals is to indoctrinate and socialize mass society according to a given class perspective.

Hegemonic apparatuses permit a variety of practices and ideologies. Indeed, the need to incorporate subordinate interests requires that hegemonic apparatuses have a certain openness and flexibility. Rather than positing a monolithic ruling class running a nation with a singular ideology, Gramsci (1967, 1947/1971, 1988) noted that hegemony can be (and often is) achieved by part of a class or social grouping. Thus, in the United States, political hegemonic apparatuses have recognizable, albeit secondary, differences depending on which politician or party controls the apparatus. Likewise, dominant ideology must be seen as plural. Within certain limits, different sections within a historic bloc or social group compete for their own ideologies. For example, debates between the "hawks" and the "doves" over the Vietnam War or U.S. aid to the Contras in Nicaragua reflected serious differences but shared a belief in the right of U.S. intervention.

In the contemporary world, historic blocs subsidize acceptable paradigms through the mass media. The media compose the primary site for promoting the theoretical and political domination of the leading social force. Fewer than two dozen corporations largely determine what passes for news, information, and public knowledge in the United States (Herman & Chomsky, 1988). In academia, a handful of journals directed by disciplinary associations mediate what passes for scholarship in the humanities, science, and politics. These apparatuses effectively control who will be spokespeople, what they will speak about, and how it will be spoken. These apparatuses essentially license the "names" that mainstream society uses for practices, events, and relations.

Gaye Tuchman (1978), Robert Manoff and Michael Schudson (1986), Lance Bennett (1988), and others have argued that by relying on the norms of objectivity, expert sources, and political pluralism, journalism reinforces hegemonic apparatuses in media and politics while marginalizing alternative presentations of knowledge and experience. Mark Hertsgaard (1992) has explained how rewards and punishments within the profession secure consent for traditional practices within hegemonic media apparatuses. The media thus confidently informed us that Ross Perot was the "leading opponent" of the North American Free Trade Agreement and that Jesse Jackson speaks for black America. Likewise, most academic journals regulate distribution of knowledge according to predominant paradigms promoted by established and respected scholars. A similar symmetry appears between standard practices, political perspectives, and theoretical justifications in education, law, religion, entertainment, commerce, and other fields.

Hegemonic apparatuses do not prevent challenges to hegemony, but they do provide an important mechanism for stemming those challenges. To avoid a collapse of hegemony, which would mean resorting to coercion to maintain power, dominant social groups often preempt demands by subordinate groups into hegemonic programs, avoiding serious conflict that might threaten those relations. Gramsci called this activity *passive revolution*. Hegemonic institutions initiate passive revolution to head off challenges before subordinate groups can politically organize.

Hegemonic apparatuses institutionalize communication, socialization, and power. For consenting individuals and groups, the apparatuses constitute efficient sites for resource allocation, ideological training, social interaction, group identification, and individual reward. When operating efficiently, hegemonic apparatuses predetermine acceptable norms and behaviors, defuse challenges, divert criticism, and disorganize opposition. On the other hand, to individuals and groups contesting the hegemonic order, hegemonic apparatuses constitute undesirable sites for dispute resolution.

## Dominant Leadership

In any social, political, or cultural endeavor, a leadership has two tasks. First, it must isolate and eliminate its enemies. Second, it must identify the interests and meet the requirements of its actual and potential allies. As a form of rule, hegemony effectively meets these two tasks. Hegemony in any field—religion, politics, philosophy, education—simultaneously widens the social base of support for the dominant leadership and narrows the social base available for any counterhegemony. To the extent that it can secure consent from other social forces, the leadership of any historic bloc builds hegemony. The leading group in any hegemony wins the battle over communication, including the power to make decisions, give meaning to social practices, and define the world.

Will dominant control contain challenges through moderate reform, or will political agitation and organization lead to social change? This ultimately is the question that attracts so many social theorists to Gramsci's (1967, 1947/1971, 1988) conception of hegemony. Gramsci takes great care to explain that any hegemony depends on social forces contending for leadership, their political programs, their organizational capabilities, and the effectiveness of their persuasive appeals to the population as a whole. Hegemony is always filled with contradictions as it recognizes and empowers subordinate group interests even as dominant forces become more sophisticated and flexible in maintaining their leadership, as long as they have sufficient resources available for bargaining. In short, the outcome of any hegemony always depends on the concrete relationships between material, political, and cultural conditions. In this mix, hegemony will be stronger or weaker depending on the leadership capabilities expressed in each sphere. Hegemony is never completely secured.

Hegemony allows us to see the construction of social relations as something other than direct domination or manipulation. We can recognize and investigate the benefits that subordinate groups realize when they consent to their second-class status. We can then analyze the political and cultural strategies used by dominant forces to preserve their power and meet the perceived needs of the mass of the population. Hegemony provides a worthwhile approach to understanding the construction of knowledge, social relations, cultural practices, and group identity. Analyzing hegemonic relationships reveals points of weakness and strength, suggesting possible sites of contention where a counterhegemony may be forged. Gramsci's conception of hegemony not only helps explain how and why capitalist society survives despite chronic social contradictions, it offers insight into the potential for future social conflict and change.

## Rethinking Continuity and Change

Gramsci was not alone in his search for theoretical and practical explanations for the staying power of capitalism. Mass unemployment, the rise of fascism, and World War II undercut confidence in capitalism, and the failure of working-class movements to resolve such historic catastrophes demoralized many intellectuals. Those active in organizing social movements—Gramsci, Karl Korsch, Georg Lukács, Rosa Luxemburg—maintained that an organized political leadership could lead society forward. Perhaps the most ambitious, practical response to the "agony of capitalism" was completed by Leon Trotsky, a central leader of the Russian Revolution. Trotsky (1938/1974) developed a cohesive "transitional program" for socialism, with immediate, democratic, and transitional demands that subordinate classes could raise to resolve existing objective social and cultural conditions. Others more removed from political activity turned their attention to communication and culture as a *substitute* for economic and political analysis.

Max Horkheimer (1972), Theodor Adorno (1945), and others gathered around the Frankfurt School set aside the material determinants of historic change to concentrate on the study of alienation, ideology, and human action. Buffeted by working-class defeats in Europe and divorced from actual social struggle, these

"Western" Marxists rejected claims about the socioeconomic basis of individual consciousness, class ideology, and national cultures as simplistic and reductive. Preoccupied with ideological domination, they admitted little possibility for change based on organized social movements, exaggerating the ability of the status quo to withstand opposition (Marcuse, 1964). Others overstated the potential for subordinate mass action to overcome objective social conditions.

## The Consciousness of Lukács

Intellectuals connected with working-class movements in Europe were more optimistic about the possibilities for social progress. German political theorist and activist Karl Korsch, for example, rejected the mechanically deterministic interpretations of Marxism and stressed the potential for social change through collective political action. As an activist in the workers' council movement in the 1920s, Korsch viewed classical versions of Marxism as out of touch with the immediate realities of working people. He held that human willpower could overcome objective social conditions. Georg Lukács (1923/1971), humanist philosopher and social critic, reached similar conclusions.

As Minister of Education and Culture, Lukács participated in the workers' government in Hungary in 1919. He witnessed the revolution in mass political consciousness and public opinion, observing the energy and enthusiasm of the Hungarian people as their political power led to new behaviors. The Hungarian revolution demonstrated to Lukács how ideas could transform society when led by a decisive social force, such as the labor movement.

In *History and Class Consciousness*, Lukács (1923/1971) presented his theoretical conclusions in what has become a classic text for Western Marxism. Lukács resurrected the dialectic in opposition to rigid determinism. In highlighting the dialectic—how things develop in response to internal and external contradictions—Lukács focused on the human potential for initiating conscious social change. Lukács (as quoted in Novack, 1978) saw that "active, working, thinking, struggling human beings were not only the products but the producers" of social progress (p. 119). Lukács emphasized the ideological consequences of commodity production, arguing that modern capitalism maintains social order and obstructs social change through cultural practices that distort human relationships and ideologies that disguise actual social conditions. Lukács arrived at this conclusion while theorizing popular consciousness in capitalist society.

In Lukács's terms, modern capitalism reifies human relations, presenting them as relations between objects. Society becomes a collection of things bound together by their connection to the market rather than relationships between humans. The relationship between those who produce wealth and those who own and control wealth is characterized in terms of expendable income or material possession. Social power and domination (called "success" in the United States) are reified in what money can buy. Given capitalist society's fetish for commodity production, it reduces all relationships to questions of the marketplace and alienates people from one another. Although we may need adequate health care, quality education, and affordable public transportation, the market frequently determines that some communities can't afford them. The so-called law of the market takes on an independence and power that individuals increasingly lose (Feenberg, 1981). Lukács (1923/1971) observed that people are objectified as workers to be purchased, humans are estranged from each other in the exchange process, and impersonal institutions govern all human activities independent of any apparent human control.

However, Lukács (1923/1971) viewed this situation dialectically: Social conditions change if people act. He believed that awareness and reflection are politically transformative: To know one's self is to transform reality. Capitalism reduces humans to commodities, but being human, these particular commodities have a capacity for self-reflection. We may passively know the world from the vantage point of our social position, but such awareness is dynamic because thought is both cognitive and creative. Thought is how we understand the world *and* how we change it. To recognize our objective condition as human "commodities" is to rise above it. Lukács believed that as workers and other subordinate groups became aware of their condition reality would be suddenly transformed and social change ushered in. Political self-awareness of subordinate classes could even overcome objective social conditions because social transformation begins at the moment subordinate classes become conscious of their plight. Armed with this insight, and witnessing its partial demonstration by Hungarian workers, Lukács optimistically anticipated large-scale social change.

Lukács overestimated the power of popular self-reflection, however. He grossly discounted structural constraints and other historically concrete conditions, such as resources, social power, political alliances, and even organizational expertise. He effectively disembodied consciousness from concrete human activity (Eagleton, 1991, p. 104). Ideas floated freely, without regard to social relationships. Consequently, Lukács left little room for the possibility that subordinate classes might possess multiple, contradictory consciousnesses. The short-lived Hungarian Commune may have warranted enthusiasm for the transformative power of collective self-awareness, but defeated and demoralized, the working classes in Germany and Italy tacitly signed on to a project of social conservatism. In resurrecting the dialectic of Marxism, Lukács abandoned materialism: Social consciousness is related to social being, and that being always exists within contradictory yet concrete circumstances.

Lukács (1923/1971) failed to note the contradictory nature of class consciousness because he did not recognize the contradictory nature of history. He found no real distinction between scientific advances that benefit humanity and social degradations, such as poverty and inequality. He considered everything associated with capitalism to be reified, artificial. Lukács's approach posed a real dilemma: How could subordinate groups become politically aware if they were overwhelmed by cultural practices that retarded and obstructed social awareness? Ultimately, Lukács relied on faith, believing that workers would spontaneously overcome the influence of capitalism and establish their own culture.

Lukács shared with Gramsci the understanding that in modern societies, dominant classes maintain power primarily through consent. Although they never communicated with each other, Lukács and Gramsci agreed on the importance of knowledge, ideology, morality, and cultural norms in propping up capitalist society. Lukács's concept of reification helps explain how consensus is constructed in consumer society. Unlike hegemony, however, the concept of reification ignores the material basis for social consensus and control. Lukács placed all his hope in subordinate classes coming to self-consciousness under radical political leadership, ready for social change. He overlooked the capability of dominant groups to renegotiate a consensus by incorporating some of the interests of the subordinate.

Contemporary investigations of popular culture by Stuart Ewen (1989), Sut Jhally (Jhally & Lewis, 1992), and others, verify many of Lukács's (1923/1971) insights: the centrality of human action in constructing social relations, the ideological effects of the commodification of popular culture, the social basis for class consciousness, and the objective possibilities for social change. Recognizing how dominant ideology reifies human relationships as relations between things helps us understand how cultural practices produce and reproduce a hegemonic social order. As a leading intellectual of his day, Lukács also had considerable influence on his contemporaries, particularly the critical theorists of the Frankfurt School in Germany.

## The Frankfurt School
## and Critical Theory

At the height of the Hungarian revolution in 1918, Lukács was optimistic about the possibilities for social change. The subsequent setbacks in Hungary, Germany, and Italy, however, affected both the enthusiasm and analysis of other social theorists. Intellectuals were confounded by how subordinate classes (so recently independent and militant) were apparently hypnotized by the culture industry. A leading center of investigation into the profound changes sweeping Europe was the Institute for Social Research in Frankfurt, Germany. Founded in 1923, the institute brought together Marxist thinkers who were concerned with the role of ideology, culture, and radical social change. At its inception, the Frankfurt School identified strongly with socialist and working-class movements in Germany. Later, when Hitler came to power in 1933, the school closed and moved to New York where it was connected with Columbia University. By the time it reopened in Germany in 1950, the institute had effectively distanced itself from popular social movements.

The critical theorists of the Frankfurt School—Theodor Adorno, Leo Lowenthal, Herbert Marcuse, and Max Horkheimer—were primarily concerned with how ideology distorted people's perceptions of reality. Borrowing heavily from Lukács's (1923/1971) conception of reification, the Frankfurt School theorists argued that social relationships and social interests were concealed by belief systems that disguised domination and power.

Horkheimer (1972) challenged empiricism's claim that knowledge is based on objectively discovered facts, arguing that it is historically and socially created by humans. This social constructionist approach recognized that ideology often passes as knowledge under the guise of rational argument and scientific proof. According to Horkheimer, traditional theory begins with descriptions, moves on to comparisons, and ends with theoretical concepts. Critical theory, however, seeks to penetrate the unfeeling world of things to show the underlying relations between persons. Traditional theory describes the world; critical theory questions and ultimately seeks to reconstruct the world. For Horkheimer, critical theory could disrupt the ideological domination of traditional thought and become a force "to stimulate change" if it interacts with the interests and practices of subordinate classes (p. 215).

Here, Horkheimer foreshadowed Gramsci's vision of a counter-hegemonic historic bloc. Unlike Gramsci, however, Horkheimer never came up with practical suggestions for applying critical theory. The unimpeded rise of Hitler in Germany demoralized Horkheimer and radically curtailed his political activity. Later, as a

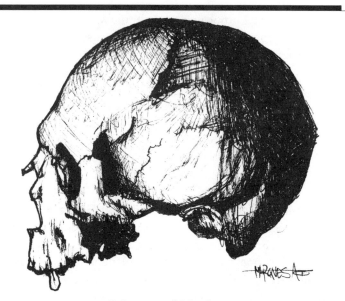

### Science and Ideology

In *The Mismeasure of Man*, Stephen Jay Gould (1981) documents how idology influences science. Polygenists who measured skull size and brain weight in the 19th century were not liars or frauds, but their data was subjecgt to cultural bias. Harvard anthropologist Paul Broca, for example, was unsurpassed in "meticulous care and accuracy of measurement" (p. 74). But his facts were "gathered selectively" and "manipulated unconsciously" according to "the shared assumptions of the most successful white males during his time—themselves on top by the good fortune of nature, and women, blacks, and poor people below" (p. 85).

Modern "scientific" claims about race-based IQ (Jensen, 1972; Hernnstein & Murray, 1994) also justify racist social policy. Science does not always blatantly serve cultural norms or biased social policies; its advances have greatly improved the human condition. Yet, because it is done by people, science always works within existing culture and its ideology.

refugee in the United States, his pessimism was reinforced by the complacency and conservatism of American workers. Although Horkheimer's critique omitted the possibility for resistance, it did encourage investigations of institutions of indoctrination.

With Theodor Adorno, Horkheimer provided an early analysis of the "culture industry." According to Horkheimer and Adorno (1975), popular music, art, movies, advertising, and other mass media provide the social cement for the status quo. The media manufacture and then serve consumer needs according to dominant social relations. They would delight in the commercial for Canon cameras that proclaims "style is everything." They would add, however, that the culture industry has perverted style so much that the substance of mass culture is nothing more than "obedience to the social hierarchy" (p. 131). For Adorno and Horkheimer, mass culture, even with its supposed fascination with the "new," consists of little more than thematic repetition and standardization of production. An evening spent watching network television confirms their critique. Despite variations of gloss and glitter, the soap operas, prime-time dramas, made-for-TV movies, and nightly sitcoms follow standardized formats, with little or no deviation. Television producers generally respond to such criticism by claiming that they are simply responding to what the public wants. Horkheimer and Adorno scoffed at such a defense, contending that the power of the latest popular music, fashion, or art "resides in its identification with a manufactured need" (p. 137). The public wants what the media promotes as desirable.

Furthermore, the media seldom deliver what they promote, perpetually cheating their audience from what they perpetually promise: enjoyment and fulfillment. Actual satisfaction is rarely fulfilled. Rather, anticipation of satisfaction becomes the commodity. Horkheimer and Adorno argue that mass culture has been reduced to a vehicle for selling cultural products. Rather than an opportunity for reflection and thought, culture has been reduced to little more than mass-produced, mind-numbing amusement (Hork- heimer & Adorno, 1975, p. 47).

The seduction of contemporary culture and its undermining of critical reflection also fascinated Herbert Marcuse (1964), who attempted to theorize alienation and society. Because he did not return to Germany after World War II, Marcuse is perhaps the best-known member of the Frankfurt School in the United States. His scathing attack on alienation and modern society in *One-Dimensional Man* (1964) attracted a big following among college students who were disaffected with traditional social theory. Marcuse was particularly concerned with individual emancipation and gratification and less concerned with collective action.

Marcuse believed that magazines, movies, television shows, and other popular cultural practices were happily embraced by the subordinate classes in Western capitalist countries because they had become docile and placated by consumer society. Cheap commodities and consumer goods—all the "stuff" available to the average person—promoted a consciousness that was immune to criticism. Capitalism must be working because so many people had so many things. According to Marcuse, Western society had become so orchestrated by dominant forces that capitalism had given birth to "one-dimensional" thought. All communication, all criticism, all practices were now within the bounds of relationships that reinforced the dominant structure and the status quo. Marcuse was convinced that modern capitalism was firmly entrenched.

His critique of society noted the interrelationship between politics and economics. The monopolization of industry influenced the state; the state worked for monopoly capitalism. Bureaucratization was necessary for the maintenance of the social order and its relations of production. Marcuse (1964) concluded that social life had become dependent on authoritarian institutions. Masses of people were organized for consumption, atomized and isolated as individual consumers. Even domination had become impersonal and anonymous. The social structure had become reified: Institutions and objects had replaced people; things had replaced relations. Humans were removed from decision-making choices, and social relations disappeared into market relations as the whole culture became increasingly impersonal.

Although he used different terms, Marcuse was describing the perfect hegemonic society. As it turns out, his description of a popularly supported bureaucratic society was shortsighted. His critique could have benefited from a deeper appreciation of hegemony, which helps identify antagonistic social forces and anticipates social change.

## The Structure of Society

In addition to those espousing Marxism and its various strands, other social theorists looked at the role of culture in society. Structuralist theories in anthropology and semiotics (the study of signs) identified cultural practices as key to socialization. Anthropologist Emile Durkheim (1916/1995) cast knowledge and religion as the product of collective consciousness. For Durkheim, knowledge was not rational nor empirical but constituted through systems of thought that arbitrarily divide the world into the sacred and profane. Society uses these systems of thought to construct and control individuals. In his model of religious formations, Durkheim insisted that each system is unchanging, discrete, and arbitrary and that individual intent is of secondary importance. Linguist Ferdinand Saussure (1916/1986) made similar structural claims about language, separating *langue* (the language system that remains static) from *parole* (individual speech that may vary in language use). Knowledge formed individuals for Durkheim; language surrounded individuals for Saussure. In either case, human intention or action was secondary to the structure. For Durkheim, society's sacred things are arbitrarily forbidden; for Saussure, the linguistic sign is arbitrary. Language, like knowledge and religion, is simply a matter of social convention. To Durkheim and Saussure, cultural practices provide systems of meaning wielding power over society because how we define, understand, and speak about our world will determine how we act in it.

Although Durkheim left room for evolution, other structuralists discarded the possibility for historic change by viewing the "system" as static. Saussure was insistent that changes never affect the

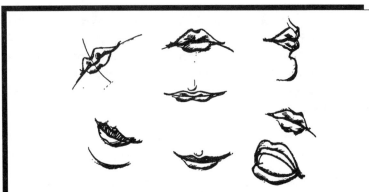

### Women Want to Look Luscious

In an interview for Bill Moyers's public television series, *The Public Mind*, the editor of *Self Magazine* explained that her attention to full-lipped models and articles on lip implants simply reflected "women's need to be more luscious." Her claim implied a spontaneous, natural yearning by masses of women to have thick lips, as well as an unexplained willingness to do almost anything to make that happen. Naomi Wolf (1991) offered another explanation in *The Beauty Myth:* The beauty industry, ranging from cosmetics and fashion to the diet and surgery business, has stepped up efforts to convince people that women have no natural beauty and must therefore spend (collectively) millions of dollars to be attractive. Throughout history and across cultures, the standards of beauty for females and males have varied widely. The central question is, Who gets to say what is beautiful and what is not—and what social purpose do those definitions serve?

larger system. Preoccupied with formal models and abstractions, structuralists seldom considered actual social relations. If static categories determine how the world functions, then human intention and action are of little consequence. Individual human subjects are thus "decentered" from society because social structures organize and control all human behavior. Following Durkheim and Saussure, structuralism was influential throughout Europe.

In anthropology, the leading structuralist was Claude Levi-Strauss (1958/1963), who wedded structural linguistics to anthropology in positing all social life to be the product of an innate language-like collective consciousness. Levi-Strauss's influence in anthropology and sociology has led researchers to investigate culture as if it were language and communication as if it were all of culture.

Roland Barthes (1972, 1977) used the semiotic study of signs to study society. A sign is simply a thing—object, word, or picture—that has a particular meaning to a person or group of people. Barthes (1972) explained that contemporary myths, from sports to advertising, support the status quo by "naturalizing" what is socially and historically constructed (p. 42). Barthes's work details how fashion, food, furniture, media, and other instances of popular culture legitimize existing social relations. Like other structuralists, neither Levi-Strauss (1958/1963) nor Barthes (1972, 1977) were particularly concerned with how society changes. However, because they were interested in explaining how subordinate groups are socialized to dominant interest, their work offers a method for "reading" social negotiations that occur in any hegemony.

## Althusser and the
## Structure of Ideology

Another structuralist concerned with representation and the creation of images was French philosopher Louis Althusser (1969). Althusser sought to express hegemony in structural terms. His attempt ultimately fell short, however, because he reduced hegemony to ideological structures that mold humans into predetermined social roles.

From Althusser's (1969) perspective, ideological practice is neither deception nor illusion. Rather, ideology has an objective social function: It provides a representational system for the way we live our life. Ideology defines the beliefs, values, and desires of individuals and groups in society. We live from our position in society, wearing the images, myths, and representations appropriate to our social role. Ideological practices provide us with explanations for what we are and what we do as mother, worker, Christian, student, or other preinscribed role. As subjects, we do not choose our identities nor are we manipulated into our social position. Rather, according to Althusser, we are "hailed" to identities that fit the roles that we have already assumed as members of a given social structure.

Life is too complex to be readily understood in our everyday consciousness, and we need some coherent explanation of how the world works. Shorthand representations are easier to understand than actual relationships. Ideology functions to maintain social order by promoting certain norms of behavior, encouraging certain social relations between groups, and justifying the conditions of life.

Ideology provides imaginary representations of real conditions. Cultural differences exist. Women exist. Workers exist. Humans have different pigmentation. The question is, what does it *mean* to be a woman or a worker? What difference does it make to have a particular skin color? Ideology delivers meaning through systems of representation: Gender roles are constructed in children's toys, clothing fashion, and occupational opportunity; in popular culture, workers are frequently depicted as beer-drinking, brawny, 4-wheel-driving, mentally weak couch potatoes; televised images of ethnic minorities feature welfare mothers, teenage gangs, and sports figures. Broadcast images explain the meaning of woman, worker, African American. Of course, television images must resonate with other practices in the workplace, at the mall, and on the street so that gender-coded and race-coded representations explain and justify inequality for society as a whole.

Organizing these systems of representation are ideological state apparatuses (ISAs), such as the family, church, media, and school. Althusser (1969) conceives of "repressive" state apparatuses—institutions such as police, prisons, and courts—that enforce dominant practices. Where Gramsci (1967, 1947/1971, 1988) saw civil society as a crucial site for battles among competing social groups, Althusser constructs his ISAs as static structures that compel human agents to accept their social position. For Althusser, ideology re-creates the preferred meaning of social relationships by creating humans that fill those social roles. In contrast to Gramsci, he disallows individual choice and social change.

In his reading of Marx, Althusser (1972) missed the premise that humans create their own social conditions, albeit out of conditions not of their own making. He passed over contradictions in individual social identity and the possibilities for struggle over meanings and resources. If we accepted Althusser's idealistic model, humans would be prisoners of ideology, and the structures of capitalism would predetermine the actions of all individuals. History would be an unchanging structure, humans only the product.

## Hegemony and Domination

Gramsci (1967, 1947/1971, 1988) wrote at a time of great social turmoil. Many of the shortcomings in social thought since World War II might have been avoided if Gramsci's insights were considered, but because he was imprisoned, his ideas were likewise locked out of the debates. His writings only became widely available during a renewed debate over culture and society that swept Europe and Latin America in the 1960s, but his ideas retain their vibrancy and urgency. For decades, European social thought stagnated along with working-class political activity. Like the radical social movements that surged forward throughout Latin America and Africa, many intellectuals grew impatient with class-based politics. Successful popular revolutions in Cuba, Algeria, Peru, Mozambique, and elsewhere attracted those enamored with direct action and eroded expectations that the industrial working class of advanced capitalist countries would lead. Revolutions in the semicolonial world resurrected Lukács's (1923/1971) argument that conscious human action could overcome objective conditions. In addition, social movements led by students, blacks, Chicanos, and women, along with the relative quiescence of organized labor in Western Europe and the United States, convinced some scholars that they had discovered new agents for social change. With the expansion of U.S. hegemony in mass communication, many of the precepts of the Frankfurt School about the importance of the so-called consciousness industry were revisited. History posed new questions and possibilities for scholars and activists around the world.

One institutional outcome was the crystallization of "cultural studies" in Britain, where sociologists, historians, literary critics, and communication scholars came together to investigate mass society, mass culture, and social power. Foremost among the early scholars of British cultural studies was Raymond Williams (1977), who sought to resolve the contradictions between structuralism's insistence on determination and humanism's emphasis on human choice in sociocultural practices.

Inspired by the first English translations of works by Gramsci (1967, 1947/1971) and Lukács (1923/1971), Williams (1977) adopted the concept of hegemony—which he saw as a major turning point in cultural theory—and Lukács's (1923/1971) definition of class consciousness. In his synthesis, Williams (1977) saw culture as a collection of practices and experiences that constitute a whole way of life. His definition underwrites the conception adopted by this text. Culture cannot be reduced to ideas or seen simply as specific practices; instead, culture is the sum of relationships between patterns of practices. Williams thought of such entities as art, industry, politics, education, family, entertainment, media, not as separate activities with separate meanings but as aspects of cultural relationships that can only be experienced as interlocking patterns, practices, and meanings. Each practice has its own norms of production and distribution, yet each practice re-creates similar relationships between subordinate and dominant groups. Collectively, these practices stitch together the concretes of race, gender, class, authority, and other social relations.

Williams (1977) elaborated on hegemony as a process of "the placing of limits and the exertion of pressures" (p. 110), describing hegemony *as* culture, as lived dominance. We cannot speak of hegemony *and* culture but must see consumer culture as a hegemonic way of life. To participate in culture is to live in hegemonic society. In contrast to economic and political theories that made cultural questions secondary, Williams saw culture as central to the constitution of society. Culture is a productive material force, the product of history, and the producer of consciousness.

Practices essential to relationships between dominant and subordinate groups and systems of meaning that explain the world are dialectically interrelated. Practices have meaning and value for our lives, whereas meanings and values influence what practices we prefer. Farm families, for example, necessarily value their relationship to the land, weather, crops, animals, tools, and work practices essential to their way of life. These connections raise up values and meanings for their daily lives. Because they value nature, production, and predictability, direct and instrumental practices have great meaning. Agricultural relations carry a particular worldview that describes and prescribes certain hegemonic practices. Suburban families, on the other hand, value freeways, train schedules, packaged goods, personal leisure, and distance from the rigors and realities of physical labor. Cleanliness, politeness, convenience, and order might be valued as a consequence. Other relations likewise suggest different practices and values.

Of course, the practices and values of any hegemony depend on what challenges and trends are accepted and which are excluded. Here, Williams (1977) made an important addition to hegemony. He argued that because hegemonic relations are always in flux, new cultural practices are frequently emerging while residual practices from earlier negotiations live on. *Emergent* cultural practices arise from the contradictions in the present order, whereas *residual* practices reflect prior and existing consensual agreements. For example, the Nike shoe commercial used the residual pull of "Revolution"—a Beatles' song of social commentary popular in the 1970s—as a theme song for personal growth and self-improvement. For Williams, all hegemonic systems are an amalgam of emergent and residual practices and their adherent value systems.

Williams (1977) further notes that emergent and residual cultural practices may be dominant, alternative, or oppositional. Emergent practices arise from contradictions between the values and interests of different social groups. Habitually and normally done, *dominant* practices tend to reinforce the status quo. We are all socialized into normative behavior by doing what has always been done, following tradition, common sense, and the accepted way of doing things. It just seems natural to do things the way they've been done before. However, different communities may have different traditions or experiences. Thus, an emergent practice often stands as an *alternative* to dominant practices, as subordinate groups practice behaviors or actions that better fit their social condition or reflect their interests. Most immigrant groups to the United States have maintained some social practices specific to their heritage as an alternative to American mass culture. These practices have not directly questioned dominant-subordinate relations and have been tolerated as alternative practices by the hegemonic powers.

Occasionally, emergent practices become *oppositional* by challenging accepted dominant-subordinate relations. At the height of the civil rights movement, for example, activists made several attempts at forming black political parties, such as the Lowndes County Freedom Now Party in Mississippi. Independent black political action in Cleveland, Oakland, and throughout the South threatened to disrupt electoral practices dominated by the Democrat-Republican two-party system. The trend to political independence directly challenged dominant-subordinate relations and thus appeared as oppositional.

Emergent oppositional or alternative practices pose challenges because they overtly or implicitly suggest different social relations. Elite groups occasionally champion alternative practices or incorporate modified oppositional practices into the dominant patterns of practices, as long as those practices do not threaten the kernel of their economic control, as Gramsci (1967, 1947/1971, 1988) said.

Williams (1977) stressed that the success of hegemony depends on whether existing institutions can accommodate emergent alternative practices and how well oppositional practices are rendered politically impotent or inconsequential—a point frequently missed by some (Cloud, 1996). Knowing how society works is in part a question of finding where the ordinarily silenced find expression. In the case of the United States, we might ask, Where are the voices of race, gender, and class heard? Mass culture appears to have representatives of each, but dominant mass culture is not produced by the majority; rather, it is produced *for* the majority, with themes that are appropriated from their many alternative and oppositional practices.

Here, communication is crucial, media paramount. Mass society is too large, complex, and active to be known through direct experience: Knowledge is literally mediated. Media don't just reflect society; they also help define it. Hegemony is conditioned by the ability of media institutions to represent popular subordinate interests. Under capitalism, voices that represent diverse groups are not included in the meaning making. Television, the dominant means for public representations of knowledge in the United States, is the medium of millions, yet production is the province of a few networks and a handful of programmers. Dominant voices in media productions include few and exclude many. Televised representations of cultural practices thus consist mostly of frames and images promoted by a handful of agents authorized by hegemonic institutions. The spokesmodels (Peter Jennings, Bill Clinton, Clarence Thomas, even Jay Leno), chosen for their service to dominant interests, appear as representative of the whole hegemonic society and are granted the privilege, right, and responsibility to make sense of the world for subordinate groups (Lee & Solomon, 1990). They tell us how to see the world. From *Dawson's Creek* and *Dateline,* to soaps, police dramas, sitcoms, and game shows, network and cable television programs provide dominant descriptive-prescriptive formats for seeing and understanding social relationships and practices. News images that are unsettling or contradict dominant explanations must be explained away.

Networks present hegemonic ideas as universally valid, but televised reality continuously appropriates alternative views, neu-

**Spokesmodels for Cultural Hegemony**

Commenting on media celebrity, ABC news anchor Peter Jennings (1989) once said, "Television seems to give people an instant set of credentials. Just appearing on the box . . . has its own set of electronic credentials, and sometimes they don't match reality" (p. 9). Reading cue cards and teleprompters, these media celebrities (news personalities, talk show hosts, and other entertainers) parlay their credentials as spokesmodels for hegemony into public perceptions about what is real, what is legitimate, and what is preferred.

tered and leashed. Comedies, dramas, and talk shows present rival ideas and practices but seldom give them an independent voice. Jerry Springer, Oprah Winfrey, Tom Brokaw, and other authorized hosts have featured an array of multicultural voices on a variety of social issues.

> We are allowed to voice our woes. We are allowed to argue, cry, shout, whatever. We are even allowed to hear about approved services and institutions that might help with this or that specific bruise or wound. But we are not allowed to rock the political or economic boat of television by suggesting that things could be different. (Rapping, 1995, p. 382)

A primary requirement for any hegemonic institution, such as network television, depends on its ability to creatively represent alternative and oppositional practices into the dominant frame. Crucial to cultural hegemony is the restriction of uncensored oppositional voices. Noam Chomsky (1987), arguably one of America's leading intellectuals, has been excluded from *Nightline*, the *MacNeil-Lehrer News Hour*, and other programs. GE, MetLife, Mobil, Pepsi, and other corporate funders have backed *The McLaughlin Report*, William F. Buckley's *Firing Line*, and half a dozen other conservative talk shows, whereas independent news shows, such as *The Kwitny Report* and *South Africa Today*, have been canceled. Lacking independent media airing alternative political views, subordinate groups more readily consent to existing conditions. Individually, we may reject certain representations in entertainment, in the news, or by politicians, but it is difficult to reject the entire dramatized consciousness of a nation. Personal life is our experience. Without collective organization, however, experience is powerless against hegemonic representations by corporate-run media.

## The Articulation of Stuart Hall

The entrance into media criticism by Williams (1977) and others positing hegemony disrupted much of the taken-for-grantedness of mass communication research. A central figure in cultural studies, Stuart Hall (1980, 1982) asserted that traditional mass communication theory and contemporary media practices support class relations in America and help justify U.S. dominance in the world. He argued that media practices and explanations have been constructed according to dominant ideology and the needs of dominant social and political interests.

Hall (1982) defined *ideology* as a socially produced system of representations resulting from the social, political, and linguistic battles over the meaning of social practices and relations. In simple terms, ideology is the communication practice that explains other social practices. But it's not that simple. Hall isn't speaking of "explanation" in everyday terms. Ideology is expressed in language, undoubtedly, but it is much more than language. Following Althusser (1969, 1972), Hall (1984, 1986) accepted the material existence of ideology in speech, in work, in ritual, and in most other human activity. According to him, we cannot ignore or escape the ideological because it isn't just someone's explanation of society. Rather, ideology is lived. Ideology is practiced daily through our actions, whether we are aware of it or not. Thus, ideologies work best through everyday practices that seem most natural.

In his discussion of ideology and consciousness, Hall bridges the gap between Lukács (1923/1971) and Althusser (1969, 1972), between culturalism and structuralism, using the concept of hegemony to explain symbolic action and the social construction of meaning. For Hall (1984, 1986), ideology is generated and produced through language—but through a language that combines the contradictory conditions of social relations. In other words, the dominant ideology is the result of a social struggle over meaning: Dominant ideology must express the conditions and aspirations of dominant *and* subordinate social groups. To express the interests of subordinate groups, a dominant ideology must incorporate significant subordinate perspectives. Hall's discussion of ideology echoes Gramsci's (1967, 1947/1971, 1988) discussion of hegemony, albeit in primarily cultural terms.

Hall (1984, 1986) emphasizes that all practices are understood through the social practice of communication. If social groups struggle over resources, relationships, and practices, then they must struggle over the meaning given to them as well. It follows then that society must constantly battle over the meaning of signs in language and symbols in practice. Communication is an arena of struggle. Ideology is an arena of struggle. Hegemony requires consent. Hegemony requires communication systems and lived ideological practices that connect dominant interpretations to subordinate conditions. Popular culture is where loyalties, sentiments, and bits of knowledge are sorted out that are as essential for the construction of hegemony in ideology as laws, jobs, and other benefits are for the construction of hegemony in politics and economics.

Hall (1984) explains that the social struggle over meaning consists of many smaller battles to *articulate* particular meanings to particular concepts and thereby establish their social significance. To articulate is to make specific connections between two distinct elements, much like a train engine is coupled to a boxcar. Any hegemony relies on articulations that connect positive meanings to existing social practices. For capitalist hegemony in the United States, liberty must be connected to property rights, freedom connected to market relations, and democracy connected to two-party elections of Democrats or Republicans. According to American foreign policy makers, elections and markets open to U.S. business signify democracy and freedom. These ideological connections explain and organize most government and corporate practices.

Ideological conceptions that are communicated according to existing hegemonic practices may be disrupted if subordinate groups can rearticulate a meaning to the dominant practice. Thus, if liberty was disconnected from private property rights and hooked to the right to a job or education or if freedom was disconnected from market relations and linked to social justice, as in freedom from hunger or want, then existing social relations would be seriously threatened—as happened during the 1960s' civil rights movement in the United States, for example.

Hall (1986) believes that the ability to change connections between meaning and practice gives human actors the potential for changing their social conditions. However, he does not slide into a world solely dependent on discourse. He admits that consciousness of conditions is necessary but does not believe it is sufficient for social change. As important as articulated meaning is for Hall, the unity that ultimately matters is the linkage between an articulated discourse and social forces capable of negotiating a different hegemony.

## Contemporary Applications

In addition to Williams (1976, 1977, 1991) and Hall (1980, 1982, 1984, 1986), dozens of other contemporary theorists have revised

## Disconnecting Postmodernism

Ernesto Laclau and Chantal Mouffe (1985) constructed another hegemony that is primarily a discursive activity: Dominant groups persuade others to accept relationships without regard to historical conditions, material resource, or social interest. They claimed that Gramsci's (1967, 1947/1971) concern with social class and economic relations was misguided because any ideology or belief is available to anyone at anyime (Laclau & Mouffe, 1985, p. 85). They argued that nothing other than discourse is significant in the construction of any political project (p. 87): Politics and ideology are solely a question of linguistic articulation (p. 86).

Claiming that ideology's power resides *solely* in its rhetorical appeal—disconnected from all other social factors—Laclau and Mouffe (1985) defeat structural economic determinism by championing a purely linguistic determinism (Amariglio, 1991, p. 535). By completely rejecting discoverable material relations and social interests, theorists following Laclau and Mouffe (1985) fancy that social movements can be constructed solely through communication practices (e.g., Nelson & Grossberg, 1988), suggesting many impossible scenarios: men leading the feminist movement, whites as the most ardent advocates of black nationalism, and capitalist entrepreneurs organizing militant labor unions. Laclau and Mouffe (1985) assert that social relations have little to do with human practice, arguing that all experience occurs through discourse (p. 115), envisioning a world that is so artificial that no human activity exists outside of language: *Everything* is discourse. Gramsci (1967, 1947/1971, 1988) understood that one's conception of the world is found, not in rhetoric or utterance, but in practical activity.

or constructed their own understandings of hegemony. Some critics have equated hegemony with domination and dismissed its usefulness as a concept (Altheide, 1984; Gottdiener, 1985; Lull, 1995; Scott, 1990). Others have muted Gramsci's (1967, 1947/1971, 1988) expectation of social revolution and reduced hegemony to a form of negotiation (Bennett, 1986, 1992; Condit, 1994) or possibly even resignation (Lears, 1985). Many more in history, communication, sociology, political science, and other fields (e.g., Boggs, 1984; Brow, 1990; Fink, 1988; Petras, 1993; Vilas, 1986; Woolcock, 1985) have used hegemony to understand and intervene in important social issues. Communication scholar Leslie Good (1990) sees hegemony as means of "understanding and potentially subverting the 'consent' of the masses to their own oppression" (p. 61). Although Todd Gitlin (1987) shaded hegemony toward dominance, he used the concept to conduct an insightful sociological study of how the mass media seduced the student movement into participating in the creation of "common sense" perceptions about student protests. Leon Fink's (1988) historical study of the Knights of Labor breathed concrete experience into hegemonic theory.

Using perspectives arising from their understanding of hegemony, other researchers have unpacked complex phenomena: Robert Goldman and Arvind Rajagopal (1991) critique media coverage of industrial conflict in the United States; Carlos Vilas (1986) analyzes the Nicaraguan revolution; Michel-Rolph Trouillot (1990) untangles the workings of the Haitian state; Stuart Hall (1986) explains the Rastafarian movement in Jamaica, demonstrating the relevance of hegemony for the study of class and race; and Richard Merelman (1992) and Cornel West (1988, 1991), among others, recognize the importance of the concept of hegemony for understanding racism.

## Conclusion

There is no hegemony on hegemony. However, our short overview should at least indicate that Gramsci's (1967, 1947/1971, 1988) concept provides an energetic means for engaging the complexities of modern society. Complementary and conflicting interpretations by scholars and activists has given rise to a political push and pull within many academic disciplines and public debates. Of course, this push and pull is also reflected in cultural practices and political actions, further demonstrating the validity of Gramsci's insights.

We intend no slight to the many unmentioned writers who have usefully employed the concept. Nor do we suggest that our critique provides an adequate account of those who have interpreted hegemony in ways outside its Gramscian framework. In this volume, we can only begin to indicate the diversity of studies and provide citations for further investigation.

In the next chapters, we turn to contemporary cultural manifestations of hegemony in the United States. Although we have divided these into distinct chapters on race, gender, and class, we realize that to dissect a living organism, such as hegemony, in any fashion is to take its life away. Yet noting distinctions and providing examples is one of the best ways to explain new concepts. We hope that the examples that follow have vitality and provoke thought leading to action.

# 2

# Cultural Hegemony and Racism

The problem of the 20th Century is the problem of color.
—W. E. B. DuBois (1903/1969)

We cannot talk seriously about contemporary culture in the United States without discussing the issue of race. Indeed, race has always defined the contours of American culture—in language, music, literature, religion, recreation, politics, humor, and more. Whereas Irish, Italian, Polish, and other immigrants from Europe have faced instances of discrimination, harassment, and abuse, beginning with genocide against Native Americans, our cultural history has been filled with consistent and pervasive discriminatory practices against Chinese, Japanese, Mexicans, Arabs, and other people of *color*. Chapters and books could be written about the complex interrelations between the multiple racial, ethnic, and national cultures in the United States. However, because the most distinctive feature of race relations in the United States has been and remains the division between black and white (Omi & Winant, 1986), in this text, we address only hegemonic relations between African Americans and dominant (white) society.

Throughout American history, there has been an ongoing debate over the definition, meaning, and importance of race, nationality, and ethnicity—especially in terms of black and white. We are not concerned with that discourse per se, except to underscore that whatever particular scientific or pseudoscientific definition has been accepted necessarily carried some social significance. Race is almost singularly and intensely ideological. The meaning of race has always been articulated through social practice, and as Gunnar Myrdal (1944) wrote, "All scientific explanations of why [blacks] are what they are and why they live as they do have regularly led to determinants on the white side of the line" (p. lxxv). *In practice*, race has regulated legal treatment, economic opportunity, and social status, and the most defining characteristic of race in the United States has been skin color.

Hierarchical racial division by color defined the peculiar institution of race-based slavery in the United States until the Civil War. In the South, the Jim Crow system of legalized segregation by color was strictly enforced until the 1960s. In each of its several reincarnations, the Ku Klux Klan has championed the cause of the "white" race. In black narrative, the significance of skin color has also been a recurrent theme—as represented, for example, in Oscar Micheaux's 1920 films about light-skinned blacks "passing" as white and in Spike Lee's *School Daze* (Bogle, 1994; Cripps, 1993; Silk & Silk, 1990). Indeed, American culture has long been obsessed by skin color. Moreover, defined by color or otherwise, race has been and remains a crucial site of social struggles over language, politics, and power in the United States. Race continues to communicate across social boundaries, interactions, and perceptions even in racially integrated communities (Anderson, 1990). Prior struggles and their outcomes, as well as changes in the social structure, have made contemporary race inequality much more complex. Likewise, the economic, political, and cultural manifestations of racial relations are more contradictory than before. Viewing race in America through the lens of hegemony, however, helps us unravel this chronic social conflict and reveals how it is negotiated and filtered through cultural practices.

This chapter looks at the incorporation of black culture into mainstream popular culture. After a brief discussion of hegemony as it applies to race, we provide a shorthand report on the socioeconomic status of African Americans in the late 20th century. We then turn to examples from popular culture that communicate and construct images and practices affecting race in American culture. We look at the negotiated messages contained in Hollywood movies, the news media, television comedy and drama, children's entertainment, music, "style," and sports. We end with an overview of contemporary political responses by African Americans and the potential for consent, resistance, and social change as related to race relations in the United States. Observations about popular culture and dominant-subordinate relations raised in this chapter also ground the subsequent chapters on gender and class.

## Racial Hegemony in Popular Culture

Hegemony posits that popular culture comes into existence through the dialectical exchange between dominant and subordinate group interests and practices. Historically, dominant cultures have attempted to dismantle and replace subordinate popular culture. Jacques Le Goff (1980) explains how the "high" culture of the elite displaced the "popular" culture of the peasants in the Middle Ages through the systematic destruction of cultural objects (temples, theaters, icons, ritual artifacts), the obliteration of subordinate practices (rites, customs, devotions, languages), and the denaturalization of beliefs (myths, narratives, themes). In time, however, opposition turned into dialogue and dominant culture re-appropriated subordinate culture through hybrid practices such as incorporating "pagan" spring rituals into Easter celebrations (Le Goff, 1980). Although we can trace a cultural "dialogue," the "exchange" between African and African American culture and the dominant Eurocentric culture of the United States followed a somewhat different trajectory. Dominant American culture did not destroy African cultural objects and practices, rather, Africans were physically removed from their culture by force. Slavery effectively destroyed communities and families, dispersing entire cultures. As chattel slaves, Africans in America could not easily maintain traditional cultural practices, rituals, or languages.

Dominant white culture mocked whatever myths and narratives survived slavery's brutality. Yet as Molefi Asante (1988), Cornel West (1988), and others have noted, a certain Afrocentric resistance was nurtured in slave narratives, themes, and holistic communication styles. A well-known example is the witty African folktales of Brer Rabbit and friends, collected and preserved by Joel Chandler Harris in the 1880s (Turner, 1994). Other African American images and practices silently appeared in dominant Southern culture in stories, music, and cuisine. Popular culture in the United States continues its dialogue with black culture.

Understanding popular culture in this way challenges traditional constructions of cultural history. Popular culture has usually been seen as the opposite of "legitimate" culture, not as the integration of cultural practices by competing social groups. History has always told us how the rich dressed, what they ate, their taste in music, and how they organized their homes—as if the dominant simply dominated, as if the elite alone made history (Taxel, 1991). In contrast, traditional "history has automatically discarded everything that smelled of the people" (Martin-Barbero, 1993, p. 73). Historically, constructions of race relations in the United States have viewed blacks as a "problem" (DuBois, 1903/1969), a "dilemma" (Myrdal, 1944), and a "burden" for whites (Jordan, 1974).

African Americans have not been seen as an integral, contributing part of American history. But this version of American history is faulty, if we understand that dominant culture can be constructed only with the contribution and participation of subordinate groups. Hegemony tells us that blacks have a centrality to history beyond the category of an elite problem. It also encourages us to consider the historic character of racism in opposition to the idea that race prejudice is an eternal or inevitable social phenomenon (Gilroy, 1987). Hegemony asks us to move beyond the simple notion of white domination and see that social relations and cultural practices have evolved out of battles, seductions, negotiations, and shared meanings between dominant and subordinate groups, white and black. To accord popular culture its rightful place in history is to see how popular culture expresses the ways of subordinate living and thinking while simultaneously promoting dominant interests.

Popular culture thus conceived has contradictory tendencies. On the one hand, popular culture has intimate links to subordinate-class practices. Subordinate cultural practices often contain conceptions of the world "in opposition (implicitly, mechanically, objectively) to the conceptions" promoted by the official, dominant world (Gramsci, in Martin-Barbero, 1993, p. 74). Culture can be a force for political and social transformation, because popular culture fuses what comes from the hegemonic culture with what comes from the subordinate group's own experiences and conditions. Yet by appropriating subordinate-class practices, dominant groups can simultaneously "experience and condemn" subordinate culture, as whites did with blackface minstrelsy during the 19th century. Minstrelsy based on black song and style actually contributed to a sense of popular whiteness by constructing a common symbolic language for racism (Roediger, 1991).

American black culture has evolved as part of the general process of cultural mediation that occurs when structural relations and social practices change. For instance, the Harlem Renaissance—the literary, political, and cultural awakening by blacks in the 1920s—arose after thousands of West Indians immigrated, Southern blacks moved north and secured industrial jobs, and black soldiers returned from the war in Europe (Huggins, 1971). The Harlem Renaissance may not have been caused by those social and structural changes, but it certainly was one consequence. Undoubtedly, changing social practices and the cultural influence of the Harlem Renaissance helped redefine what it meant to be black. Capturing the spirit of the times, Cyril Briggs, William Colson, Marcus Garvey, W. E. B. DuBois, and other black leaders and journalists debated the tasks of the "new Negro patriotism" (Vincent, 1973). Garvey's Universal Negro Improvement Association recruited over 200,000 members to "African" social clubs, marching bands, and cooperative societies, as black nationalism and self-organization became as popular as NAACP campaigns for political and social rights (Vincent, 1980). Similarly, in the early 1970s, at the crest of the civil rights movement, another discussion on the meaning of race swept black communities across America. Disappointed by the failure of civil rights legislation to change their quality of life, many young urban blacks rejected the goals of integration and the term *Negro*. Black pride and black nationalism became the new themes. James Brown sang, "I'm Black and I'm Proud," and Stokely Carmichael and the Black Panthers advocated "Black Power." Independence movements in Guinea-Bissau, Mozambique, and Angola militarily advanced "black" power against European colonialists. Politically, black power ruled in newly independent Ghana, Zimbabwe, and Tanzania. To be black was to be African. Afro hairstyles, African pendants, dashikis, and other African wear became a political statement, then a fashion trend as culture merged with politics. Things look different in the 1990s, absent effective political leadership and under the pressures of unemployment and poverty, black cultural styles reflect an urban "gangsta" look, exhibited in the hip-hop fashion of baggy pants, baseball cap, and sports shoes (Poulson-Bryant, 1994).

Popular culture in the hegemonic sense never "overcomes" subordinate cultural practices. In the United States, popular culture is the site where dominant-class forces construct cultural hegemony, where they lead subordinate groups, including African Americans, toward relations and practices based on racial inequality. Economically and politically dominant groups have always used the cultural creations of subordinate groups to manufacture a popular mass culture that promotes practices, relations, and ideologies conducive to the cultural hegemony of the dominant groups. In fact, we would argue that dominant-class forces could not construct the popular culture necessary for their hegemony without the contribution and participation of subordinate artists, technicians, and performers. (Try to imagine American popular culture without jazz or hip-hop, for instance.)

Most of the creativity in popular culture comes from subordinate groups. Recognizing the market potential for new artistic forms, corporate interests simply modify and mimic the authentic creations of musicians, choreographers, writers, filmmakers, and other artists. Until recently, black culture had to be made palatable for whites. Like so many white minstrels with black-painted faces, Perry Como sang Little Richard, Elvis performed Memphis blues and those "Blues Brothers," Dan Aykroyd and John Belushi, rode the energy of Aretha Franklin and 1970s soul music. In recent years, however, black cultural images and practices appear prominently in mass popular culture and are valued because of their "black" identity. Not only does this trend indicate a wider acceptance of black culture, especially by American youth, but it also reflects a growing awareness by established hegemonic institutions that black interests must be represented in dominant practices.

To the extent that popular culture uses positive African American images, blacks (to some degree) can recognize their own interests in dominant cultural practices, values, and relations. Thus, hegemonic institutions strive to produce images and coordinate practices that support the status quo and are appealing to blacks and other subordinates. For instance, some 40 years ago, to oppose the spread of communism among blacks, Congress minted a commemorative half-dollar celebrating two African Americans—educator Booker T. Washington and scientist George Washington Carver. Demonstrating their commitment to democratic pluralism, every state (except Arizona) now recognizes Martin Luther King, Jr.'s birthday as a national holiday. Schools and universities celebrate February as Black History Month by featuring films and stories of black entertainers, sports figures, and politicians. Capitalizing on the popularity of black athletes, Nike, Reebok, and other sports shoe companies promote their products by using black "street talk" and style. These are only a few examples of what Richard Merelman (1992) calls black "cultural imagery"—prominently featured persons, places, and events important to African Americans. Merelman argues that black cultural imagery increasingly permeates popular culture because dominant groups recognize the importance of black participation in American life.

Merelman's insights reveal the contradictory tendencies that lurk within every cultural practice. Encompassing subordinate interests in dominant practices is the hallmark of hegemony. Schools,

### King's Holiday

As a national holiday, Martin Luther King, Jr.'s birthday reflects an accommodation by the status quo to demands of African Americans for social equality. Unfortunately, this response is mostly imagery without political substance. Official celebrations limit the occasion to discourses about King's nonviolence, patience, and moral character. Although such odes to King may be well-intentioned, they cover up his intransigence against racism, his opposition to the war in Vietnam, and his willingness to take direct, mass action against established institutions. To focus on King the man downplays the historic significance of the civil rights movement and obscures continuing race discrimination. As one student said at a recent Loyola University celebration, "We got the holiday, now how about the pay day?"

Despite the whitewashing, King's birthday allows some social struggle over meaning. In the context of deepening socioeconomic inequality, rescued meanings of King and the civil rights movement can become the basis for new political perspectives, alliances, and strategies.

media, and advertising agencies fulfill their hegemonic function by promoting black cultural imagery. Neutered of oppositional articulations through capitalist control over production and distribution, black cultural imagery advances the existing cultural hegemony, including its race inequality. Yet familiar images provide a sense of self-worth and group solidarity for African Americans. The struggle continues. Will African American cultural imagery advance equality, or will whitewashed cultural imagery substitute for political substance? Will cultural imagery bring group solidarity and provide a basis for resistance as Merelman anticipates, or will appropriated representations divert and demobilize independent black political action?

Due to the capitalist monopoly over media production and distribution (Bagdikian, 1990; Herman & Chomsky, 1988; Schiller, 1990), most cultural images will be encoded with hegemonically "preferred" meanings. As Celeste Condit (1989) argues, cultural images are never completely boundless in meaning. Images, practices, and meanings are always linked to existing social relations in some manner; they are never completely independent. On the other hand, because every hegemonic relationship can be reflected in numerous cultural forms, it is often difficult to empirically identify tendencies as clearly subordinate/oppositional or clearly dominant/preferred. Fortunately, when we look at the interaction between subordinate and dominant practices in American popular culture, many of them are "color coded" in black and white, making observation and analysis easier.

## Consent for Inequality

Two separate yet related questions are immediately posed by viewing popular culture as a negotiated relationship between dominant and subordinate, white and black, especially if we admit the race-mediated nature of cultural hegemony in the United States. The first question is perhaps easier: Why do whites consent to social relations that permit race inequality? The most obvious answer is that most whites, only superficially aware of black social conditions, think that race inequality in America is a thing of the past. Recent polls by the University of California confirm that most whites believe that "racism is all but gone" (Winkler, 1991, p. A8). Thus, discrepancies in income, housing, education, and quality of life, if even recognized as significant, are considered the result of individual choice, merit, or luck, but not race discrimination.

Ironically, most whites can still rightly perceive that they are better off relative to blacks. What the Kerner Commission (1968) so thoroughly documented in 1968 holds true today. Whites hold a material advantage over blacks in access to job trusts, educational opportunities, housing preferences, and other social arenas where whites are the primary decision makers. This relative economic advantage will be maintained as long as political leaderships tolerate or legally protect race-based social inequality. Just as important, these economic and political advantages are ideologically secured and justified through religion, literary stereotypes, "common sense," popular humor, language, and other cultural practices. On the other hand, even when whites gain no economic advantage from racism, they are "compensated in part by a . . . public and psychological wage" as W. E. B. DuBois argued (1903/1969, p. 70). At any rate, in news and entertainment media, an abundance of images substantiates white belief that race inequality has either been resolved or is the consequence of black incompetence.

The more intriguing and important question for hegemony is, Why do African Americans consent to race inequality? Pat Buchanan, William Bennett, or Rush Limbaugh might answer by denying that such inequality exists in the United States, but the evidence (some of which is presented below) overwhelmingly suggests otherwise (Feagin, 1991b, 1994; Usdansky, 1991). Another answer might be that blacks either don't care or don't know any better. Such an answer is tinged with racial prejudice. Another answer might be that blacks, like other subordinate groups, have been deceived, manipulated, or brainwashed. This view presumes that subordinate groups are especially susceptible to ideological manipulation. Such a view discards hegemony in favor of the more reductive and limiting notions of domination and deceit. We suggest that the answer to why blacks have consented to racially unequal social relations in the United States is more complicated but nonetheless understandable if we employ the perspective of hegemony.

First, we note that African Americans have consistently and repeatedly *not* consented. Most high school history books grossly understate black resistance to racism (providing instances of dominant articulations of meaning?), but Foner (1970), Genovese (1979), Moses (1978), Vincent (1973), Weisbrot (1990), and others have presented substantial evidence of black revolt. Their collective work shows that over the decades, periods of relative tranquility have been punctuated by dramatic moments of resistance and social action. Second, in responding to episodic black revolt, dominant capitalist groups have made significant concessions on occasion, but federal, state, and local governments (and vigilante groups such as the Ku Klux Klan) have just as frequently resorted to repression. In other words, race relations in the United States have not been primarily consensual. Rather, racism has been institutionalized in America through a combination of systematic coercion *supplemented* by infrequent attempts at winning subordinate (black and white) consent for unequal relations. Racism, in this view, is not simply an ideology of genetic superiority. Rather, racism occurs in practices and structures that enforce and reinforce distribution of resources and opportunities according to racial preferences, which are of course, ideologically coded.

Still the big question remains: Why would African Americans consent to a system of inequality, even if intermittently? Indeed, although blacks have repeatedly withdrawn their consent, they have also repeatedly signed on to the American way of life, as exhibited by the Tuskegee Institute, the Urban League, the NAACP, various churches, fraternities, business and social clubs, and the race movies of the 1920s, among other examples. So why? The workings of hegemony direct us to an answer. Significantly, we have found that whenever African Americans (in numbers large or small) have contingently consented to American social relations, they have been convinced by their material, political, and cultural conditions—the three requirements for hegemony outlined in Chapter 1. This discovery can be demonstrated by showing the relative "benefits" that African Americans perceive and receive when they "consent" to the status quo.

### Consenting to Coercion

Why do blacks consent if conditions are so bleak? Most don't. The majority continue to face gross economic and political discrimination. Still, 1 in 6 black families are realizing the American Dream: 16% of black households have incomes over $50,000. Black professionals, entrepreneurs, managers, and others recruited to capitalist hegemony have fairly clear reasons for their support of the status quo. This new black middle class willingly consents to and participates in established hegemonic institutions, including the Democratic Party, public schools, local governments, churches, and social service agencies, providing a sizable buffer to any organized resistance by the 25 million African Americans who are working class and poor. Talented, articulate black professionals now service dominant interests, disorienting, demoralizing, and betraying the black majority.

Supreme Court Justice Clarence Thomas and authors Thomas Sowell (1975) and Shelby Steele (1990) attacked affirmative action. The sole black representative on California's Board of Regents spearheaded the effort to dismantle affirmative action in that university system. Los Angeles Mayor Tom Bradley defended police actions against the black community, and in Detroit, New York, and other cities, black mayors have engineered cuts in public education and social

## Hegemony and Race

Our aim here is not to apply hegemony mechanically but to use the concept to gain insight into the complexities of social relations that are heavily mediated by racism. Stuart Hall (1986) offers several suggestions for looking at cultural hegemony in the United States: (a) Each social formation may construct many different hegemonies; (b) racism arises under concrete, specific conditions; (c) racial differences divide subordinate groups; and (d) consent for racism is culturally constructed.

services. Former Senator Carol Mosely-Braun initiated legislation criminalizing black youth. Black ministers and politicians frequently single out black parents for a decaying civil society.

Sought out by mass media, this black political and intellectual leadership has focused on the breakdown of the moral fabric of the *black* community, blaming poverty, drug abuse, and declining academic performance on African American cultural values and absolving American social structures and government policies from responsibility and from race discrimination.

A new black professional class *and* impoverished black communities are the results of changes in U.S. capitalist hegemony. In response to the massive civil rights movement, dominant social forces renegotiated their relationship with the subordinate black minority. With little cost and great benefit, corporations, government agencies, and other hegemonic institutions recruited thousands of black representatives through material reward, political involvement, and cultural seduction. Ironically, even as they face continued discrimination themselves, our contemporary black overseers legitimate more overt forms of coercion against the majority of African Americans.

*Each social formation has the capacity for many different combinations of economic, political, and cultural practice.* Because dominant groups must continually negotiate relationships with subordinate groups, the hegemonic relationships are continually changing. On the other hand, each social formation is also limited by its historic development and productive capacity. Dominant groups will not negotiate away their power, and any concessions they might be willing to give are always dependent on existing material resources. In short, each social formation is culturally specific.

Hence, although not claiming that economic conditions are the sole determinant of cultural practice, we should nevertheless be able to identify some of the objective relations within the United States that structure the "horizons of possibilities" for social and cultural activity (Hall, 1986, p. 13).

*Racism and its cultures are historically specific.* In the United States, as in many other capitalist countries, race has become a distinctive feature of economic development, but race in Europe or South Africa has a different social dynamic than does race in the United States. U.S. capitalism did not invent racism, but it has used and reproduced the racism from slavery as an economic and ideological prop. Economically, racism has been profitable because it permits lower wages, longer hours, worse working conditions, and simultaneously, more unemployment for blacks. Consequently, racism has been ideologically useful and necessary. Racism justifies discriminatory economic practices by reference to racially biased stereotypes such that blacks are seen as unmotivated, lazy, inferior, and uncultured, for example. In other words, we can say that "capital requires racism not for racism's sake but for the sake of capital" (Gilroy, 1987, p. 21). Because capitalist hegemony functions through differences between and within subordinate groups, in many respects, it functions best in a multicultural setting. Dominant social forces can "lead" by presenting themselves as the universal arbiters of social order and by exploiting differences between racial and ethnic groups.

The significance and consequence of race within any given society also changes over time. The racism of the antebellum South is not the racism of the race riots in the 1920s, nor is it the racism of Jim Crow segregated lunch counters in the 1960s. As we enter the new century, U.S. racism has not disappeared; it has taken on a "new age" form.

Just as racism is historically specific in its form and appearance, so, too, black culture develops along historically diverse lines, changing as it goes. Black culture evolves "in complex dynamic patterns in which new definitions of what it means to be black emerge from the raw materials provided by black populations elsewhere" (Gilroy, 1987, p. 13) and in response to dominant socio-cultural changes. American black culture has been influenced over the decades by West Indian, African, and British black cultures, distinct cultures with their own histories, practices, and meanings. Hairstyles such as the Afro, dreadlocks, and the "fade" are markers of such cultural influences on African American culture.

*Racial differences within subordinate groups, such as the American working class, have political consequences.* Subordinate groups are often split by gender, race, and religion—each of which has political ramifications. Although black and white workers may share interests that conflict with their corporate employers, black and white political opposition may vary in their expressions. Contending social forces confront a variety of restraints and possibilities for social action that should also be discernible: economic strength, social and economic position, political organization and expertise, cultural history and capital, ideological sophistication, relationship to other social forces, and so on. Whites generally believe that racism has ended and are positive about progress toward racial harmony (Winkler, 1991). Blacks, on the other hand, focus on the pervasiveness of structural racism. Although many studies have demonstrated that whites are less *overtly* prejudiced, results from California's Survey Research Center indicate that the odds of blacks facing discrimination are high (Winkler, 1991). In short, contemporary race relations are highly contradictory.

David Duke and Pat Buchanan tap into the populist opposition to "big government and big companies," but they lace their appeals with white racism. In contrast, Louis Farrakhan of the Nation of Islam roundly criticizes white racism but encourages his followers to work with capitalist banks, businesses, and government agencies. Politically speaking, the contradictions caused by racial practices within subordinate groups can provide an opening for a new historic bloc to challenge dominant capitalist groups, a flash point for demagoguery, or even an instance for political leaders from the dominant groups to arbitrate in the "interests of all society."

*Consent, including consent for racial hierarchies, is always con-*
*structed through the practical application of cultural practices.* To represent the interests of all society, hegemonic institutions and leaders must win consent from subordinate groups throughout
society. The construction of racism, like all cultural development,
occurs in and through practices, representations, languages, and
customs. Segregation may be unlawful, but realtors, teachers, and
neighborhoods still maintain the custom of "looking out for their
own." Such practices are not necessarily racially motivated, but
because prior conditions have left a legacy of segregation, neighborhood patterns of friendship, worship, recreation, and other
social relations tend to re-create segregation by default, if not by
intent.

## The Double Edge of Hegemony

Measures to correct discriminatory practices against blacks are
often viewed as undemocratic by socially and politically subordinate whites. In the California survey, 51% of whites expressed hostility to policies meant to counter discrimination (Winkler, 1991).
Notice here that government coercion is not only directed at those
attempting to renegotiate the hegemonic terms, but can also potentially be used against other subordinate groups within the historic
bloc that are reluctant to make adjustments desired by dominant
groups. For example, in 1965, the federal government sent troops
to Selma, Alabama, and elsewhere when state and local forces
failed to recognize the necessity for adjusting legal segregation. To
satisfy the demands of a growing civil rights movement, dominant-class forces were compelled to contradict the expectations of
some subordinate white groups. Accustomed to one set of hegemonic relations, many Southern (and Northern) whites were un-
willing or unprepared to accept new terms. Thus, Southern racists
were coerced by federal authorities to desegregate schools, lunch
counters, transportation, and other public services. In the aftermath, the government used social service agencies (education, em-

ployment, welfare, arts and recreation, etc.) as hegemonic institutions to organize and maintain the new status quo. Of course, the new arrangements were less than expected. Jim Crow segregation was dismantled, but integration and equality were muted. Voting rights were granted, but policy decisions were reserved for national administrators from the two major political parties. Discrimination in hiring was outlawed, but not enforced. Meanwhile, administrative spokespeople were selected and trained who would represent the good intentions of the new hegemony in its schools, agencies, and media.

Whereas renegotiating race relations required significant coercion against subordinate white groups, a more subtle, but equally effective, form of coercion has been used against blacks who expected more substantial reform. Populist rhetoric about "merit," "reverse discrimination," and "government intervention" along with media depictions of unwed black teenage welfare mothers or black criminals puts negative spins on measures intended to end discrimination. Facing animosity on the job, in the media, and in the community, many blacks decide the efforts for desegregation may not be worth the price. Bolstered by a rhetoric of self-help, they may even consent to separate but equal social relations (Jones, 1994). Understandably, racism in practice and structure often appears insurmountable. African Americans may "consent" as they recognize the odds or tire from the battle. In short, the force of normative behavior protects and reinforces existing racial relationships.

To ensure the legitimacy of such everyday cultural practices, "race has to be socially and politically constructed and elaborate ideological work [must be done] to secure and maintain the different forms of 'racialization' which have characterized capitalist development" (Gilroy, 1987, p. 38). As Gramsci (1947/1971, 1988) argued, the ideological work necessary for maintaining dominant interests in economic relationships is organized politically. To lead society, dominant groups must enlist the positive participation of different parts of society. In this case, capitalist classes must lead by winning consent and "taking into account subordinate (black) interest" (Hall, 1986, p. 17). Undoubtedly, in the United States, where blacks are a minority, coercion is always possible, but for smooth functioning, consent is preferable. Blacks provide a pliable workforce, a lucrative market for goods, and a convenient scapegoat for social problems. Conversely, orchestrated black resistance in major urban areas would be politically disruptive and economically costly. It would be more effective and less disruptive to minimally satisfy black material needs, to maximize participation by African Americans in the political process, and to integrate black cultural images into dominant discourses, wherever and whenever feasible. The future of hegemony in the United States depends on how well these preconditions are realized and how they interact in American culture. We begin with the material realities and socioeconomic conditions of black America in the 1990s.

## The American Dream in Black and White

The conditions of life for the majority of black Americans reveal not just the legacy of *past* discrimination but also underscore the malevolent reality of current racism in well-established institutions and practices (Feagin, 1991b). This claim sounds harsh and strident compared with reports in *Time* and *Newsweek* and arguments presented in some other scholarly works. Thomas Sowell (1975), William Julius Wilson, Nathan Glazer, Shelby Steele, and Charles Murray, for instance, have moved the discussion away from race discrimination back to a "refurbished blame-the-victim focus" (Feagin, 1991a, p. A44). Texts, editorials, and news reports are using a new language with terms such as the *underclass, reverse discrimination,* and *ghetto pathology,* which turns attention away from structural social relations and back toward blacks as a problem. Two common themes run through these discussions: (a) Blacks have failed to progress in society because of their "culture of poverty," and (b) a growing black middle class has achieved the American Dream. If so many blacks are doing so well, the argument runs, achievements in education and employment must depend on merit, not race. Accordingly, white racism cannot be the cause of persisting inequalities, because failure on the part of individual African Americans is due to their own inadequacies or cultural proclivities. Although diverse scholars, media pundits, and politicians play down the importance of racism as a major factor in continuing social inequality, the reality of race discrimination is actually much different.

From the perspective of hegemony, this debate is important because we must be able to ascertain the material benefit a subordinate group derives from any hegemonic relationship. Sifting through the empirical evidence should help us construct explanations for social relations and communicative practices. We are particularly interested in the relationship between material conditions, political actions, and cultural perceptions. If black America has finally and fully joined the Great Society, then questions of political consent are resolved, and either urban social unrest and cultural antagonisms will disappear or our explanations will have to be revised. On the other hand, if blacks continue to experience injustice and inequality, then recurring social discontent and antagonistic cultural distinctions make sense, and widespread political consent or inaction would have to be explained more completely. Obviously, we cannot speak of black America as if it is a monolithic totality; social conditions that characterize a subordinate group cannot simply be foisted on each individual.

African Americans are the most highly subordinate racial group in the United States. More than any other such group, blacks historically have experienced unusually severe and chronic constraints from slavery to Jim Crow to current institutionalized racism. They have faced multiple legal exclusions, political disenfranchisement, vigilante and legal harassment and physical abuse, enforced geographic isolation, economic discrimination, little social respect, and much social discrimination, including in particular, "submission to the authority of whites in most important spheres of life, such as occupation, residence, schooling, and politics" (Merelman, 1992, p. 317). There is an ample body of work to justify this general depiction of life conditions for blacks (Anderson, 1990; Essed, 1991; Jaynes & Williams, 1989; Omi & Winant, 1986).

In 1989, the National Research Council (NRC) released *A Common Destiny: Blacks and American Society* (Jaynes & Williams, 1989), a 608-page report based on research of over 100 social scientists—the first comprehensive study since the Kerner Commission's (1968) *Report on Civil Disorder* 20 years earlier. Remarkably, the NRC conclusions reinforce previous findings of black and white disparities in infant mortality, poverty, and access to quality education and health care. The NRC concluded that although blacks had made major gains in the last 50 years, by every indicator, blacks continue to face major inequities (Jaynes & Williams, 1989). In 1991, the Population Reference Bureau (PRB) released *African-Americans in the 1990s*, which bolstered the NRC's findings. The PRB concluded that blacks lag behind whites in nearly every measure of economic and physical well-being, as racism and discrimination remain. In 1999, a Harvard University study found the widening wealth gap dramatically affecting blacks—median black worth is about $7,400—12% of white median worth (Muwakkil, 1999).

The NRC presented overwhelming statistical indicators showing that the status of blacks relative to whites has stagnated or regressed in the last 30 years. Gains that blacks have made were in place by 1970—a time when the civil rights movement was still politically powerful and shortly after the Kerner Commission policies were enacted by federal and state governments.

Improvements in the socioeconomic conditions for blacks occurred at a time when the hegemonic relations had been substantially renegotiated between the subordinate (but politically active) black population and dominant white capitalist institutions. Following adjustments by hegemonic institutions such as schools, governments, political parties, and the media, a working consent was reestablished between black America and established power, removing the motivation for the civil rights movement, which went into decline. Now, given the absence of an organized political opposition, hegemonic institutions have reneged on their social agreements, policies on civil rights have been gutted, and economic and social conditions for the black communities have deteriorated.

## Housing

Housing remains a prevalent and stable sign of discrimination. Realtors' maps may no longer be marked in red, but the policies are just as prevalent: The vast majority of the nation's 30 million blacks are as segregated now as they were at the height of the civil rights movement. Even the much-touted black middle class confronts major discriminatory obstacles. A nationwide study of 120 financial lenders in 23 cities found that qualified black families with employment, income, and credit histories equivalent to whites were rejected for home loans from 6 to 12 times more often (Stangenes, 1993).

## Employment

One of the most glaring inequities between black and white remains that of employment. The capacity to have and hold a good job is the traditional test of participation in American society, and there has been improvement in the last three decades. Still, the overwhelming majority of African Americans continue to be concentrated in low-skill and low-pay jobs, if they have a job at all. Young blacks are worse off now than young blacks were 25 years ago (Gordon, 1996; Wicker, 1996). In Chicago, Detroit, Newark, and most other major cities, almost half of black youth from 18 to 25 years old are unemployed. Some will never have a job. The tenets of the American Dream—work hard, play fair, be rewarded—have no meaning, no existence for most of black America.

The percentage of all black families earning over $50,000 rose to 16% in 1992—about one in every six families, whereas the proportion of whites with comparable earnings increased to over 35%. Economic gains have gone exclusively to the relatively small black middle class.

Finding a job is no guarantee of upward mobility. With the real average hourly wage rate lower than at any time since 1964, 8 million workers work full-time and are still poor. And finding a job is only half of the story. Black workers face discrimination on the job, in job assignment, pay, treatment, and other subtle, covert, and even unintentional discrimination (Feagin & Feagin, 1978). Blacks who begin in the secondary labor market tend to stay there as they age, whereas young whites tend to move to better-paying primary positions (Boston, 1990). Even blacks with college degrees and professional positions face continuing discrimination, which limits their income, and the "effects of discrimination on blacks is cumulative" (Thomas, 1990, p. 340). In the end, black elderly are about four and a half times more likely to be poor than whites ("Study Finds," 1993, p. 3).

*Education*

Under pressure from the massive civil rights movement, significant changes were proposed for public schools; with the decline of the movement, initial plans have been dismantled. Evidence gathered by the NRC and the Urban League demonstrates that racial inequality persists in education. A 1993 Harvard study found that 66% of the 6.9 million black students in the nation's public schools attended segregated schools—the highest proportion since 1968. To speak of urban public schools is to speak of segregation, "where every face is black, where there are simply *no white people anywhere*" (Kozol, 1991, p. 5). Even in schools where some restructuring has taken place, the fact of racial segregation has been, and continues to be, largely uncontested (Kozol, 1991). Public schools are chronically overcrowded, understaffed, poorly maintained, and mismanaged. There is literally no major urban school system that does not face a continual, permanent crisis financially and educationally. Reading Jonathan Kozol's (1991) descriptions of public schools—doors guarded, police patrolling halls, leaking toilets, peeling paint, windows covered with steel grates, and perimeter walls lined with barbed wire—we hear echoes of the Kerner Commission's warning that education is a symptom of racism and one cause of urban unrest. As industries "downsized," neighborhood property values declined, tax bases shriveled, and the quality of urban public schools declined. In short, education for black students has been gutted.

Changes in higher education have also been inadequate. More blacks attend college now than 30 years ago, but fewer finish and fewer still pursue postgraduate degrees. The American Council on Higher Education reported that the number of doctorates earned by blacks during the 1980s dropped to about 5% of degree recipients, prompting an NAACP official to call black men in higher education an endangered species (Mannegold, 1994).

*Law and Order*

There are more black men in their 20s in prison than in school. Biased practices in law enforcement ensure that the war on drugs and crime is disproportionately focused on the black community. A *USA Today* analysis of drug arrests related that in 1989, 41% of those arrested were black, although blacks are only 15% of the drug-using population compared with whites, who make up 80%. The National Association of Alcohol and Drug Abuse reports white male students are more likely to use alcohol, cocaine, and marijuana than their African American counterparts ("Did You Know," 1992, p. 7). Even the former director of President Reagan's "War on Drugs," William Bennett, agrees that "the typical cocaine user is white, male, a high school graduate, employed full time, and living in a small metropolitan area" (Gettye, 1993, p. 4). Yet police and the courts target black youth. In Chicago, the *Sun-Times* reported that youth from the North Side are twice as likely to get off without prosecution as black kids from the West or South Side. For such practices to be so consistent, they cannot be inadvertent. More likely they reflect the coercive intent of hegemonic institutions, led by people like Frederick Goodwin, head of the Alcohol, Drug Abuse and Mental Health Administration who compared urban blacks to monkeys, describing them both as hypersexual and overly aggressive (Gettye, 1993).

These facts do not appear in media headlines or televised sound bites, however. Rather, through consistent stereotypical media representations, the black community retains its identity as a "problem" (van Dijk, 1991). Negative representations permeate mainstream popular culture (Bogle, 1994; Broderick, 1973; Turner, 1994) and mesh with racially segregated social activities (Anderson, 1990). Not surprisingly, the NRC concluded that a color-blind society is unlikely in the foreseeable future due to existing social and economic segregation (Jaynes & Williams, 1989).

Although the NRC study and American Sociological Association studies continue to find large majorities of blacks and whites who embrace principles of equal opportunity and access, whites remain less amenable to integration in social settings. Indeed, whites perceive blacks to have a lower social standing compared with "native white Americans," according to a 1992 National Opinion Survey (Lewin, 1992). Blacks are regarded as less hardworking, more prone to violence, less self-supporting, and less intelligent compared with other groups, such as Irish, Swedes, Hungarians, and British. Although commissioned by the American Jewish Council, researchers were surprised to find that the major conflict uncovered was between black and white. Color clearly continues to mark American cultural beliefs and influence our practices.

## Black Images in Popular Culture

For hundreds of years, American popular culture has been filled with themes, tensions, and humor based on race. In the late 18th century, blacks dominated community festivals and heavily influenced white popular entertainment (Roediger, 1991), but racial segregation and "blackface" entertainment by whites combined to create many of the racial stereotypes of blacks that we have today. Minstrel shows, which became the most popular form of 19th-century entertainment, popularized "dehumanizing racist stage stereotypes" exemplified by the "coon song" craze that swept the nation (Roediger, 1991, p. 98). Sheet music, scripts, and posters featured Uncle Tom, mammy and pappy characters, Zip Coon, and the now famous Jim Crow—a laughably grotesque caricature of a happy slave. The selling of caricature began in real earnest after 1865, when black-white relations were revolutionized with the abolition of slavery. Repeated caricatures of blacks became prevalent stereotypes, such as the contented slave, the comic, the brute, and the exotic primitive (Brown, 1968).

Many of these stereotypes—developed in popular theater, minstrel shows, and racial artifacts over 100 years ago—still appear on *Martin, Saturday Night Live,* and other network shows. The popularity of these images and the resurgent appearance of replicas of pickaninnies, Aunt Jemima cookie jars, and other "contemptible collectibles" at crafts fairs (Turner, 1994, p. 27) illustrates the enduring appeal of negative presentations of blacks, the control that whites have over production, and the continuing subordinate position of African Americans.

## On Language

Race images in culture, especially in literature, theater, and mass entertainment, necessarily have included a racialized language. Words reflect social standards, social relations, and social hierarchies. Sociolinguists have verified that dominant social groups influence public discourse by encoding social hierarchies of race, gender, and class into the language (Lakoff, 1975). As Martin Luther King, Jr. noted, "Even semantics have conspired to make that which is black, ugly and degrading" (Bosmajian, 1983, p. 46). Indeed, the English language refers to black as "soiled," "wicked, evil," "cheerless and depressing," "marked by anger and sullenness," and attended with "disaster, calamitous" (*Merriam-Webster's Collegiate Dictionary,* 1993). Synonyms for blackness are mostly offensive, whereas terms for whiteness are more favorable, which is not to say there are not negative connotations for white, as in *whitewash, pale,* and *weak.* The point is simply that language is both a product of social relations and a tool for organizing them.

### *"Words Can Ever Hurt Me"*

"Language as a potent force in our society goes beyond a merely communicative device. Language not only expresses ideas and concepts but it may actually shape them. Often the process is com-

### White Coons

The language of race developed in tandem with race relations. The words *coon* and *buck,* for example, were not always used as derogative racist put-downs. Before 1848, the word *coon* referred to a white country person who was especially sharp and sly. To identify with rural common people, the Whig party adopted the symbol of the coonskin cap and used raccoons as party mascots. Under the influence of black-faced minstrel shows, however, the meaning of coon gradually evolved from signifying sly rural whites to become a signifier for shiftless, deceitful rural blacks. The minstrel

pletely unconscious. . . . so powerful is the role of language in its imprint on the human mind that even the minority group may begin to accept the very expressions that aid in its stereotyping," says Simon Podair. (Bosmajian, 1983, p. 47)

Derogatory slang terms for black and white reveal the starkly racial bias of the English language. Synonyms for blacks include *colored, Negro, coon, darkie, jungle bunny, sambo, ape, pickaninny,* and worse. There is no serious racial insult to whites. "Poor white trash," for instance, implies living below standards acceptable to average whites. *Honky, whitey, cracker, redneck,* or *ofay* just don't ravage the same tear on one's dignity as the "n-word"—the most enduring symbol of oppression—even if rap artists claim otherwise.

Since the beginning of African slavery, derogatory terms for blacks appeared in popular communication, complementing official definitions of black identity and justifying discriminatory character Zip Coon and the "coon song" craze of the 1830s helped popularize the term as a racial slur.

During the American Revolution, *buck* described a dashing, young, virile man, presumably white. In the early 1800s, buck came to signify a dandy and womanizer. Popular usage gradually rearticulated buck to mean a man preoccupied with personal appearance who forced his attentions on women. During the rising segregation of the 1830s, buck became an adjective for black men associating with white women. Within a few years of such racially charged usage, buck easily became a noun referring to crudely sexual black men.

Words such as coon and buck have had more than ambiguous meanings; they have had trajectories that led from white to black during periods of intense social change. Such an evolution of language suggests that the very concepts of black and white address highly stressful social anxieties (Roediger, 1991, pp. 98-100).

treatment. As heathens, Africans "could be transported to the colonies like animals," wrote historian Winthrop Jordan, and "whenever the shipmaster had to preserve the safety of the ship, he did not hesitate to jettison his human cargo. . . . for insurance purposes the men, women, and children thrown to the sharks were designated as goods or chattels" (Bosmajian, 1983, p. 37). The Catholic Church in the 1850s explained that the "negro is what the creator made him—not a rudimentary Caucasian, not a human in the process of development, but a negro" (Roediger, 1991, p. 140).

Likewise, the language of law has always been racialized for blacks. In 1857, Chief Justice Taney explained that "all men are created equal" was never meant to include "Negroes" and that "the only provisions which point to them and include them, treat them as property" (Bosmajian, 1983, p. 38). Historically, the racialized language of law was used by state institutions to keep blacks separate from whites. Until 1954, racially segregated education was legal. Until 1966, almost half the states in the United States had laws forbidding marriages between whites and blacks. Legislators and judges justifying these laws relied on phrases such as "to preserve racial integrity," "to prevent a mongrel breed of citizens," "to prevent the obliteration of racial pride" (Bosmajian, 1983, p. 44). Such communication contributed to the construction and defense of institutional racism.

Contemporary government spokespeople and media reports continue to racialize law and order by categorizing certain crimes such as "mugging," drug dealing, or "riots" as "black" (Hall, Critcher, Jefferson, Clarke, & Roberts, 1978; van Dijk, 1991). Of course, "the ability of the law and the ideology of legality to express and represent the nation-state and national unity precedes the identification of racially distinct crimes and criminals" (Gilroy, 1987, p. 74). But racially coded language helps dominant hegemonic institutions legitimately mete out coercion against specific subordinate groups. In the United States, criminality has been cast as an expression of black culture through the gradual replacement of "gangs" as a central sign for urban black teens. To construct a racial discourse and language around drugs, violence, and crime develops new definitions of the "black problem" and prompts coercive social solutions. The idea that black crime is expressive of black ethnicity not only mobilizes popular support for increases in police force but also is likely to "drag the political energies of the white working class down into the depths of racism and reaction" (Gilroy, 1987, p. 111). Ironically, the language and lyrics of "gangsta" rap reinforce stereotypical depictions of black youth as dangerous, violent, and antisocial—images not unacceptable to the major record companies that promote the music.

## The Hollywood Version

Managers of cultural hegemony have historically produced and distributed representations that meet dominant interests by incorporating acceptable images from black culture. The movie industry's use of black images in film provides a clear illustration of hegemonic control and adjustment. It also sheds some light on how blacks are recruited to American cultural hegemony through the reworking of the images they create or identify with into mediated images that simultaneously accept subordinate values and reinforce dominant interests.

Mainstream film has cast black characters as "toms, coons, mulattos, mammies, and bucks" (Bogle, 1994), essentially the same stereotypes that dominated literature and culture a century ago (Brown, 1968). As early as 1904, in movies such as the *Ten Pickaninnies* (1904) " 'nameless' Negro children romped and ran about while being referred to as snowballs, cherubs, coons, bad chillun, inky kids, smoky kids, black lambs, cute ebonies, and chubbie ebonies" (Bogle, 1994, p. 7). But D. W. Griffith's *Birth of a Nation* (1915) "constitutes the grammar book for Hollywood's representation of blacks" (Diawara, 1993, p. 3). Griffith had the requisite toms and mammies, but "it was the pure black bucks that were Griffith's really great archetypal figures . . . violent and frenzied as they lust for white flesh" (Bogle, 1994, p. 13). Hollywood still relies on these stereotypes—albeit in more subtle, modernized guises.

Storytelling and moviemaking have to rely on standard types; after all, most movies follow standard genre formats: Western, gangster, and crime films have the requisite villain and hero; comedies, musicals, and romance flicks have boy-meets-girl themes. The point is that depictions of blacks in movies have been singularly negative and less than creative, but successful black-oriented films of the 1920s, by Oscar Micheaux and others, demonstrated that stereotypically negative images of blacks are not necessary. Yet Hollywood continues to present blacks as a problem or existing primarily for the comfort and understanding of white spectators (Diawara, 1993, p. 3).

By the end of World War II, blacks were moving into mainstream American life. Black workers had become an essential part of industrial production in Chicago, Detroit, Cleveland, and other cities. Stable working-class black neighborhoods were established from Newark to Los Angeles, as 3 million blacks moved north. Black median income doubled between 1940 and 1960, as postwar prosperity "eased fears that black gains would threaten white affluence and security" (Weisbrot, 1990, p. 10). Jackie Robinson, the first black in major league baseball, won rookie of the year honors in 1947. In 1948, Harry Truman was elected president with a civil rights plank and 2 million black votes. The U.S. armed forces were desegregated in 1950 and U.N. diplomat Ralph Bunche won the Nobel Peace Prize. The NAACP lawsuit against segregation led to a 1954 Supreme Court ruling that "separate but equal" had no place in America's schools. The American Dream seemed a little less of a fantasy.

## Integration Hollywood Style

Hollywood reflected the ambivalence of a nation accepting a newly vigorous and productive black community but reluctant to upset established racial patterns. Three black actors tapped into this contradictory public consciousness in the 1950s: Ethel Waters, Dorothy Dandridge, and Sidney Poitier. Poitier was the model integrationist hero. "He spoke proper English, dressed conservatively, and had the best of table manners. For the mass white audience, Sidney Poitier was a black man who had met their standards" (Bogle, 1994, p. 175). More important, the film image of Poitier helped reinforce capitalist hegemonic leadership for the black minority.

Politically, the 1960s was probably the most important decade for black America in the 20th century. It featured sit-ins, mass demonstrations, significant desegregation, and other striking legal changes, as well as a series of dramatic assassinations—President John F. Kennedy, Malcolm X, Martin Luther King, Jr., Robert Kennedy, and Black Panther Fred Hampton (Hampton & Fayer, 1990). "The decade moved from the traditional goal of cultural and academic assimilation to one of almost absolute separatism and the evolution of a black cultural aesthetic. The movies of the period reflected the great transition" (Bogle, 1994, p. 195).

By the end of the decade, the integrationist civil rights movement had been superseded by various shades of black nationalism and militancy (Carmichael & Hamilton, 1967), and black style permeated youth culture and college campuses. Eventually catching up, the motion picture industry overcompensated with its own version of black power.

## The Black Superhero

The turn of the decade could be known as "the age of the buck," given the prevalence of tough blacks in movies such as Melvin Van Peebles's (1971) *Sweet Sweetback's Baadasssss Song*, MGM's *Shaft* (1971) directed by Gordon Parks, Sr., and *Superfly* (1972) independently produced by Sig Shore and directed by Gordon Parks, Jr. The success of these three black films, creatively directed by black artists "snapped the industry moguls to attention" (Bogle, 1994, p. 241). Hollywood responded with a series of format-driven black films, now known as "blaxploitation" movies. Talented blacks were recruited as producers, actors, even technicians, as movie studios moved to cash in on the latest film fashion. Among the dozens of films produced were *The Mack, Cleopatra Jones,* and *Slaughter,* appearing in 1973, and *Black Belt Jones, Black Samson,* and *The Black Godfather* in 1974.

These films helped rebuild cultural hegemony on dominant terms. The movie industry's sudden interest in black themes came at a time when hegemonic institutions were under political attack by an increasingly radical black movement. From universities to local governments, hegemonic institutions were renegotiating the terms of domination-subordination. Adjustments to black demands were pragmatically cost-effective, socially and politically. The changes in the film industry were no exception. With its "blaxploitation" films, Hollywood successfully articulated the political tenor of black power into a new cultural hegemony. Black heroes who defiantly challenged authorities were held in "admiration and awe" in black folklore (Scott, 1990, p. 41), so movies that starred tough, black heroes were well received. Hollywood packaged these modern-day characters in images that glamorized the ghetto and elevated the pimp/outlaw/rebel to folk hero while failing to address the social conditions of black life (Bogle, 1994,

p. 236). Old stereotypes of black bucks "simply resurfaced in new garb to look modern, hip, provocative, and politically relevant" (Bogle, 1994, p. 232)—all for hegemonic effect. Dominant studios "played on the needs of black audiences for heroic figures without answering those needs in realistic terms" (Bogle, 1994, p. 242). "Black" power was always embodied in *individual* heroes who invariably dealt with social and community ills as personal obstacles. As Richard Dyer (1993) observes, in most black movies, the world is a ghetto, blacks don't get out, and racism doesn't stop.

Despite the distortions, patronizations, and service to dominant interests, black-oriented films from this period retain a certain edge. "Often political and social messages crept through, providing insights and comments on the quality of life in America. They touched on the mass hope for an overturn of a corrupt racist system" (Bogle, 1994, p. 242). Above all, the films of the 1970s illustrate how hegemony was constructed through the incorporation of black concerns (racism, discrimination, power) and black-oriented images (urban scenes, strong males, ghetto life) in representations that carried concepts (individualism, family values, hard work, authority) preferred by dominant groups. However, for many of the political and economic reasons touched on above, the decade closed without a politically active black community. And without political organization, black resistance and black voices got weaker.

Not surprisingly, in the conservative 1980s, Hollywood was out to rid films of the rebellious black character. Having largely been marginalized in daily life, such figures could no longer exist in movies, or if they did, they must be "tamed, disposed of, or absorbed into the system" (Bogle, 1994, p. 269). Crude stereotypes resurfaced in films such as *Caddyshack* (1980) and *Weird Science* (1985) and "neo-minstrelsy" appeared in *The Blues Brothers* (1980) and *Soul Man* (1986), but the new practice was to use black stars such as Richard Pryor, Louis Gossett, Jr., and later, Eddie Murphy and Danny Glover in supporting roles in big-budget releases. The 1980s became the era of the "buddy film," as pairs of white and black men were depicted as the best of friends.

*Fantasy Friends Forever*

Opening the decade, audiences were treated to Sylvester Stallone and Carl Weathers in the *Rocky* series and other buddies. Billy Dee Williams was Stallone's buddy in *Nighthawks* (1982) and then buddy to the Star Wars heroes in *The Empire Strikes Back* (1980) and *Return of the Jedi* (1983). Gregory Hines teamed with Mikhail Baryshnikov in *White Nights* (1985) and with Billy Crystal in *Running Scared* (1986). Dan Aykroyd befriends Eddie Murphy in *Trading Places* (1983), Donald Woods helps Denzel Washington fight apartheid in *Cry Freedom* (1987), and among other black buddies, Bruce Willis aids Damon Wayans in *The Last Boy Scout* (1991). However, of all the buddy flicks of this era, the most popular with audiences, black and white, were the Eddie Murphy vehicles, *48 Hours* (1982), *Beverly Hills Cop* (1984), and the sequels to each. Then, in 1987, audiences were introduced to what must be the model interracial couple of the new age—Danny Glover and Mel Gibson as partner cops in the *Lethal Weapon* series. With *Lethal Weapon* and *White Men Can't Jump*, the buddy genre turned itself inside out; black characters stabilized their white counterparts as if to say racial conditions are secondary to life's more personal problems.

Beyond their attraction as action-adventure pictures, all of these buddy films are "wish-fulfillment fantasies for a nation that has repeatedly hoped to simplify its racial tensions" (Bogle, 1994, p. 271). With occasional variation, these interracial "buddy films" follow an identifiable format that can only be characterized as a narrative and visual "strategy of containment" that subordinates black characters and images and "subtly reaffirms dominant society's traditional racial order" (Guerrero, 1993, p. 237). In other words, we return to the question of why and how blacks consent to this order. The answer, in cultural terms, lies within the representations and readings of images intended to present existing hegemony as preferred and natural. Given their popularity, the answer lies within the multiple meanings and interpretations of buddy films (Artz, 1998).

In considering why interracial buddy films as a whole might be popular with black audiences, four general characteristics stand out.

1. Black culture is recognizable—in language and style—and important to the story. In *Beverly Hills Cop*, Eddie Murphy sports a Detroit high school jacket, sneakers, and a hip urban style—loud talk, sprinkled with vulgarity and a cool posture smacking of insubordination.

2. White characters often appear inferior to black stars, like the two dippy cops in *Beverly Hills Cop*, or socialite Dan Aykroyd in *Trading Places*.

3. Black stars exhibit strength, dignity, and intelligence. Louis Gossett teaches Richard Gere to be a man in *An Officer and a Gentleman*, Richard Pryor and Eddie Murphy are always clever and successful, and Danny Glover helps stabilize Mel Gibson in *Lethal Weapon*.

4. Black-white cooperation appears possible. Even Nick Nolte grudgingly respects Murphy in *48 Hours*.

These ingredients vary from film to film, are buffered by certain dominant readings, and are overturned in several instances. Still, in general, these ingredients predominate in buddy films and explain black consent for the narratives and themes appearing in these films.

The four characteristics of buddy films that invite black appreciation are usually complemented by other aspects that invite white audience approval according to hegemony's "preferred" reading.

1. Featured black culture appears as stereotypically "jive." With some exceptions, such as Danny Glover in *Lethal Weapon*, black characters are hustlers, criminals, or athletes.

2. Despite black character aptitude, white authorities are ultimately in charge. Murphy is literally in "protective custody" to Nolte for 48 hours, and his escapades in Beverly Hills always restore the "natural" order of white authority. Pryor has been most successful at the box office as a "meek clown in the protective cultural custody of a white buddy" (Guerrero, 1993, p. 241).

3. Black stars are separated from their community. Pryor, Murphy, Hines, Wayans, and other black heroes have few, if any, black friends. Seldom do black stars have a love interest, although white

buddies often have girlfriends, wives, and families. In *Lethal Weapon*, Glover's family is made acceptable for the mass white audience "by carefully scrubbing it 'clean' of too strong an ethnic identity" (Bogle, 1994, p. 276).

4. The fantasy of black-white cooperation appears possible on white majority terms. Race provides the tension for the movies' success, but the complex and contradictory dynamics of real interracial friendships are never explored. Either black characters penetrate "clearly demarcated white cultural, social, or physical space" (Guerrero, 1993, p. 243), like Pryor in *The Toy* and Murphy in Beverly Hills, or white characters find themselves lost in a stereotypically defined black cultural space, like Wilder in prison or Kline in South Africa and in an urban black neighborhood. Whites are "simultaneously portrayed as both victims of cultural change and the only gatekeepers of society which appears on the verge of self-destruction" (Giroux, 1994, p. 81).

These two apparently contradictory sets of ingredients illustrate how buddy films build on negotiated dominant terms to attract a wide audience. "The popularity and number of these films is due, in part, to their ability to transcode, even into terms of fantasy, social unease over rising racial tensions" (Guerrero, 1993, p. 240). Throughout the 1990s, Hollywood continued to downshift social and political meanings into escapist narratives—adding new black buddies such as Will Smith.

The narrowness of ideology and creativity displayed in Hollywood's buddy films should be compared with the work of the handful of independent black filmmakers, led by Spike Lee and Mario Van Peebles, who have brought a different cultural perspective to the cinema. For the first time in almost a century of cinema, distinctly African American stories are being widely distributed. Yet independent producers still face the dominance of the Hollywood studios and the cultural hegemony of consumerism. Popular images such as urban gangsters reinforce stereotypical beliefs about black incivility, and "issue" movies such as *Boyz in the Hood* and *Do the Right Thing* thrash away in the politics of personal heroism. The relevance or necessity for political group struggle is conveniently denied (Merelman, 1992, p. 331). In short, while the hege-

### Pryor and Murphy

Black culture cannot be read simply as oppositional. Popular culture has a way of integrating and diffusing resistance. Some black cultural images carry less social critique than others; subordination does not inherently breed rebellion. Despite similarities between Richard Pryor and Eddie Murphy, for instance, the two comedians represent radically different takes on the African American experience.

Pryor was the comic of the streets, foulmouthed and outspoken but also "blistering with pain and pathos" as he slammed discriminatory race relations (Bogle, 1994, p. 259). Because of his humorously biting social insights on race, Pryor had a large black following long before he became a movie "buddy." As white audiences "discovered" him, Pryor tempered his ethnic humor because he realized it was reinforcing racist attitudes. Notably, he became a star to white audiences only after Hollywood trimmed his social critique and cast him as a bumbler.

Eddie Murphy, in contrast, had a large white following from the very beginning, perhaps because his comedy has lacked the social outrage of Pryor's. Murphy may be a "loose, jivey, close to vulgar black man," but he doesn't "threaten the white audience's feelings of superiority. Nor does he challenge (through insightful anger) racial attitudes" (Bogle, 1994, p. 281). One look at Murphy as "Farina" on NBC's *Saturday Night Live* should demonstrate that although he gives some lip service against racism, his comedy represents images that bolster race prejudice.

monic institutions in film production make adjustments and offer new motifs, the established social (and racial) order appears natural and inevitable on the silver screen.

## Black and White in Color

Representations of established race relations have also predominated on the smaller screen of television from the very beginning. Whether news, drama, soap opera, situation comedy, or children's show, television as the major hegemonic medium in contemporary America has consistently presented images supportive of dominant capitalist interests (Schiller, 1990). Of course, from a hegemonic perspective, television has also struggled to work in black cultural images whenever possible to solidify subordinate consent for the status quo.

For cultural hegemony, the introduction of television as a mass medium was not a question of technology or art form. Rather, television transformed the social experience of millions of people as the mode and manner of sensory perceptions changed dramatically (Martin-Barbero, 1993). No longer dependent on print or aural communication, public access to information and events could be witnessed immediately in sound and sight. Suddenly, there was less distance between cultures, and the possibility for significant cultural interaction appeared. However, dominant control of the medium ensured that cultural interaction between black and white (and America and other countries) would be mediated according to dominant interests. As Michael Marsden (1980) writes, television provides "a series of common, shared experiences and images which have become part of the collective shared traditions of society" (p. 124)—traditions that bolster existing hegemonic relations. The impact of the media monopoly on cultural production will become clearer as we look at examples from television past and present.

Television began as an entertainment medium and has remained that above all. Yet it has also become the principal socializing institution in the United States. Len Masterman (1984) contends that because television continually manufactures "a seamless, plausible, authentic flow of 'natural' images," it "outdoes all other media in its effortless production of cultural myths, 'realities' that go-without-saying" (p. 5).

Not only does TV uncritically reflect the social structure of society in its selection and presentation of characters associated with class divisions, but it also reinforces the notion that there is a fixed order in society, and that whoever tries to upset that order will meet with tragedy. (Taylor & Dozier, 1983, p. 109)

Prime-time images of race thus help validate and "naturalize" established political and social understandings about race relations. Given the history of race relations in the United States, stereotypical portrayals of blacks may well be accepted by the white majority. On the other hand, black recruitment to hegemony will likely require more complex characterizations, especially when we note that blacks on the average watch more television than whites (Bales, 1986) and prefer and depend more on television for their information (Becker, Kosicki, & Jones, 1992; Licata & Biswas, 1993).

Television thus becomes a key site for the construction of black consent for the existing social order. With the increasing fragmentation of television audiences, "black-oriented" programs have become particularly important for advertising products and for marketing hegemonic perspectives. Images and concepts on black-oriented shows demonstrate the hegemonic process of cultural production particularly well.

## The News White Out

As should be clear from the presentation on blacks in American cinema, one of the main ideological strategies is to downplay the prevalence of racism by focusing on blacks as a problem or featuring stories of individual blacks isolated from actual black social conditions. This same framing can be found in the practices of the news media.

Even where blacks are reporters, "social control in the newsroom" limits stories about blacks and the choice of black perspectives on the news. Black leaders and institutions "are still considered less credible sources," and blacks are "portrayed negatively or stereotypically by the press" (van Dijk, 1991, p. ix). This is not to say that news reporting has not changed over the years, but the changes have been "modest" and "cosmetic" (van Dijk,

1991, p. 15). As in the movies, there are more black faces on the news, but they are not always treated fairly.

In reviewing dozens of media studies, Carolyn Martindale (1988) concluded that news media still remain focused on stereotypical and negative issues such as crime and conflict. In *Minorities and the Media,* Charles Wilson and Felix Gutierrez (1985) also observed that coverage of minorities has remained stereotypical: Minorities are still often portrayed as too lazy to work and involved in drugs and more generally as "problem" people. In contrast, as van Dijk (1991) and Johnson (1981) so thoroughly illustrate, "racism" as a topic is never broached by the media. The media convey the impression that racial problems in fact have been solved. Van Dijk (1991) argues that television, newspapers, and magazines

> have their own white agenda, which remains focused on minorities as problem people, who tend to be covered especially when they satisfy a number of stereotypical conceptions or expectations. Issues of concern to black community, such as segregation, discrimination and racism, lack of affirmative action, and the fundamental condition of poverty, tend to be ignored or explained away. (p. 15)

Contemporary television reporting has become little more than "drive-by journalism." A convenient new story line is black pathology (Drummond, 1990). News reports frame blacks as drug lords, crack users, subway muggers, and gang members. TV newscasts routinely cover the black community in hit-and-run fashion with images of criminals, crack addicts, and illiterates (Perkins, 1994). Van Dijk's (1991) study of news headlines found that black violence gets much more coverage and more negative attention than white violence. He identified word choice, syntax, relevance, ordering, racial identification, and racial comparisons as characteristics of news reporting used to persuasively define and convey the preferred reading of any event involving blacks (p. 64). The main focus of news about blacks was violence and crime, not social conditions. News has since made a "cultural link between crime and politics . . . making criminality an expression" of black culture and placing "gangs and crime as the central sign of urban black teens" (Gilroy, 1987, p. 109). Even events that could be construed as social revolts against intolerable conditions were headlined: "Blacks Riot" or "Rioting Mobs Shoot Police." Such descriptions serve to explain existing race relations in terms amenable to dominant social groups.

Social groups remain hegemonic leaders only if they have the resources to reproduce their dominance, economically, politically, and also culturally and ideologically. The reproduction of racism, like other social relations, occurs in the repetitive practices of everyday life (Essed, 1991), and watching television (several hours a day) is perhaps the most universal social practice in America. In terms of news reporting, Scott's (1990) point about society's need for "discursive affirmations of a particular pattern of domination" (p. 46) is applicable. Given that television watching has become the "primary interpreter of American life" (Taylor & Dozier, 1983, p. 107), the selection of themes and topics for television news must influence popular knowledge and belief. To prove such a claim, much more research and analysis would be required. There is, of course, an abundance of research on media depictions of blacks that has not been mentioned here (Smitherman-Donaldson & van Dijk, 1988). Each year, evidence comes in that news coverage of African Americans serves to reinforce racially prejudicial beliefs and justify existing hegemonic social relations and political and economic practices—dragging the "political energies of the white working class into the depths of reaction" (Gilroy, 1987, p. 111).

Not surprisingly, blacks have little regard for news reporting (Drummond, 1990). We conclude that because the news media has failed to adequately recruit blacks and positively represent black America, it has not yet fully responded to the needs of hegemony. Winning black consent for dominant relations has fallen to other television productions.

*Laughing Matters*

Situation comedies have long been a staple of television programming and the primary format for black representation, indicating that they are a good place to observe cultural negotiation. Analyzing comedy is risky business, however. We all know that to

explain a joke is to make it not funny. Yet because comedy is socially constructed, political, and an important part of popular culture, it is an essential ingredient to hegemonic consent. British film
critic Andy Medhurst (1990) writes, "If you want to understand the
preconceptions and power structures of a society or social group,
there are few better ways than by studying what it laughs at. Comedy is about power: there are those who laugh and those who are
laughed at" (p. 15). One of comedy's chief functions under the established order then is to "police the ideological boundaries of a
culture, to act as a border guard on the frontiers between the dominant and subordinate, to keep the power of laughter in the hands of
the powerful" (Medhurst, 1990, p. 16). Medhurst does not go far
enough, though. In terms of negotiating hegemony, comedy cannot simply speak for the dominant. Nor does comedy have a single
political tendency. Like other cultural practices, comedy has contradictory potential. It can be used by dominant social groups to
embarrass and put down subordinates, or comedy can be used to
disrupt the social order and ridicule power. The direction and social function of comedy depends on *who* constructs humor and *how*
they circulate it. "Hegemonic" comedy must appeal to a universal
audience; it must laugh at existing social relations in such a way
that dominant and subordinate groups "lighten up" and find pleasure in the world as it is.

It is not enough to simply say popular comedy serves hegemonic
interests; we need to find out how. Television situation comedies
(sitcoms) furnish a dominant comedic form that allows us to investigate some of the ingredients that go into constructing cultural hegemony. Horace Newcomb tells us that the world of the domestic
comedy "creates the illusion of being lived in rather than acted in,"
providing "a sense of involvement" by the audience in the construction of meaning (Fuller, 1992, p. 148). The audience feels involved and can construct a variety of meanings, but potential articulations are nonetheless limited. Janet Woollacott (1986) regards
situation comedy as a fictional genre with recognizable patterns,
styles, structures, and forms. With its half-hour time slot, limited
character development, cheap sets, and predictable story lines, the
situation comedy "limits not only possible narratives but [also]

possible solutions" (Ibalema, 1994, p. 205). Conforming to conventions, the sitcom genre "may be constantly varied but rarely exceeded or broken" (Woollacott, 1986, p. 196), letting producers and viewers know what is possible and what to expect. The conformity of the genre also allows us to identify how cultural tensions between dominant and subordinate groups are resolved in these particular texts.

The narrative form limits the plot of sitcoms. Predictable comedic disruption must be followed by quick resolution. The audience knows that everything will be made right in the end through amusement, laughter, and comfortable closure (Woollacott, 1986, p. 200). Misunderstandings, unlucky mishaps, and predictable accidents are somehow made right.

Sitcoms are also limited in their setting. For the sitcom to continue week after week, "the characters and their mode of interaction must not be allowed to evolve . . . the ideal situation therefore is one that is both open to outsiders and other discourse but closed to experience and modification of these discourses" (Atallah, 1984, p. 239). Events or characters from the outside can be allowed to enter the situation but "only in such a way that the outsiders don't affect the situation so it can be maintained for future weekly episodes" (Woollacott, 1986, p. 198). Rebecca never sleeps with Sam on *Cheers*, Fred and Lamont never get rich on *Sanford and Son*, and none of the *Friends* ever maintain a love interest. Not only does "the plot for each episode have to be developed and resolved within 23 or so minutes" (Ibalema, 1994, p. 205), but writers must also avoid developments that will affect the story lines of other episodes.

Comic disruption, insularity, and predictability define the structural limits of character development and story line. Sitcom characters are caricatures—dumb blond, girl-obsessed young man, authority-challenging teenager, overbearing (or understanding) father, precocious toddler, dippy neighbor, and other predictable character "types" reflective of existing social relations. Such stereotypes are necessary for comedy.

Every "joke needs an object, a butt, a victim, and that object needs to be recognizable" (Medhurst, 1990, p. 21). Socially constructed and popular stereotypes make for easy and convenient targets. The issue is why certain "victims" are so stereotypically recognizable and so humorous. Of course, viewers come to sitcoms expecting to be amused, adding to the likelihood of acceptance and pleasure of any joke or stereotype (Woollacott, 1986, p. 206), but "a joke is seen and allowed when it offers a symbolic pattern of a social pattern occurring at the same time" (Douglas, 1991, p. 298). Producers emphasize characters and situations that reflect existing hegemonic social relations. Viewers recognize stereotypical character types and situations from their daily lives that are organized racially. In short, dominant comedic themes reflect and reinforce familiar social hierarchies.

Subordinate groups in the existing social hierarchy make for convenient and effective "objects" of sitcom humor. Common victims of jokes are thus likely to be victims of social inequality as well. Indeed, as a popular form of social communication, comedy depends on dominant norms, values, and expectations being seen as "natural"; otherwise, the audience wouldn't "get the joke." Thus, to the extent that humor employs dominant ideology, it becomes a social glue for cultural hegemony.

Although hegemony depends on the degree to which subordinate discourses can be articulated to dominant interests, subordinate groups do have alternative comedy. Richard Pryor triggered laughter talking about white dudes, Southern "crackers," or even racist stereotypes, satirizing black culture without elevating white society as a model. So could Dick Gregory, who always got a laugh when he asked if Native Americans could say they "discovered" the white guy's Cadillac. The crucial question for a hegemonic institution such as television is which stereotypes will black characters play? To fulfill television's hegemonic function, writers and producers must come up with acceptable stereotypes and situations that will attract blacks while comforting whites because popular culture "secures positions [only] with the active consent of readers and viewers" (Woollacott, 1986, p. 213). The most successful characters let white audiences "see inside" black culture without being threatened and let black audiences think they are always a step ahead of white domination—in short, black characters that maintain the "natural" order of the status quo with dignity. It is a difficult assignment and television has not always been successful.

## Have You Heard the One About Race?

Before *Amos 'n Andy*, the first all-black TV show, premiered in June 1951, the NAACP was in court seeking an injunction to prevent CBS from airing it. Played by two white actors, *Amos 'n Andy* had been popular comedy on radio for some 20 years, but as the one and only show with an all-black cast to appear on TV, it came under severe attack by civil rights groups and their supporters. The characters were classic minstrel figures conceived by white writers and producers: Amos the "low-key, compliant Uncle Tom"; Andy the "easy-going dimwit," who "never ceased to be duped by his supposed friends"; the "feeble-minded janitor," Lightnin'; and "Kingfish," the "stereotyped scheming 'coon' character, whose chicanery left his pals distrustful and the audience laughing" (MacDonald, 1992, p. 28). Blacks laughed at *Amos 'n' Andy* along with whites, although they recognized that the representations had nothing to do with black life (Riggs, 1987). The NAACP objected to the show because blacks came across as "inferior, lazy, dumb, and dishonest" and black women as "cackling, screaming shrews, in big mouth close-ups using street slang, just short of vulgarity" (MacDonald, 1992, p. 29). The program made a clear social statement that although everyone aspires to the American Dream, blacks were comically short of the skills needed to succeed but were nonetheless happy with their plight (Riggs, 1987). The series was produced for only two seasons, 1951 to 1953.

For years, no other shows with prominent black characters were broadcast. Segregated America had segregated entertainment. Occasionally, a black entertainer appeared on the Ed Sullivan or Steve Allen shows in the 1950s, and black audiences eagerly greeted them. It wasn't until the late 1960s that programs regularly featured black actors. As with the movie industry, and other hegemonic institutions, television responded only under the pressure of social unrest, and like the movie industry, television had little comprehension of black perspectives.

## Black as White

In 1968, *Julia* appeared on network television, giving the United States a positive image of blacks (Riggs, 1987). Star Diahann Carroll described her character Julia as "a white Negro, the overly good, overly integrated fantasy projection of white writers, acting they felt, in a manner sensitive to decades of TV prejudice" (MacDonald, 1992, p. 125). Blacks saw it differently. There were major racial rebellions in 1967 and 1968 from Detroit to D.C., from Newark to Memphis. The nation was embroiled in racial conflict, but Julia lived in a friendly all-white world. *Julia* was "unrepresentative of social reality . . . to assuage white consciences and make the curtailment of social programs and the repression of riotous ghetto dwellers palatable to white society" (MacDonald, 1992, p. 126). Producer Hal Kanter protested, "This is not a civil rights show. What we're driving at is escapist entertainment, not a sociological document" (MacDonald, 1992, p. 126). But as we understand cultural practices, everything about subordinate and dominant interaction, including entertainment, has social implications. *Julia* repelled many blacks and was such a "whitewash" that socially conscious whites were embarrassed.

*The Bill Cosby Show* coincided with *Julia* from 1969 to 1971 but had a black ambiance that was missing in *Julia*. Cosby as a high school track coach worked in an integrated environment like Julia, but his life contained black images and sounds—from the jazz sound track to Cosby's afro hairstyle. This was not a show about the realities of black life, but *Cosby* included black actors, themes, and images to appeal to black audiences. Of course, content alone does not make comedy. Delivery, timing, and structure also make for humor. In Cosby's case, his demeanor was comically disarming and comfortable to white audiences.

## Flipping Off Race

By the 1970s, the problems of race prejudice, social injustice, and government bureaucracy appeared more complicated than the public had been led to believe. Hegemonic institutions made political adjustments to the civil rights movement, removing much of the motivation for political activity, whereas the movement itself fractured into a more militant black nationalist wing and the accommodationist perspective of the new black Democrats. Equality had not been won, but demands were dulled.

On television, viewers found escape, not relevancy. News programs resorted to "happy talk," and television shied away from serious issues. Avoidance of social concerns in the 1970s had a particularly chilling effect on black roles. Representations of blacks on television were once again limited to derisive stereotypes. Comedies claiming to be satires featured loud, insulting, and self-deprecating black comedians. It became "riotously funny to joke about skin color, hair texture, race riots, poverty, welfare checks, and minority social customs" (MacDonald, 1992, p. 177). Emblematic of what became a new minstrelsy, *The Flip Wilson Show* brought inner-city stereotypes into American homes from 1970 to 1974.

Wilson acted out characters creatively drawn from the black community: a gospel-shouting Rev. Leroy; a tactless and loud "devil-made-me-do-it" Geraldine; and Sonny, the janitor. By performing classic stereotypes before a predominately white television audience, Wilson "helped reinstate the racist joke in television" (MacDonald, 1992, p. 178). The show's popularity with black audiences also permits an "oppositional" reading. Black pride was growing, and these caustically "authentic" characters struck a chord in the black community. Black audiences watched Wilson exaggerating the traits of recognizable characters and laughed at the satire. Television critic Les Brown rejected this argument, saying that Wilson's "satire" "fed, rather than dispelled, racial bigotry" (MacDonald, 1992, p. 179). Indeed, an oppositional understanding of Wilson's popularity with black audiences is not meant to negate the more serious consequences of his humor. It only seeks to explain how images that permit alternative understandings can also shelter dominant interests.

## The New Minstrelsy

Flip Wilson's success encouraged producers and writers to exploit racial humor, as seen in *All in the Family, Sanford and Son, Good Times, The Jeffersons, Carter County,* and *What's Happening!!* among others. There were suddenly more roles for blacks on television but almost exclusively as comic entertainers for white America.

> Here was the coon character, that rascalish, loud, pushy, and conniving stereotype, strongly achieved in types such as Sherman Hemsley's boisterous George Jefferson, Jimmie Walker's grinning J. J. Evans on *Good Times,* and Whitman Mayo's lethargic Grady Wilson on *Sanford and Son* and *Grady.* Here, too, was the resurrection of the loud-but-lovable mammy, its roundest modern embodiments being Isabel Sanford's shrill Louise Jefferson, LaWanda Page's overbearing, purse-swinging Aunt Esther on *Sanford and Son,* and Marla Gibbs's caustic character, Florence, the wisecracking maid on *The Jeffersons.* (MacDonald, 1992, p. 182)

Each character and each show are rich in cultural negotiation. For reasons of space and because any illustration broadly implicates the others, we focus on *The Jeffersons,* consistently the most popular show with black audiences during its 10-year run.

A Norman Lear-Bud Yorkin production, *The Jeffersons* (1974-1984) was a spin-off of *All in the Family. The Jeffersons* related the events in the life of a black family that "finally got a piece of the pie," as the series' theme song goes. Sherman Hemsley starred as the successful dry cleaning businessman-buffoon-bigot, George Jefferson, formerly the neighbor of Archie Bunker. Having made his fortune, George moves with his wife and young adult son into a "*de*-luxe apartment in the sky" on New York City's East Side. The Jeffersons have a black maid, and an interracial couple lives upstairs. *The Jeffersons* adheres to the common characteristics of the sitcom genre discussed earlier—comic disruption, insularity, and predictability.

The comic disruption in each episode consists of George making a fool of himself as he tries to influence his son's life, increase his wealth, or control "his" household. The series revolves around the family Jefferson, and most scenes take place within their apartment, the insular setting for the program's tension and resolution. Finally, the show is filled with predictable characters, narrative, action, and resolution. George will inevitably and loudly insult his interracial neighbors, especially the naive and wimpish white husband. Louise will invariably save George from some embarrassing situation or forgive him afterward. Whatever intrusion or accident befalls the family, within 30 minutes they overcome it.

It doesn't take much to recognize that stereotypical characters have been written into *The Jeffersons:* the wise-cracking, lazy black maid; the henpecked, naive white liberal husband; the understanding, wise, large black wife. And then there's George. Hemsley's George has probably been the most criticized of all the characters. Lance Morrow (1978) of *Time* magazine described George as a little black bigot who shrieked when he talked and bullied all other characters. It wasn't hard to dislike George: He was loud, arrogant, obnoxious, insulting to women, and self-centered. Ironically, George Jefferson wasn't always so, which reveals his stereotypical role even more clearly. On *All in the Family,* George demonstrated his biases (as a foil for Archie Bunker), but more important, he was seen as devoted to his family and a successful businessman—disproving Archie's claim that blacks were lazy. On *The Jeffersons,* however, the audience sees little of George's business sense and is treated instead to episode after episode of "George's unmitigated arrogance and obnoxiousness" (Turner, 1994, p. 144).

Despite negative stereotypes, *The Jeffersons* always ranked in the top three most popular shows by black audiences during its 10-year run. The construction of themes and characters on *The Jeffersons* served black audiences hungry for nonsubservient black images. As a successful upwardly mobile black businessman, a millionaire even, George Jefferson contrasted with negative stereotypes of black poverty. Likewise, with a loving wife and well-behaved, self-sufficient son, George Jefferson disproved stereo-types about black male irresponsibility. Finally, although George was not always dignified, he always had dignity. He was black and did not shuffle with head down in front of white folks. Expressing a complete disdain for white decorum, George didn't defer to whites, nor did he serve whites, but still he was "movin' on up." For black audiences, the "frustration, tension, and control neces-sary in public" interactions with white authorities gave way to "unbridled retaliation" in the safe setting of television comedy (Scott, 1990, p. 38). Symbolically at least, the accounts between dominant and subordinate were balanced. George's situation was enjoyed by millions of poor and working-class black Americans.

In negotiating cultural hegemony, *The Jeffersons* was one of the best of the 1970s sitcoms at bringing subordinate views into domi-nant frames. *The Jeffersons* also carried messages that brought comic and social pleasure to the racially biased. The characters, ac-tions, and narratives reinforced racist beliefs and kept blacks at a comfortable distance from "white" culture. By drawing George so crudely, the show also said that black people are different, that even though they can be successful like any other American, they will still be crass and uncultured.

*The Jeffersons* promoted the ideological and cultural needs of dominant capitalist America. The show blatantly advocated the American Dream—from its theme song to its display of material success to its privileging of the problems of economically success-ful black families—implying that hard work is duly rewarded, even for a black buffoon like George. Each character in each epi-sode demonstrated the importance of and reward for taking indi-vidual responsibility, one of the primary themes of capitalist hege-mony, which obscures evidence that social conditions have bearing on race inequality. This ideological and social bias is not restricted to *The Jeffersons* but appears in other black-oriented shows of the 1970s. In analyzing black male roles in *Benson, Webster, Different Strokes,* and *The Jeffersons,* Herman Gray (1986) concluded that all four sitcoms emphasized images of blacks who have "achieved middle-class success, confirming in the process the belief that in the context of current political, economic, and cultural arrangements, individuals, regardless of color, can achieve the American Dream" (p. 224). Because black-oriented sitcoms follow the tenets of the sitcom genre, other realities and experiences of black America are not mentioned or addressed, the effect of which is "to isolate and render invisible the social and cultural experiences of poor and working-class black Americans" (Gray, 1986, p. 239). Black-oriented sitcoms throughout the 1980s advanced the same ideological and social message, although several negotiated the cultural forms differently.

### Can Positive Images Be Negative?

In 1984, the new *Cosby Show* raised the universal themes of family and child raising to a new sitcom art form and also demonstrated that "a program about a black family could keep the audience laughing *with* rather than *at* the situations in which modern American families find themselves" (Turner, 1994, p. 133). The show centered on Bill Cosby as the father, Dr. Heathcliff Huxtable, a successful obstetrician, his escapades, and his interactions with his family. Education, financial security, and family relations prevailed as themes in the series. *The Cosby Show* consistently ranked at the top of the Neilsen ratings: Every Thursday night at 8 p.m., 29 million homes with 60 million viewers tuned in to watch Cosby, "the father of our nation" (Fuller, 1992, p. 15).

The public responded favorably to *The Cosby Show* because it humorously presented positive images congruent with well-established beliefs, especially about family and child raising. The father was in charge. The family loved and respected each other, and all problems were solved by the family. *The Cosby Show* promoted individual responsibility and materialism. Hard work and merit were rewarded. The purchase and possession of consumer goods was an indication of success and self-worth. Racism was not an issue, because as intelligent, hardworking, talented individuals, the Huxtables rose above racism. As a black-face version of the American Dream, the Huxtables idealized a family that just happened to be black.

*The Cosby Show* also fulfilled the expectations of audiences used to the standard sitcom formula. It was uniquely insular, even compared with other sitcoms. As Mark Crispin Miller (1986) observed, "Nothing happens, nothing changes, there is no suspense or ambiguity or disappointment" (p. 209). The setting was tightly drawn. The "nothing" that happened each week, happened inside the Huxtable home; events outside the home were always hearsay by or to Cosby. We seldom see Cliff or Clair at work, nor do we see the children at school. It was predictable. Each week, one or another child would violate family expectations, be comically discovered, and be lectured with love and humor by Cosby. *The Cosby Show* gave America cotton candy for the eyes and America ate it up (Riggs, 1987). *The Cosby Show* represents one of the finest hegemonic cultural products ever produced for black and white audiences, weaving the American Dream and American nostalgia into the pleasure of the moment, which never changes.

*Good Times* showed poor ghetto folk, ignoring black contributions to society. *The Jeffersons* characterized George's blackness as bigotry. Other shows appealed to black audiences, but none presented black culture in such a continuously positive manner as *The Cosby Show*. However, *The Cosby Show* presented black culture like it presented the Huxtable family—hermetically sealed in an "idealization of racial harmony, affluence, and individual mobility" (Gray, 1986, p. 239) that is beyond the reach of millions of black Americans. The real problem, as critic Terry Teachout (1986) writes, "is that it fails to dramatize its vision of black assimilation in the context of the world outside of the four walls of the Huxtable household. Not only are the answers too easy, the questions never get asked" (p. 59). There is little connection between the actual conditions of black America and the artificial images of the Huxtables. The Huxtables are not black in anything but skin color. But this deception allows black audiences to enjoy *The Cosby Show*. Not that the average black viewer believes the Huxtables are a typical black (or white!) family, but in consuming pleasurable and familiar cultural images, viewers are also willingly consuming dominant framings of those images.

Paul Gilroy (1987) reminds us that subordinate cultures, including black cultures, are not "mere aggregations of oppositional statements" (p. 159) but are negotiated in relation to the dominant culture. Cultural forms, like much of the art, music, and fashion featured on *The Cosby Show*, were created over a long period of time "inside and in opposition to the capitalist system . . . by those who experienced subordination at its most vicious and degrading" (p. 159). Yet worked into the sitcom genre, these cultural artifacts are not oppositional. Instead, this "cultural imagery" provides the background ambiance for ideological and social constructions beneficial to the status quo. As commodities purchased by the Huxtables, featured black cultural artifacts appear only as evidence that blacks can be successful competitors and consumers of *all* American culture.

Henry Louis Gates, Jr. (1989) argues that *The Cosby Show* suggests that black people are solely responsible for their social conditions, with no acknowledgment of the constricted life opportunities most black people face. In the view of communication researchers Sut Jhally and Justin Lewis (1992), *The Cosby Show* tells people that "there really is room in the United States for minorities to get ahead, without affirmative action, anti-poverty, education, housing, and employment programs" (p. 19). The Huxtables replaced the stereotypical image of the black family but, intentionally or not, in a manner supportive of the dominant culture.

## Hegemony in Living Color

Meanwhile, two other shows, *Frank's Place* and *Brewster Place*, "dramatic" comedies featuring working-class, respectable blacks, interacting in larger social settings, were not supported by the networks and were quickly canceled (MacDonald, 1992). Producers and advertisers seemed uncomfortable with richly drawn representations of black America. New comedies returned to caricatures of inner-city black humor, crudely drawn but seemingly authentic.

*In Living Color* came to Fox television in the 1990s, pushing "race" humor to the limit. An African American cast satirized and parodied a wide range of familiar black characters: the militant, the "snap-queen," the busybody, the "Uncle Tom," and even ghetto thieves on "The Homeboy's Shopping Network." Throughout, white actors mimicked white liberal guilt and the callousness of racist behavior (Berger, 1991, p. 17). Black audiences relished the irreverent skits and the hip-hop music.

Distorted images once termed racist appeared as black artistic license, naively ignoring the social consequences of cultural practices. "Its scathing, sometimes vicious parody of real and imagined black characters may feed the very stereotypes the show attempts to undermine. If white members of its audience are apprehensive about black people, the show [*In Living Color*] may leave them feeling they are right" (Berger, 1991, p. 17). What was true of Flip Wilson 20 years earlier still applied to Wayans's show, *Martin*, and several other 1990s comedies. Self-deprecating comic portrayals trivialize social issues. At a time when antidiscriminatory social programs are under attack, television images of ghetto thieves, sex-hungry black females, and uncouth black clowns—all products of "black" artists—help verify the dominant social and political stereotypes of black inferiority and incivility.

Other sitcoms in the late 20th century give credence to DuBois's lament about continued race segregation while delivering material rich in cultural negotiation. The relatively innocuous *Fresh Prince of Bel Air* aired the same contradictions so necessary to hegemonic constructions of race relations in America. Will Smith, as the Prince, "initiates a hip-hop sensibility into the mainstream" in a clash between inner-city culture and affluence, says producer Quincy Jones (MacDonald, 1992, p. 292). When a Philly rapper takes on the black "bougies" of Beverly Hills, "There is no way a glamorized hip-hop dude can lose to an accomplished, but dull businessman" (MacDonald, 1992, p. 291). The white writers of *Fresh Prince* split the George Jefferson character into two. The Prince kept George's flamboyance and boisterousness; his uncle had the success. The power to challenge existing (white?) values fell to the ill-mannered, insensitive street kid; as usual, black success comes at the expense of black culture. African Americans recognize the language, style, and culture attached to Will, but throughout the series, these signs of black culture "are mainly used to make him look silly and cartoonish" (Bogle, 1994, p. 42), reassuring white audiences that black inequality is the result of black cultural difference. To be successful like Will's Beverly Hills relatives, blacks must adapt to dominant cultural values and norms. Once again, cultural hegemony has been aided by working subordinate images into dominant framings of social relations.

### Sitcoms as American Culture

An important hegemonic institution such as television must constantly negotiate with diverse social audiences to ensure the continuation of a social order that maintains existing hierarchical relations. Contemporary U.S. capitalism depends on mass consent. The population has to support or at least tolerate its living conditions. An important part of subordinate consent is dominant-group acceptance of subordinate value and contribution. Cultural imagery in television helps validate social values for subordinate groups. Television willingly receives and uses black cultural images in its productions, productions that function primarily to promote dominant values and relations, including race relations. This process is complicated but still clear.

Networks produce shows that advertisers will sponsor. And advertisers sponsor only those shows that will attract (and not offend) a large audience, shows that carry images that reinforce existing beliefs, including beliefs about cultural distinctions. It's a neat arrangement that on the surface appears to include cultural diversity. As the "intellectual" leadership of the hegemonic institution of television, however, corporate owners and their hired producers, writers, and advertisers make every effort to include cultural images conducive to hegemony and exclude cultural images that challenge that hegemony.

Comedy featuring black characters and images has shifted with changing social relations and practices. Positive representations are frequently appropriated and retuned by network producers. Positive images that reinforce stereotypes (*The Jeffersons*) and positive images that promote dominant cultural values (*The Cosby Show*) are not only recruited, they are marketed. Positive images that challenge dominant cultural values are frozen out (without identification) or segregated as much as possible (*Frank's Place*). Whatever redeeming social value they have as entertainment, network sitcoms are a vehicle for the construction of cultural and racial hegemony in the United States.

## The Color of Violence

Largely segregated to comedy, African Americans have had fewer dramatic roles on television. The number and type of dramatic roles indicate the social status of blacks on television and in America, validating the reality of discriminatory social practices (Taylor & Dozier, 1983, p. 110) as well as demonstrating the workings of cultural hegemony. Drama critic Jim Pines (1990) has argued that black representations are easily assimilated into the generic conventions of drama through a "recognizable repertoire of conventions" that tend to create a "reality effect" (p. 63). We could demonstrate this by reviewing the history of dramatic black characterization on network television, which parallels the history of blacks in movies and blacks in sitcoms, but the work of Henry Taylor and Carol Dozier (1983) on TV violence provides a suitable commentary on much of that history.

Taylor and Dozier (1983) surveyed dozens of shows, from 1950 Westerns such as *Hopalong Cassidy* to police shows such as *Kojak* and *Police Story* and "seemingly innocent situation comedies" such as *Barney Miller* and *Mayberry, R.F.D.* in the 1960s and 1970s (p. 118). Whatever the network or the genre (action-adventure, drama, comedy, variety), all shows "invited viewers to see policemen as individuals, with human strengths and weaknesses, rather than merely as impersonal members" of the established order (p. 119). Taylor and Dozier argued that because audiences believe that "on some level" television is truthful, it is an important source for learning about political objectives and occupational roles and identities (p. 111). They concluded that TV violence thus is a form of social control—legitimizing the use of violence by law enforcement personnel.

### "Down Shaft"

The portrayal of legitimate uses of violence reveals the ideological perspective of network television and reveals the social status of the characters. Taylor and Dozier (1983) found no black "surrogates" in television from 1950 to 1976. Blacks could legitimately use violence if they were cops, as infrequent private investigators, such as *Shaft* and *Tenafly*, but *never* as citizen heroes. Justifiable vigilante response was reserved for white characters only.

Hegemonic institutions must contain independent subordinate social action; thus, television conveyed the message that "blacks can use socially sanctioned violence only when they are operating in defense of the status quo and are acting under the direct orders of whites" (Taylor & Dozier, 1983, p. 128). Moreover, most black police characters lacked any serious connection to the black community. Little has changed since Taylor and Dozier's study: In the 1980s, Mr. T on the *A-Team*, T. C. on *Magnum, P. I.*, and Hawk on *Spenser for Hire* operated as black-buddy accomplices for more dominant white decision makers; in the 1990s, networks confined black physical force within sanctioned institutions on *NYPD Blue*, *Homicide*, and *Law and Order*.

In television shows with violence, every social and racial group had representation—black, white, Mexican, Asian, Indian, female, elderly, handicapped, handsome, and ugly. However, whereas official *and* vigilante action by whites appeared as legitimate and just, force by workers or blacks struggling for equality or advantage was never portrayed positively. "The message was clear: Anyone who defends the status quo can be a hero, and will be given social sanction to use violence" (Taylor & Dozier, 1983, p. 125). The legitimate use of violence on network television is reserved for official representatives of government agencies and supportive white independents. Positive portrayals of blacks were limited to a few characters who served established institutions.

African Americans are not randomly projected but presented in a framework of "heroic blacks" who defend hegemony's status quo and the unwashed, unnamed mass of African Americans deserving of disrespect and violence. In his extensive overview of blacks in television, J. Fred MacDonald concluded that fictional television "practically never offers respectful portrayals of the black disadvantaged" (1992, p. 285). Rather than depicting working-class and poor blacks, prominent black roles in dramatic television have an overabundance of cops and lawyers. Viewers are shown "the policeman . . . as a heroic, successful, middle-class person, and the character always achieved a happy ending" (Taylor & Dozier, 1983, p. 131). Network television seems to be saying that police and courts are good friends of black America.

Little has changed since Taylor and Dozier completed their study. During the 1980s and 1990s, *Picket Fences, Law and Order, NYPD Blue, Homicide, The Practice,* and other series featured a number of attractive and talented black characters in respectable roles—mostly as cops and lawyers. Without other images, these roles are "falsely emblematic of minority respect for the criminal justice system" and send the message that "the system works and that racial oppression can be overcome through the strength of individual personality" (MacDonald, 1992, p. 285). Yet because these black actors fleshed out these roles, appreciative black (and white) audiences were attracted to programs touting hegemonic values.

*Talk Is Costly*

Cultural hegemony must be won constantly and universally, because in a socially stratified society, subordinate classes and groups are prone to challenge the status quo. Even the most obscure social practice or cultural activity must be attended to by dominant social classes. Hegemonic institutions are constantly on the prowl to squelch any possibility of oppositional cultural practices constructing alternative meanings. Accordingly, in the late 20th century, corners of broadcasting were filled with a variety of new formats, including "narrow-casting" to target audiences, which sought to extend consent for our happy consumer society: home shopping, cooking, house and garden, sports, science fiction, romance, and a multitude of talk shows.

Talk shows have become common fare on American television, appearing 24 hours a day in some cities. Sometimes it seems as if anyone can have a talk show. Since *The Oprah Winfrey Show* went national in 1986 with her "confessional" and "public healing" format (Cloud, 1996), daytime talk shows have proliferated with the same formula. Although Oprah has backed away from crude displays of public humiliation, others have taken it to hideous extremes. "Today's talk shows celebrate victim and victimizer equally; they draw no lines and have no values except the almighty dollar" (Nelson, 1995, p. 801). In reflecting on the negative social effects of "humiliation" television, cultural critic Jill Nelson (1995) observed that the mission of talk show hosts is "not to get beneath our assumptions and stereotypes but to exploit and solidify them" (p. 801). Guests are overwhelmingly young, mostly black and Latino, apparently poor and unemployed. Out of all the television formats, blacks are overrepresented on talk shows. "In the world of talk, young black men are portrayed as arrogant, amoral, violent predators. . . . a few pathological individuals are presented as representative of the group" (p. 801).

Given the predominance of black and other minority group guests and the prevalence of blacks in studio audiences, we assume that black viewers also watch these shows. Why? Because the guests are presented as "authentic" people with "real" stories to tell, stories vaguely familiar to black television audiences, related in life contexts, styles, and languages that are obviously "black." Yet this is staged authenticity. Talk show producers prepare and promote the loudest, most obnoxious, and most demonstrative guests and audiences available. As viewers, we shake our heads in disbelief or judgment over the stupidity and crassness of the guests, finding some perverse pleasure in the experience.

"All of this has a profound political effect," writes Nelson (1995). Daytime talk shows "erase the line between the anecdotal and the factual . . . focus attention on the individual, aberrant behavior of a small number of citizens and declare them representative of a group" (p. 802). Most talk shows seek out the exception; media and legislators castigate "black welfare cheats," and soon a young black woman with four children appears as a guest of Ricki Lake, Sally Jessy Raphael, Geraldo Rivera, or Jerry Springer. Nelson (1995) says watching TV talk shows is "like being caught in a daylong downpour of fear, hostility, and paranoia. . . . television gives not only a voice but a face to our fear and rage, enables us to point the finger of blame at the tube—at 'them'—and roar for punishment" (p. 802). Corporate control of television broadcasting ensures that the voices and faces chosen do not reflect the decisions or interests of subordinate groups but, rather, the representations that the directors of cultural hegemony believe will best attract audiences, sell products, and advance the status quo.

## Race, Representation, and Reality

The end of the century found network television caught in another controversy over black representation: None of the lead characters in over two dozen new network prime-time programs in 1999 were black. Meanwhile, two smaller networks, UPN (Paramount) and WB (Warner), broadcast a number of second-rate, all-black sitcoms. After 50 years of broadcast, network television had succeeded in resegregating black from white.

This is not an issue of numbers. The problem is one of representation. Although some roles have been more positive, negative roles are cast as equally "authentic." Controlled by a handful of corporations dedicated to advertising revenue, network and cable TV will continue to air "authentic" shows such as *Amos 'n Andy*, *Flip Wilson*, and *Martin*, whenever audiences permit. Likewise, under pressure or to expand their advertising revenues, programmers will create more Jeffersons and Cosby-type programming that insinuates that black progress is possible. Networks may even go so far as to allow an undercurrent of resistance to leak out of a show such as *In Living Color*, as long as it maintains its classic typecasting. But prime-time TV will give no tenure to shows that deviate from the American Dream.

Hegemonic institutions recognize that a little disrespect for dominant values goes a long way. Chastising liberals, satirizing contemporary black politicians, and reveling in hip-hop styles, the "feel" of *In Living Color* is an affront to the status quo. It reinforces dominant prejudices while implying opposition. The very implication of opposition attracts black audiences and solidifies network and advertising support. Of course, hegemonic institutions know that social change does not occur through insinuation or implication but only through political action leading to social transformation. Network television thus lulls audiences to sleep politically and dulls their social awareness.

Television breaks daily life into fragments and repetitions, into rituals and routines. Every day at 2 p.m. is the soap; at 3:30 is *Jeopardy;* Thursdays at 8, it's *Friends.* Through a favorite news anchor, soap, or sitcom character, or even through a talk show guest, television offers a discourse of familiarity in simple story form to white and black audiences. "In this immediacy and directness, the stamp of hegemony is at work, precisely in the construction of an appeal that speaks to people out of the familiar conditions of daily life" (Martin-Barbero, 1993, p. 218). Understandable and predictable, images repeatedly aired by television service hegemony. Here, the "aesthetic of repetition" affects the televised cultural images as well. Over the years, repetitive images of stereotypical characters and situations have bolstered established race relationships and social practices.

As part of the cultural negotiation between dominant and subordinate, black sensibilities have forced their way onto network TV in the last two decades. But at what price? The hegemonic leaders of culture have welcomed black contributions but successfully censored out shows, images, and characters that might encourage boldness in "gesture, speech, and carriage" by black Americans.

Over the years, television has perfected the marketing of black desire for recognition and power as "black-oriented" sitcoms, crime dramas, talk shows, and other programming that promotes the American Dream in its "colorized" version.

## The Color of Style

Most Americans experience black culture through the mass media, the version of black culture prevalent in the current hegemony. Although one cannot find a "pure" black culture unadulterated by dominant influences, for African Americans, the culture of daily life is nonetheless more immediate and less mediated than mass-produced depictions. The social role assumed in daily life is still an "acting" role, but the character is the actual self. We thus look at the culture acted out and lived by African Americans, not because of its authenticity but because of its social significance, because daily life is where hegemony becomes naturalized and supported or resisted.

Black style is nurtured in daily life by repeated individual actions that seek public approval. Because a person's self is constructed through social interaction with others, as social psychologist Erving Goffman (1959) explained,

> The individual typically infuses his activity with signs which dramatically highlight and portray confirmatory facts that might otherwise remain unapparent or obscure. For if the individual's activity is to become significant to others, he must mobilize his activity so that it will express *during the interaction* what he wishes to convey. (p. 30)

Style is how one highlights identity and communicates self in social interactions. For subordinate groups, style is the struggle for their own culture, an "attempt to defy" dominant cultural values. Whether it was Malcolm X and his zoot-suited "running" partners in the 1950s (X, 1965) or the hip-hop "B-Boys" of the 1990s, "black style has always played a starring role in the development of black culture, which emerged in direct opposition to the dominant cultures" (Tulloch, 1993, p. 84). As an alternative and oppositional culture, black culture has been a culture of resistance with a style that sought "to create an exclusive identity for a people who desperately wanted to achieve a sense of community" (p. 87). Significantly, this struggle for black identity takes place more *culturally* because political and economic outlets have been largely closed for African Americans.

Culture has been how blacks have expressed their ways of living and thinking in American society. And because social relations shift, black culture constantly changes as it "actively makes and remakes itself" (Poulson-Bryant, 1994, p. 57). In the process, black culture interacts with and helps construct hegemonic cultural practices. We have tried to stress the interrelationships between dominant and subordinate social groups in the development of hegemonic institutions. Although we may mark certain actions and interests as dominant or subordinate, we recognize that those distinctions do not always indicate their interactions. We do not assume that everything produced by a subordinate group means resistance or that everything that comes "from above" represents the values of the dominant class (Martin-Barbero, 1993, p. 76).

Traditional dominant culture appears in the lifestyles of the subordinate classes, in what Jaynes and Williams (1989) termed "residual" practices. Malcolm X "conked" his hair in the 1950s because straight and shiny hair was a dominant cultural value. However, each cultural practice has contradictions with predominant tendencies, some residual and some emerging as alternative or oppositional (in Williams's terms). The tendency toward opposition or consent reflects the weakness or strength of existing hegemonic relations. A subordinate group's consent is contingent on its interests appearing in hegemonic practices; a strong hegemony will likely influence subordinate cultural practices. Conversely, subordinate resistance to hegemony will likely include greater independence in subordinate cultural practices. Over the decades, the cultural styles of black America have reflected as much.

According to Martin-Barbero (1993), subordinate group cultures convey a sense of coherence, moral certitude, a certain cynicism, and an ability to live for the day with much improvisation and enjoyment (p. 76). Such cultures are coherent because group members collectively acquire their "culture" by participating in the same practices, experiencing similar relationships to the social order, and sharing similar perceptions—what Pierre Bourdieu (1978) has defined as *habitus*. It is in the structuring of everyday life that hegemony effectively programs the expectations and tastes of a particular social group such as African Americans (Martin-Barbero, 1993). Art, music, language, sport, and "style" affirm specific race, gender, and class distinctions. Accordingly, we can speak of "black" art, music, language, and "style" to the extent that we can identify practices, relations, and perceptions characteristic of black Americans.

## Black Urban Style

The general character of black urban style has been recognized by Cornel West (1993) as "male styles of walking, talking, dressing, and gesticulating" (p. 88). Richard Majors (1994) extends this to the "expressive life style" of African Americans, which "is a passion that invigorates the demeaning life of blacks in White America. It is a dynamic vitality that transforms the mundane into the sublime and makes the routine spectacular" (p. 474). Majors sees "cool pose" exhibited in many public instances, including sports and entertainment.

For West and Majors, contemporary black style is primarily a black male response to "the words and actions of dominant white people" (Majors, 1994, p. 473). Being tough is a response to the incredible social pressure exerted on black males. Posturing is a survival response of the "invisible" young men. Today, however, black males are pushed beyond invisibility and toward disappearance. Efforts to remove young blacks from the public sphere have heightened. Expelled from school, denied employment, black youth are harassed, jailed, and pushed toward despair. West (1993) adds that today,

> For most young black men, power is acquired by stylizing their bodies over space and time in such a way that their bodies reflect their uniqueness and provoke fear in others. . . . This young black male

style is a form of self-identification and resistance in a hostile culture; it also is an instance of machismo identity ready for violent encounters. (pp. 88-89)

Majors (1994) claims that "cool pose" is "an aggressive assertion of masculinity. . . . through the virtuosity of performance, [the black male] tips the socially imbalanced scales in his favor" (p. 474). The creative demonstration of the "cool pose" accomplishes what Goffman (1959) says is the primary function of dramatic representation in everyday life: "a means of vividly conveying the qualities and attributes claimed by the performer" (p. 31). In the guise of pose and posture, the black style that West and Majors speak of communicates strength, control, danger, and disregard for authority.

Watch the "gangsta" teen hip walk: His posture is limp; one shoulder is dropped; he walks with a strut and an occasional dip; one arm follows the dips in an exaggerated swing; his hands are extended rakishly from his body with fingers folded and pointed; every once in a while, he grabs his crotch to adjust for movement; his head is cocked, and if noticed, he dons a combination smirk-sneer-scowl-smile. This posturing pimp-roll of a walk can also be stalled and adapted for leaning, standing, or riding. Add the appropriate fashion accents—low-hung khakis or denims, a box-cut fade, loose high-tops—and this "posing" connotes "control, toughness, and detachment" (Majors, 1994, p. 473).

To be "bad" like this is good in that "it imposes a unique kind of order for young black men on their own distinctive chaos and solicits an attention that makes others pull back with some trepidation" (West, 1993, p. 89). "Cool pose" frequently accomplishes its purpose of giving young blacks some "power" over their personal space, if none other. "Cool pose" appeared in the zoot suit in the 1940s, in black leather and berets in the 1960s, in afro hairstyles and African dashikis in the 1970s, and in baggy pants and "gangsta" looks in the 1980s and 1990s. In each instance, the nonverbal codes, the language, "the objects, and the 'gear' used to assemble a new subcultural style" had to be "organized into a system coherent enough for their relocation and transformation," writes John Clark

(Tulloch, 1993, p. 93). In each case, black culture worked dominant culture into new forms.

The "gangsta" style and "cool pose" in general have achieved their goal of communicating power for blacks to whites due to the social distance between the races. According to Goffman, social distance is one way in which awe can be generated and sustained. Because race discrimination has segregated black from white, restrictions have been placed on interracial contact. "Cool pose" would be unnecessary and unworkable if there was more social contact between blacks and whites and less intimidation of youth in general, but in a segregated society such opportunities are rare outside of sports, work, or other compulsory settings. Instead, movies, television, and print provide an illusion of closeness where social distance is the norm.

Today, the "artifacts" that accompany hip-hop's "cool pose" include mass market commodities such as baseball hats, NBA T-shirts, name brand athletic shoes, and an eclectic group of designers, such as Tommy Hilfiger. Capitalist economic hegemony produced these goods, and then capitalist cultural hegemony appropriated them back as symbols of the hip-hop style for further marketing. It is very difficult to identify where black style begins and corporate marketing ends. At any rate, what we have now is the further African Americanization of youth culture, as white teens "buy" into the "black" look. Moreover,

> Like all Americans, African-Americans are influenced greatly by images of comfort, convenience, machismo, femininity, violence, and sexual stimulation that bombard customers. These seductive images contribute to the predominance of the market-inspired way of life over all others and thereby edge out non-market values— love, care, service to others. (West, 1988, p. 17)

In short, the attempt to create a distinctive black style simultaneously profits capitalist enterprises and the hegemonic values of consumption. Thus, although this distinctive style provides an identity and sense of solidarity for young blacks and other youth

(Tulloch, 1993), it is not anchored by a clear political project and gets pulled into the marketplace.

## Selling of Black Style

Fashion designer Carol Tulloch (1993) argues that the meaning of black style lies behind its expressive exterior. Black style cannot be reduced to its tangible elements—this jacket, that sweater—but is a "quality born from within the courier" (p. 84). The "ostentatious armor" of the overly well-dressed black "Dandys" in the 1940s indicated how urgently and seriously they wanted to be accepted as legitimate citizens but nonetheless wanted to maintain their own identity. Subsequent black styles have shown more disregard for hegemony and its social styles of dress as "costumes are used to convey an essentially class and ethnic message," the very opposite of mainstream men's wear, which Neil Spencer (1993) has characterized as a "revolt into conformity" (p. 40).

Following a brief Black Muslim "dress for success" influence, black style has gone through the black power-black nationalist-Pan-Africanist period of the 1970s, been influenced by the Rasta movement as demonstrated by the emergence of braided dreadlocks and female African garb, and is currently moving through a 10-year hip-hop fashion trend. Hairstyles today still include "dreads," but more frequently, black male youth sport shaved "fades" with furrows around the head, diagonal lines at the side, or occasionally even blond, short-cropped afros.

Unlike the black power look or African-inspired fashion, fashion goods that make up the hip-hop style are easily accessible and transferable to other ethnic groups. Whereas the sports-inspired influence in hip-hop style is a big business for Nike, Reebok, Champion, and a few other giants, the availability of black style has been adopted by other groups intent on making a statement of social dissatisfaction—from South Africa to Japan. In the United States as in Britain, black styles have become "a determining force in shaping the style, music, dress, fashion, and language" of the urban scene. Gilroy (1987) argues that this is because "black expressive cultures affirm while they protest"; the cultural assimilation of blacks "is not acculturation but cultural fusion" (p. 155). The penetration of black forms into dominant culture manifests past and present social struggles and illustrates how hegemony accommodates subordinate group interests in nonpatronizing ways.

## The Sporting Life

Although here we cannot accord sports its cultural due as others have done (Huizinga, 1938/1950), we would be remiss not to include some mention of sports in our discussion of race and culture in the United States because sports has been one of the few sites where blacks have been welcomed. Black participation in sports has followed the same story line of segregation that plagues all of American culture from exclusion to reluctant acceptance and tolerance to widespread recruitment on dominant terms. Participation in sports has also been predicated on racial stereotypes as mouthed by Los Angeles Dodgers baseball executive Al Campanis and gambling commentator Jimmy "The Greek" Snyder of CBS Sports. Campanis justified the lack of black managers and executives in baseball on the grounds that blacks are athletically skilled but intellectually inferior. Jimmy "The Greek" explained to a TV reporter that blacks were physically superior to whites because they had been "selectively bred" by slave owners mating strong blacks to produce hard workers (MacDonald, 1992, p. 258). Such displays of ignorance may be excused as individual prejudice, but the practices of major league sports and network sports teams suggest otherwise. Blacks are woefully underrepresented as announcers, technicians, and producers. In 59 NFL broadcast positions at Fox, for instance, there is only one black (Shuster, 1994, p. C2). Most often, blacks are relegated to sideline "color" commentary.

Sport is important to race and culture because it advances hegemonic relations in its recruitment of black youth, its inclusion of black-targeted commercials, and its legitimization of the suitability of blacks for sports to the exclusion of other occupations. Pamela Wonsek's (1992) study, "College Basketball on Television: A Study of Racism in the Media," explains that sports advances the preferred portrait of blacks in America and suggests that black recruit-

### Jumping Men Shouldn't Think

College administrators defend the so-called student-athlete, unless being a student gets in the way of being an athlete. When Rutgers University President Francis Lawrence was heard to say that black students were genetically incapable of doing as well as whites, students organized protests and speak-outs on campus, including a sit-in at a Rutgers-Massachusetts basketball game. According to the *New York Times*, six or seven basketball players wanted to boycott the game, but the athletic department reportedly threatened their scholarships. The students wanted to speak out, but they were intimidated. Rutgers stripped away the myth of the student-athlete. At a time of serious discussion about racism, they sent the athlete back to the gym and away from the university forum.

The contribution of sports to the stereotyping of blacks was clear at the basketball game that night. In the first half of the game, fans were cheering black athletes carrying the pride of good old Rutgers U. At halftime came the sit-down against racism. Suddenly, some of the fans showed their true colors, as taunts of "Niggers!" and "Spics!" filled the arena (Herbert, 1995). Students who sat peacefully on the court to protest the university president's racist remark about their inferiority found out that much of the student body shared his beliefs. Apparently, many thought that blacks made good entertainers, but if they can jump, they should stay away from political and social discussions.

ment to sports is "an accommodation by a white majority which recognizes the exploitation potential of blacks in organized sports" (p. 452). Cultural hegemony needs black athletes to entertain audiences and release social pressure. The hegemonic institutions of high school sports, colleges, and the media collectively encourage black youth to concentrate their energies on developing athletic prowess at the expense of education and self-development.

"The allure of professional sports is hard to resist by black students who see it as a ticket out of poverty" (Wonsek, 1992, p. 452). Black athletes romanticize sports as a means to attention, adulation, and financial reward. Hegemony encourages this romantic version through the ritual practices surrounding sports (Bourdieu, 1978). Consider the spectacle of big-time sports in the United States—fans, cheerleaders, televised contests, high-spirited commentators who keep score and replay highlights, and the distribution of artifacts such as jackets, T-shirts, hats, and shoes. What youth desirous of self-worth and recognition can resist? "Ironically, if the hours spent preparing to get into the NBA or NFL were spent preparing to get into medical school, the odds of the young black male becoming an M.D. would be significantly greater than of his becoming a professional athlete" (Gaston, 1986, p. 377).

## Dissing Rap

The public debate over rap music focused, in part, on whether lyrics represent reality or shape it (Leland, 1992). Does rap music encourage criminal behavior? Does it encourage disrespect for women? Is it too crude? Reducing rap in this way to its most disturbing antiwoman and antisocial lyrics ignores the social context. Cultural production is contradictory. Rap creatively reflects the anger and desperation of black youth and the influence of dominant culture's fascination with violence and sex. It is simultaneously challenging and reinforcing, liberating and reactionary.

Rap is a musical "cool pose" that is a cultural response to the political and social realities of race, gender, and class relations in America. Rap was born in New York City in the late 1960s, as deejays such as Kool DJ Herc adapted the techniques and styles of the Jamaican "sound-system" culture to the subculture of the South Bronx—scratch mixing, break-dancing, rapping, and graffiti (Gilroy, 1987). Rap music was "experienced" through audience response and stylized posturing by the deejay. It was built around the "pleasures of using exclusive or specialized language in a cryptically coded way which amused and entertained, as well as informed the audience" (Gilroy, 1987, p. 194). "Word up," "def," "dope," "diss," and other words made their way into popular culture, advertising, and teen slang. Early rap critiqued American society, poverty, unemployment, and racism. Rappers incorporated quotes from Martin Luther King, Jr. and Malcolm X into their presentations, drawing on black power and its emphasis on fraternity, solidarity, and Pan-Africanism. Early rap also celebrated black life and expressed hope in the future. As Gilroy (1987) puts it, "Black expressive cultures affirm while they protest" (p. 155).

The vulgarity, the rage, the antihumanness expressed in later "gangsta" rap culturally signifies the movement toward political hopelessness and social nihilism of black youth (West, 1993). Yet rap anticipates social unrest; lyrics about gang-bangers, dead police, and civil war were graphically realized on April 29, 1992, when Los Angeles exploded. The posturing of rap may be disarming to a naive America weaned on televised images of black comics and heroes, but because politics and culture cross, rap communicates volumes about race relations in this country.

The posturing in rap music echoes Adorno's (1945/1977) insights into subordinate responses to domination: Most rap artists live and work around an "abundance of real suffering which tolerates no forgetting," and "it is now virtually in art alone that suffering can still find its own voice, consolation, without immediately being betrayed by it" (Gilroy, 1987, p. 212). There is no affirmative action for the black poor; there are no economic incentives, political programs, or even organizations that give voice to their condition. Rap music gives voice to that frustration, anger, and fear. But as such, rap music must be tamed or channeled by hegemonic institutions.

One response is outright hostility, expressed by the likes of Tipper Gore, U.S. Senator Bob Dole, and former Education Secretary William Bennett. The dominant "class affirms itself by denying to another its right to participate in the culture, declaring openly that another aesthetic or set of sensibilities has no value" (Martin-Barbero, 1993, p. 81). Blacks who have squeezed into middle-class society, such as C. DeLores Tucker of the National Political Congress of Black Women, are embarrassed by rap and share the perspective of Gore et al. They recognize as Gramsci did that cultural practices are arenas of struggle that must be entered because cultural practices, including music, "are themselves material forces" (Gramsci, 1947/1971, p. 165). Critics of rap certainly want to defend the decorum of public discourse, but they also want to quiet the pounding challenge to the status quo. Democratic President Bill Clinton, for example, used rap as an excuse to politically distance himself from efforts on behalf of black America (Leland, 1992).

There is an irony in the posturing confrontation between Tipper Gore and rappers such as Snoop Doggy Dogg and Ice-T—a double irony when rapper Easy-E donates money to the George Bush campaign or when rappers unite in a "Hip-Hop Coalition for Political Power" and promote voter education. The hegemonic system that rap critics defend is the same system that has chosen to promote the most offensive rap music. The early "soft" rap of M. C. Hammer was too whitewashed and could not compete with the social critique of Public Enemy, N. W. A., or even Arrested Development. Consequently, mainstream record companies and video producers came out with a harsher version. Somewhere in the sound editing of rap by Warner Brothers and other record labels, the oppositional politics of early rap were mixed out and the "gangsta" edge was sharpened. Politically charged rap was marginalized in the recording industry, leaving "gangsta" as the "authentic" sound of black street life. Rap still appeals to black audiences, but socially relevant messages have become politically weak, nonexistent, or focused on black responsibility for drugs, crime, and other social ills. In addition, with direct challenges to institutional racism deleted, the tough posturing, antiwomen lyrics, and loud vulgarity appeals to disaffected white youth as well. Indeed, more than 60% of rap music is purchased by whites.

There is nothing new about whites embracing black culture. It has been happening since community festivals of the 1800s. It happened during the Harlem Renaissance in the 1920s; it happened in the 1960s with Motown and the civil rights movement. This time, however, the lyrics and the posturing of black artists is mediated by hegemonic institutions intent on "segmenting the market" that segregates the races even as whites purchase and watch rap music. Rap's racial interaction occurs in music and video, not on the dance floor, not with actual people. Whites "experience" black lifestyle from a distance. Mercury Records president, Ed Eckstine, refers to rap as a new minstrelsy that white youth can play with and yet divorce themselves from real social conditions of racism and discrimination (Leland, 1992).

Another response to rap follows the direction of MCA Records, which markets music with the beat and rhythm of rap but carries romanticized lyrics (Watrous, 1993). Black music means money— $1.5 billion in 1992—and MCA has become expert at marketing youth culture and making black music part of the mainstream. The entrance of black culture into the mainstream has been at the expense of black artists, whose music sounds generic when studios produce it. This hybrid "black" culture has been adopted, confirming its value and contribution to American cultural hegemony.

Rap artists who oppose gangsterism and include black politics do not get the attention of record companies, video networks, or commercial radio deejays. Rap that takes an overtly oppositional stance to racism and social inequality is ignored or excluded from promotionals. Censorship is subtle and almost unnecessary because distribution and advertising are corporate controlled. Although cultural hegemony chastises "gangsta" rap, major labels willingly manufacture the records. The effect is to recruit artists and audiences alike to a mediated black culture that fits the economic and political requirements of hegemonic institutions, music that sells and conforms to stereotypical representations of black life acceptable to dominant interests—in other words, MCA-type ge-

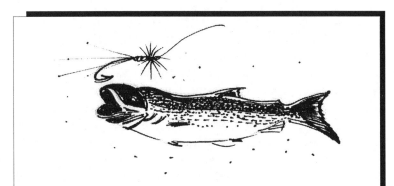

### The Revolutionary Potential of Rap

Not all rap hard drives an antisocial message. Not all rappers revel in self-degradation, directionless violence, and the abuse of women. Lyrics from Arrested Development's song, "Give a Man a Fish," are sharp, confrontational, and overtly political, calling for organized activity against racism: "This government needs to be overthrown." The lyrics don't shy from aggression but advocate a positive political direction: "Save those rounds for a revolution" and "Raise your fist, but also raise your children." The song also implies interracial solidarity and hope: "poor whites and blacks bumrushing the system" so "direct your anger, love"—themes largely absent from the recording industry's rap promotions.

neric music or the antiwomen, antisocial "gangsta" sound. After all, hegemony is not well served by too many songs like Kool Moe D's, "I'm Ashamed of My National Anthem."

## The Politics of Culture

Expressed through music, style, entertainment, language, and many other daily negotiations between dominant and subordinate groups, hegemonic cultural practices and institutions seem natural and inevitable. Furthermore, dominant cultural practices comfortably surround existing economic and social relationships, cloaking

them in legitimacy and respectability. Of course, economic and social conditions are not simply camouflaged by cultural practices
but must develop according to concrete struggles and conflicts
over material resources and social relationships—the outcomes of
which are resolved *politically*. In the dialectical, contradictory interrelationship between cultural, economic, and social relations and
practices, Gramsci (1947/1971, 1988) argued that the political was
crucial. Cultural practices exist only in relation to socioeconomic
and political practices. We have already outlined some of the economic realities of black America, and here we want to very briefly
note some of the political conditions that relate to cultural, social,
and economic practices.

Cultural practices may express the aspirations and interests of a
subordinate group, such as slave songs and stories that implied the
desire of African Americans for freedom. Likewise, actions such as
boycotts, rent strikes, or factory occupations communicate economic demands. But neither cultural practices nor economic actions by themselves organize the subordinate group and its allies
into a political force. Gramsci held that a subordinate group remains subordinate unless and until it is capable of politically organizing a *counter*hegemonic historic bloc. To be capable of rearrang-
ing existing social relations, a "leading" subordinate group must
present a political program that better represents the interests of
other subordinate groups than do existing political practices. A
subordinate group constructs and leads a new historic bloc by per-
suading other social forces of a new way of seeing and living in the
world. Thus, political organization incorporates cultural practices
and proposes new social and economic relations. This requires,
above all, that the subordinate group and its potential allies remain
*politically independent* of dominant social groups and their hegemonic institutions, which exist primarily to recruit subordinates
toward dominant interests. Independence from existing hegemonic institutions does not necessarily mean that subordinate
groups do not participate in those institutions but that subordinate
groups participate only with the singular goal of building a different hegemony. To achieve new social relations, subordinate groups
need to develop new hegemonic institutions that advance the in-

terests of a new historic bloc that resolutely challenges dominant social power.

Gramsci (1988) explained that the material conditions of and relationships between different social forces influence the development of political responses by subordinate groups. In the case of blacks in the United States, momentous social and economic changes have had recognizable political ramifications. Freed from slavery, blacks became literate and politically active. However, confined by Jim Crow and legal discrimination, blacks were economically and socially segregated and politically handicapped. Following World War I, industrial expansion, and northern migration, blacks launched powerful social and political movements, best expressed by the NAACP and Garvey's Universal Negro Improvement Association, which had over 200,000 members. Then, black political action was swept into the labor movement of the 1930s and 1940s. Following the post-World War II prosperity, black Americans redoubled their demands for the political and social equality. The modern civil rights movement emerged at the height of black economic progress. At each instance of black social and political unrest, hegemonic institutions responded with a combination of repression and reform. The most recent and significant changes occurred in the 1960s and 1970s with the abolition of de jure segregation and the promulgation of several civil rights laws affecting education, voting, and job discrimination.

This sketchbook history of black political activity illuminates Gramsci's understanding of the process of resistance that subordinate groups pass through on their way to constructing a new hegemony: (a) self-identity and self-interest, (b) identity and interests shared with other subordinate groups, and (c) hegemonic alliances with other subordinate and middle-class groups for a larger social project (Hall, 1986, p. 14).

From the Civil War until the 1920s, black politics vacillated between accommodation and separation with dominant white society. Integration was expressed militantly by the NAACP and more cordially by Booker T. Washington and the Tuskegee Institute (Foner, 1970); Black nationalism was championed by the Garvey movement, the African Blood Brotherhood, and others (Vincent,

1980). For African Americans, black nationalism has been the primary political expression of self-identity and self-interest.

In the aftermath of the Harlem Renaissance and following the Great Depression of the 1930s, black workers recognized their working-class status (curbing their nationalist sentiments) and enthusiastically joined unions such as the United Auto Workers that opposed segregation. The civil rights movement expressed an awareness of black self-interest and an acute understanding of the need for alliances with other subordinate social groups, especially poor and working-class whites. Martin Luther King, Jr. occasionally moved beyond the civil rights focus as he challenged U.S. involvement in Vietnam, launched a "Poor People's March," and helped organize city workers in Memphis. Upon leaving the Black Muslims, Malcolm X made contact with African leaders, the civil rights movement, and looked to the United Nations for some redress of black grievances in the United States. Following the assassinations of Malcolm and King and well-publicized federal civil rights legislation, many whites (and blacks) were persuaded that civil rights had been resolved. At the same time, black nationalism came back with a fury as black youth dissatisfied with legislation that did not touch their lives turned to the solace of cultural and political self-identity.

Throughout the history of blacks in America, new cultural practices have arisen as social conditions changed and political projects emerged or receded. For example, Negro spirituals and gospel music were supplemented by "New Negro" militancy in the poetry and literature of the Harlem Renaissance in the 1920s. During the wave of black social protest in the 1960s, Motown Records turned out socially conscious songs such as Marvin Gaye's "What's Going On?," Stevie Wonder's "Living for the City," and Edwin Starr's "War." At the height of black power in the early 1970s, James Brown sang, "I'm Black and I'm Proud." Today, rap expresses the frustration and rage of alienated black youth. Cultural practices such as music, fashion, and language have let African Americans "fight the power," as Radio Raheem's music box blasted in Spike Lee's *Do the Right Thing*, but at no time has a black sociopolitical movement successfully led or participated in a larger social project that could transform society and its race relations. Blacks have had a significant influence on American cultural practices. Even powerful hegemonic institutions such as the movie industry and network television have responded favorably to black participation. The brief outline of economic conditions confronting the black community also suggests that hegemonic institutions have not simply ignored black demands but have made some significant adjustments, leading to the emergence of a black middle class. Likewise, government agencies and institutions have made political adjustments—but with an important difference. African Americans have largely been able to determine their own cultural practices. Indeed, their independent creativity has nourished American culture as a whole. Economically, it has been more difficult, but some black Americans have been able to move ahead. The collective buying power of African Americans has encouraged advertisers and programmers to attend somewhat to black needs and interests. Capitalist hegemony "is motivated to mobilize African-American culture" (Merelman, 1992, p. 336), encouraging independent black cultural activity, and the marketplace accepts any independent black economic activity as a source of profits.

In contrast, political power has been closely guarded by dominant capitalist classes. Independent black political activity threatens the policies, programs, and legitimacy of dominant political practices. In times of economic and social crises, black political organizations would provide leadership for a disaffected population that would otherwise be left floundering. All attempts at independent political activity have been marginalized by the media and obstructed by coercive government action.

## Leadership and Political Action

The civil rights movement intimated the possibility of black and white alliances that could challenge the status quo, but hegemonic institutions made historic adjustments to undercut that possibility. No political leadership responded to the new social arrangements in a way that would further advance subordinate black interests.

### Organizing a Collective Counterhegemony

In the last days of his life, Malcolm X was intent on founding
the Organization of Afro-American Unity (OAAU), which
would socially, culturally, and politically lead the black community forward. The OAAU set coalition building as one of
its top priorities. Other goals included independent political
activity, cultural and educational programs, and community
building.

Malcolm explained his turn to alliance building as preparation for a clash between oppressed and oppressor, between
those who want freedom, justice, and equality for everyone
and those who want to continue capitalist cultural hegemony.
In explaining that the fight for a better society would not be
based on skin color, Malcolm was advocating a political alliance among all subordinate groups—black and white—
against dominant structures and their hegemonic relations.

King frequently hinted at larger social challenges to capitalism,
and in the last year of his life, Malcolm X outlined a program for his
Organization of African American Unity that implied
counterhegemonic alliances. Other independent black movements
were less insightful. The Black Panthers, for instance, got side-
tracked into a combination of local social welfare programs (such

as the "Breakfast for Children" project) and ill-advised physical confrontations with police (an extreme form of "cool pose"). Hegemonic leaderships were clearly more successful as they alternately crushed militant opposition and recruited malleable black representatives to the dominant order. Both the Republican and Democratic parties have made overtures and provided openings for black participation, the Democrats being more successful.

Believing they could advance the interests of their black constituencies from "inside the beast," tens of thousands of black activists joined the Democratic Party—the primary hegemonic institution of dominant politics in the United States. Today, the new black middle class gives political support to some 4,000 black elected officials (BEOs) of the Democratic and Republican parties, but the majority of African Americans have simply withdrawn from political activity out of frustration. Coincidentally, there are few independent, self-governed black political organizations.

Without engaging in a full discussion of black political action, we would suggest that the political effectiveness of black America has depended on persuasive education, independent organization, and mass political action. Political activity channeled into the two-party electoral system has essentially reinforced hegemony. Two-party electoral campaigning functions not to elect candidates, but to convince citizens that they are participating in a democracy. Such political "participation" serves to negotiate subordinate needs in favor of dominant interests. In contrast, the movement leaders of the 1950s and 1960s did not try to elect "good" Democrats or Republicans but demanded that black civil rights be guaranteed. New civil rights laws came only after hegemonic leaders saw that *independent political action* was becoming too massive too ignore. Mass action—not electoral politics—brought change.

Today, no significant independent political leadership exists to build a counterhegemonic project of social change. Without some organized opposition to channel African American social dissatisfaction, we should anticipate that as social conditions reach the breaking point, more rebellions on the scale of Los Angeles will break out. Of course, hegemonic institutions have been able to find useful black representatives such as ex-Los Angeles Mayor Tom

Bradley (now deceased), Supreme Court Justice Clarence Thomas, former U.S. Senator Carole Mosely-Braun, State Representative (and ex-Black Panther) Bobby Rush, and thousands of other BEOs. These hired subordinates administer the rules, practices, and penalties on behalf of the status quo, providing a political shield for hegemonic race relations. In short, severe political contradictions exist. As the primary political and economic beneficiary of civil rights legislation, the black middle class consents to the status quo (West, 1993, p. 41) but is increasingly frustrated and outraged by the new racism (Feagin, 1994; Scott, 1990). The disenfranchised majority have little political outlet. In some cities, such as Los Angeles and Chicago, gangs have become an important political vehicle for the black community by default.

The Gangster Disciples' political arm, 21st Century V.O.T.E., led the public protests to keep the Chicago public schools open and funded in 1994 (Johnson, 1995). The Crips and the Bloods' "truce" in Los Angeles following the release of the police oficers who beat Rodney King kept the lid on violence and dissipated the police department's best excuse for a crackdown on the black community. The Crips and Bloods also prepared a comprehensive program for rebuilding Los Angeles that was millions of dollars less than proposals by Mayor Bradley, President Bush, or the Democratic Party. The plan included black youth involvement and a gang truce. But as Mike Davis (1992) wrote in *The Nation*, "A Crips/Bloods truce is the L.A.P.D.'s worst imagining: gang violence politicized" (p. 744). Apparently it was not well imagined by the news media either: Major media "whited out" any mention of the truce or the program. At present, however, gangs have no clear political program to fight racism and certainly lack the credibility necessary for building cross-racial alliances.

At the end of the 20th century, DuBois's observation remains valid: Race relations remain the most divisive issue in America. A survey by Loyola University's Center for Ethics in Chicago found that business leaders still consider racial and ethnic divisions, affirmative action, and education the most crucial issues in Chicago ("Survey," 1992, p. 1). Affirmative action, in particular, has become a flash point that hegemonic institutions are using to politically separate black from white and the black middle class from the working poor. Lacking an independent political leadership, African Americans are ill equipped to defend the gains of the civil rights movement, let alone resolve the economic atrophy that is crippling the black community. Given the decreasing economic resources of American capitalism, social programs that have secured black consent for hegemony are threatened. Cultural practices alone will not forestall political and economic adjustments undertaken by the dominant capitalist classes. Social rebellions should be expected, with physical coercion against African Americans more prevalent. The future of racial political hegemony is at stake.

## Conclusion

Mass culture is successful because it inserts itself into popular experience and transforms that experience from within. Mass culture provides us with representations of black life that adhere to popular stereotypes and simultaneously allow black appreciation. The culture industries that control the production and distribution of movies and television rely on black cultural practices and productions for many of their creative inspirations, thus encouraging and to some extent subsidizing black culture, albeit on hegemonic terms.

Since the Civil War, blacks have been recruited to the American Dream through a combination of significant political reform, modest economic enticement, and widespread cultural participation. We cannot give a statistical balance sheet on which of these three conditions for hegemony will be most prevalent at any given time, but we do note that social conditions, political conditions, and cultural conditions are very rarely in "balance." Importantly, the resulting social contradictions have provided sites for renegotiating the terms for hegemony. We hope we have demonstrated some of that in this chapter.

We have not discussed art, dance, children's entertainment, religion, the family, workplace relations, and many other aspects of human activity that constitute culture as a whole way of life. We did not speak much about politics or exhaust the history of the struggle for racial equality in the United States. Representations of race and cultural and social practices that reflect and reproduce race relations are so pervasive and ubiquitous that we could not begin to address them in a single chapter. We hope that what we have presented illustrates how the concept of hegemony might be helpful in understanding the complexity of contemporary culture and race relations. More investigations of hegemony and race in the United States are needed, especially in those "sites" where we directly experience articulations of race. Some of the sources noted provide an excellent starting point.

# 3

## Hegemony and Gender
### *Breakthroughs and Entrenchment*

> Goodness has nothing to do with it.
>
> —Mae West

The efforts of women in the United States (and other Western democracies) to achieve equality is a unique test of hegemony's tenets. It has been possible for those in power to sustain their domination of certain ethnic and economic groups through physical separation and, at times, overt power. The upper classes can afford to live in different places than the working class and the poor. There are still suburbs and sections of cities where the only black faces are those of the help and urban neighborhoods where the only white faces are those of the police or landlords. The sharper the separation between those with power and those without, the less incentive there usually is for the former to understand and negotiate with the latter and the more possible it often is to stop "insurrection" with unmasked force. Witness the violence surrounding numerous labor strikes and attempts at racial integration. But it's nearly impossible for most men to live separately from women. And with the notable exception of continued domestic violence, physical force—certainly in any organized or official sense—has rarely been attempted in the United States. Most men have daily contact with women, profess love for women, construct intimate lives with women, entrust critical decisions such as those about child rearing to women. Thus, men and women, both individually and collectively, have agreed (generally speaking) to whatever economic, political, and cultural relationships they have had over the decades. During those various time spans when women couldn't own property, couldn't vote, couldn't attend college, couldn't partake in public discourse, couldn't enter certain professions, and couldn't play certain sports or join certain clubs, large numbers of women as well as men thought the situation was fine. And when these situations were finally challenged, the resistance, although strongly sustained by men, was necessarily based on gaining widespread female support. Opposition of some women was a critical factor in delaying change or blocking it altogether.

This chapter examines the reaction in the United States to the ongoing struggle for women's rights as an explicit challenge not simply to the power and privilege of men but also to the traditional structures of patriarchy embedded in family, church, government, and business. The first part of this chapter establishes a historical and ideological context with a brief overview of significant issues and events in the American women's movement. We do this to show the ongoing patterns of resistance, co-optation, change, and retrenchment. Second, we focus on one of the current sites of cultural negotiation, the "working mother," to illustrate in more detail the strategies of hegemonic opposition.

## The Women's Movement(s) in the United States

Most Americans learn very little about women's social movements in the United States or their particular contributions throughout world history. Although this situation has changed somewhat since the 1980s, most U.S. citizens believe that "the women's movement" started sometime in the 1960s. They have little knowledge about the barriers to women's equality, including the fact that it took American women over 70 years of concerted effort to obtain the right to vote (Buechler, 1990; Lerner, 1979; Simon & Danziger, 1991). A 1976 survey of general U.S. history texts indicated upward of a 45:1 ratio of men to women chronicled. One book mentioned 278 men and 5 women, 4 of whom were covered in the only three paragraphs focused on "women's history" (Riley, 1987).

Without an understanding of various women's issues and the structures of resistance, it is easy to believe that the development of women's aspirations and rights was (is) the product of some sort of "natural evolution" rather than a conscious challenge to widely held ideologies and practices. This attitude appears in corporations of the 1990s when people assume that the "glass ceiling, " although very much in evidence, will simply take care of itself over time—no need to reexamine traditional beliefs and structures. Even a cursory look at the history of women in the United States reveals that change has occurred as a result of collective struggle against collective resistance. Moreover, a critical part of that resistance has been significant groups of women themselves.

Like most efforts in large-scale social change, women's progress has not been uniform and steady but a series of starts and stops, overt rebellion and opposition, co-optation and accommodation. The most obvious markers, such as the women's eventual right to vote in 1919, have not necessarily been the most effective in challenging systemic oppression of women. Although officially sanctioned violence against women has sometimes been used, by far the most common form of resistance to change has been making the status quo seem normal.

*First Wave: Suffrage, Temperance, Education, and Independence*

Although suffrage (the right to vote) and economic independence (the right to own property) had been called for by American women since the 17th century, the most concerted effort occurred in early 1800s and found its most widely known statement in the Declaration of Sentiments issued from the Seneca Falls Convention of 1848. Although often cited as the "opening shot " in the battle for women's voting rights, the declaration was actually more focused on domestic issues such as property rights, marriage and divorce, child bearing, and custody. Then, as in the late 20th century, many women saw the institutionalized incompatibility between private (e.g., family) and public spheres (e.g., workplace) as the primary field of contention (Johnston, 1992, pp. 26-49). Simply put, women wanted more control over their own lives, wanted to be valued in their own right as whole human beings rather than as subsidiaries to men.

By far the most prevalent objection to this position at the time was the argument that women, at least middle- and upper-class white women, held a spiritually higher position than men but were physically and intellectually weaker. Thus, they must be protected from the vulgarity and harshness of public life (i.e., political, economic, and intellectual power). Very often, therefore, opponents to women's rights argued that they only had the best interests of women (and children) at heart.

This position attained some of its validity from the widely promoted ideology of "true womanhood." According to this precept,

> Women were supposed to embody four cardinal virtues: piety, purity, submissiveness, and domesticity. A woman's power was supposed to reside in the home in her role as wife and mother. A proper woman was always charming, sacrificed herself daily for her family, and did not bother with politics or education. She found her fulfillment through serving others. The angel in the house was emotional rather than intellectual, spiritual rather than cardinal. She was morally superior to men. Her influence was subtle but pervasive. (Johnston, 1992, p. 17)

Critics of true womanhood, then and now, saw its emergence as a way to keep women from gaining such rights as articulated at Seneca Falls. True womanhood depended on increasingly separate spheres for the most economically and educationally advantaged men and women. Women's ascendancy in the home was predicated on her absence everywhere else as well as her abdication of overt power. Moreover, a real "lady" was not only dependent on the economic and political prerogative of men but also on the cheap labor of working-class women. As the social gap between classes widened with the Industrial Revolution, the material extravagance and physical fragility required of a lady became an occupation in and of itself; what 19th-century economist Thorstein

Veblen called "a means of conspicuously unproductive expenditure" (Lerner, 1979, p. 133). Thus, the social construction of the 19th-century lady as a norm for all women kept society's most educated women out of the most desirable professions (to work signaled your husband's failure and your own lack of femininity) and kept paid domestics as second-class women (by definition, because they worked!). It also fueled men's desire to earn enough money so that their wives wouldn't "have to work."

Several scholars have observed that this social system's eager acceptance by men, particularly industrialists, was perfectly understandable because it clearly supported a system of capitalism and patriarchy. The ruthless world of 19th-century capitalism—robber barons, exploitative labor practices, and socially destabilizing hiring practices—were supposedly balanced by the genteel world of "the lady." The angel in the house redeemed the devils outside and thus sustained them (Ewen & Ewen, 1982; Johnston, 1992; Lerner, 1979).

It must be noted that many women embraced the system as well. After all, the image of an angel was very attractive, and the threat of not being feminine (i.e., "truly female") was daunting. Unlike being an ethnic minority or a common worker, being a lady was construed as a status symbol. As important was the fact that many women found pockets of genuine strength within the confines of "true womanhood." For one thing, the system did offer a domain that was, theoretically, absolutely hers—the home. Child-rearing decisions, for example, became mother centered. And volunteer work through churches and other community organizations devoted to the poor and the sick not only gave women a larger sense of purpose but protected those most vulnerable to the indifference of capitalist culture. If women abandoned home and community for the uncaring world of business and government, society would suffer. Thus, as Buechler (1990) observed, certain 19th-century opposition on the part of women to their own emancipation was both rational and altruistic (pp. 171-188).

Of course, few ever questioned whether business and government had to continue as they were. Thus, a significant part of the resistance to social change with regard to women came in the form of creating and celebrating cultural practices that were largely viewed as good and normal. For example, the aforementioned assumption that women were solely responsible for all of the child care coupled with the assumption that only men should engage in public life encouraged the daily practice of such separation. Such accepted practices allowed *Harper's Weekly* to run a cartoon in 1868 opposing women's suffrage that consisted simply of two scenes and an underlying phrase, "How it would be if some ladies had their own way."

One scene showed men taking care of babies and sewing. Next to it was a drawing of women properly dressed and posed in every way except that they were in a saloon and smoking. The mere juxtaposition and caption was apparently considered enough to make an effective argument against removing barriers to women in public life.

A corollary of believing that women's natural place was in the home was (is) the conviction that women who don't agree are *un*-natural. Thus, it is no surprise that suffragists were ridiculed in word and political cartoons as mannish, man-hating, or even monstrous. Even the seemingly innocent move by Amelia Bloomer and her followers to abandon harmful corsets and encumbering skirts met with vicious rebuke (Johnston, 1992, p. 42). As one observer explained, "Trousers were the symbol of the male and of male domination, and the proposal that women should adopt them (almost entirely concealed by the skirt as they were) was seen as a threat to the whole structure of society" (Johnston, 1992, p. 13).

Also the targets of derision were temperance advocates whose arguments about economic dependency were often portrayed as shrill and narrow-minded campaigns about drinking per se—a dismissive stereotype that continued well into the late 20th century. What was obscured by public ridicule in the 19th century and continues to be omitted from discussion in most current high school texts were the critical links that united many in the suffrage, temperance, and abolition movements: (a) the conviction that certain rights were due all human beings and (b) opposition to practices that undermined or denied human dignity. Temperance figured into this picture because of most women's (and children's) dependence on men for survival, dependence that was clearly linked to the cultural practices of marriage and the limited opportunities for women to gain economic self-sufficiency. Dependence on a man who drank heavily (a cultural practice seen by many as a "natural expression of masculinity") was often a direct threat to a family's safety and other basic needs. However, this understandable sociopolitical stance was often reduced to the caricature of Carrie Nation with her little hatchet. Indeed, a significant aspect of past and present opposition to women's rights is the tendency to portray them as isolated and bizarre.

In addition to ridicule, opponents of suffrage used more ominous tactics. Antisuffragists raised alarm about increased domestic strife and an increase in ignorant (read: immigrant) voters (Simon & Danziger, 1991, p. 13). Long prohibited from attending institutions of higher education, women founded colleges of their own and were finally admitted to land grant colleges in the mid-1800s. However, when "coeds" began to match and even exceed male counterparts in academic achievement, they were restricted by enrollment quotas and prohibited from taking certain "masculine subjects," such as science, math, and philosophy (Riley, p. 164). When female mill workers began to use company boardinghouses (in which they had been ordered to live) as sites of solidarity, the boardinghouses were shut down. And in perhaps the most overt use of power against suffragists, peaceful protesters were arrested and subjected to inhumane prison conditions and brutal force-feeding. This last tactic was used during the final years of the suffrage movement, arguably because all other methods of co-optation and persuasion had failed to turn away the demand for the vote.

By the 1920s, after decades of struggle and setbacks, American women had achieved much in the way of legal rights. They could vote, own property, attend college, and hold a wider array of jobs than ever before. Moreover, they were beginning to break down certain social double standards, most noticeably in the area of sexuality. But the demands of domestic responsibility, the obligation to be ornamental, and the prohibitions against professional careers continued. A small but noteworthy number of women, most of whom had attended the prestigious women's colleges of the East, saw traditional marriage as so restrictive that they never married. But their challenge to patriarchy remained essentially private.

Meanwhile, social patterns and practices were shifting to accommodate the "new woman" of the 20th century without disrupting too many core assumptions. Popular magazines extolled the progressive virtues of the "companionate marriage," which acknowledged mutual needs for romance, sexual pleasure, and respect.

> Responsibility for such relationships, however, rested primarily on the shoulders of women, who had the most to lose. Male identity and economic security still rested primarily on work, whereas women understood that their economic security, emotional fulfillment, and social status all depended on a successful marriage. (Evans, 1989, p. 178)

More and more women proved themselves to be accomplished athletes, but many colleges heeded warnings to curtail female athletic programs lest such "masculine" activity make women unacceptable as wives. Careers were encouraged in the mass media but only as a means of finding the right husband (Evans, 1989, pp. 182-183). The growing consumer economy targeted women as primary consumers and enlisted the burgeoning advertising trade to convince women that there was a host of heretofore unknown problems that they needed to worry about and corresponding products that they needed buy. Childbirth, mothering, and homemaking were ceded to male "experts" who reduced women's control of the first and expanded responsibilities in the last two categories. Birth control became a "professional issue," but the development of successful children remained the mothers' responsibility (Johnston, 1992, pp. 120-125, 220). Women were told (not for the last time) that they could "have it all"; failure to do so was strictly their choice rather than the result of social forces. In the 1920s wake of women's political, educational, and economic victories, Miss America was created—a contest limited to young, unmarried women who did not submit transcripts or other evidence of intellectual or creative

**Miss Oklahoma 1995**

Contestants for Miss Oklahoma 1995 competed in the traditional categories of talent, swimsuit, and evening gown. Despite announcers' claims that this was much more than a beauty contest, contestants seemed to be judged primarily on their physical appearance. "Talent" was so uniformly bad that only clips of actual talent winners were included; a finalist tap-danced to the William Tell Overture wearing a matador costume—without irony. The swimsuit competition was labeled "health and fitness," but all the contestants did was walk across the stage in swimsuits and high heels. The evening wear competition (try to imagine men "competing" in evening wear) had been merged with the pithy question event. Each contestant glided to center stage in a slinky, low-cut dress, gave a 2-minute answer to a question such as, "Why is public education necessary?" and turned around to give the judges a rear view. The winner of this contest went on to win the title of Miss America 1995.

ability but did compete against each other wearing swimsuits. In sum, although women had made significant advancements from the beginning of the 19th century to the beginning of the 20th century, they were still "kept in their place" largely through convincing most of them that their primary obligations were to look attractive, create and manage the household, and above all, be supportive of their husbands.

*Second Wave: World Wars,*
*Economic Depression, and Aftermath*

U.S. involvement in World War I and World War II had a profound effect on many social patterns, including gender relations. In both cases, the U.S. war effort benefited greatly from women's involvement in traditionally male spheres, and in both cases, the government joined hands with mass media, educational, and even religious institutions to see that women returned to their "proper place" once the crisis was over.

Perhaps because U.S. involvement in World War I was less extensive than in World War II, its impact on social relations has been less noted. Nevertheless, during World War I, women entered the workforce in record numbers. Even more striking was their role during the economic depression that followed. With so many men deprived of their traditional roles (neither soldier nor breadwinner), society looked to both women and men to create new ways to hold families together. But it was World War II that really laid the groundwork for modern feminism by giving women experiences that could no longer be contained by old paradigms (Johnston, 1992).

Strong women were necessary to dominant interests during the 1930s and 1940s, so it is not surprising that images of strong women became prevalent, especially in film. This was the heyday of Katherine Hepburn, Rosalind Russell, Bette Davis, Claudette Colbert, Joan Crawford, Carol Lombard, Myrna Loy, and Barbara Stanwyk. On screen, they were smart, independent, and funny. There has not been another era like it in terms of roles for women. To be sure, their characters often reflected some ambiguity about strong women. The noir films of the 1940s were especially cautionary about the treachery that lurked behind female independence. And career women, no matter how competent, were eventually convinced to sacrifice job for family (*Woman of the Year*, 1942) or pay the consequences (*Mildred Pierce*, 1945). Citing hundreds of examples, Haskell (1974) argues that these ebbs and flows and crosscurrents in U.S. movies, during the 1940s and throughout the history of mainstream film, reflect widely shared beliefs and contribute to popular assumptions and public discourse about gender construction and relationships. In essence, she contends that strong women on screen were welcomed when their real-life counterparts were needed by established interests. But these same images were shunned when the actual women started to challenge that establishment.

The ambiguity about working women could be seen in other widely disseminated messages as well. On the one hand, government and industry exhorted women to "do their part" by taking on jobs from which they had once been prohibited. Suddenly it was no longer "mannish" to be a welder but patriotic. But there were many signals of caution and resentment as well. Ads and articles assured the female welders and their counterparts that looking feminine was part of their duty. Union officials and other male blue-collar workers openly longed for the return of the all-male workforce (Evans, 1989).

This era is particularly interesting from a hegemonic point of view because the desired behavior on the part of the subordinate group changes so dramatically in such a short period of time and the messages from dominant interests are so overt.

In the 1940s, women were told that they shouldn't work outside the home if they were married, then that it was patriotic to work outside the home, then that their real job was to cook and take care of their kids and husband. In the 1950s and 1960s, movies glorified male war heroes and the sweethearts they left behind. Hollywood and the country selectively forgot women in the factories and the armed forces. It was as if their jobs as riveters, welders, nurses and pilots—along with the emergent feminism—never happened (Douglas, 1994).

Moreover, at least one analysis contends that the women who experienced the least resistance to their new roles were middle- and upper-middle-class women whose husbands weren't threatened when their wives took working-class jobs (Honey, 1983). Apparently, it's easier to think Rosie the Riveter is cute when you're not a male riveter.

The deluge of messages telling women to return to full-time domesticity is well documented (Douglas, 1994; Evans, 1989; Johnston, 1992; Rothman, 1978; Simon & Danziger, 1991) and played a critical role in one of contemporary feminism's most well-known calls to arms, *The Feminine Mystique* (Friedan, 1963). Articles and ads extolled the glory of family togetherness, made possible by a mother devoted to elaborate meal preparation, the latest in home decoration, constant child supervision, and the ongoing arrangement of social activities. This carefully crafted togetherness was presented in word and picture as the essence of what was normal and good—a fundamental requirement for the happiness of all concerned.

What is contested about these messages by most feminists is not the desirability of a warm family life or good meals. The objections have to do with the virtual requirement to marry and the overwhelming domestic responsibility assigned to women as well as the equally overwhelming requirement for material goods—thus the corresponding need for men to dedicate their lives to earning money. Many critics have noted ironically that the proliferation of appliances and other timesaving products (e.g., cake mixes, frozen food, and no-wax floors) did not result in diminished household chores but expanded what could be expected. The time saved with an automatic washer and dryer was supposed to be used to make gourmet dinners; the time saved with TV dinners was supposed to be used to drive the kids to Little League.

Like their 19th-century foremothers, women were told to create their own special sphere, which would support their husbands' careers. Moreover, they were supposed to look exquisitely feminine while doing it. Gone were the comfortable slacks and flat shoes of the war years that alleviated self-consciousness and facilitated physical activity. Very high heels and voluminous (or unduly tight) skirts were de rigueur. Even housekeeping required that women "look their best."

Women in magazines were always stylishly and impractically dressed. In advertising, they sometimes wore a glove to press the button of the latest household machine. More often than you would expect, they were shown in striking poses in the kitchen while wearing a tiara. . . . This fit in with the women's other cherished role, as "glamour girl" for her weary husband, as well as counselor and confidante. "The two big steps that women must take are to help their husbands decide where they are going and use their pretty heads to help them get there," wrote Mrs. Dale Carnegie in the April 1955 *Better Homes and Gardens.* "Let's face it girls. That wonderful guy in your house—and in mine—is building your house, your happiness and the opportunities that will come to your children . . . through success in HIS job." (Hine, 1986, pp. 30-31)

Appearance is a particularly good site for exploring how constructed social practices become so normal that the fact of their construction and the nature of their consequences become invisible. Consider the adjective *feminine.* Although many women during the 1950s refused to conform to the new fashions (and *very* few wore tiaras in the kitchen), they usually refused on the basis of individual preference. In other words, although they might eschew spike heels and gloves, they did not, for the most part, argue for a new definition of femininity. They simply thought of themselves as individually opting out of an unassailable truth.

Although women were still entering college during the 1950s, there was much teasing about the "Mrs. degree." Female students (largely referred to as "coeds" as though they were some sort of appendage to real students) were encouraged to major in subjects that would make them interesting wives and good mothers. Talk of career preparation usually centered on teaching or nursing as "something to fall back on" in case you couldn't be supported by a husband right away. Even the most prestigious coeducational universities encouraged this idea. The University of Chicago, for example, concentrated on pictures of male students when depicting intense study in their promotional material. Women were largely featured in dating scenes and other social activities. Some schools restricted the number of women admitted to ensure room for returning G.I.s, and of course, some of the "best schools" (e.g., Harvard and Yale) continued to exclude female students altogether.

Most of the women's colleges founded in the 19th century to counteract such practices seemed eager to join the domestic surge. The president (male) of Radcliffe told the class of '65 that their reward for studying hard could be an Ivy League husband. Mount Holyoke allowed seniors to use wedding pictures (complete with husband) in lieu of traditional graduation portraits. Smith alumnae marching in a homecoming parade held signs proclaiming how many in their respective graduating classes were already wives and mothers.

As has been noted, grade school texts did little to acknowledge women's roles outside the home. Churches stressed the centrality of virtuous, caring, saintly mothers and the need for young girls to "save themselves" for marriage. *Playboy*, founded in 1953, celebrated women who didn't save themselves but stayed in the bedroom anyway. TV shows of the 1950s largely abandoned previous images of working women (albeit in "pink-ghetto" jobs) and spunky wives (e.g., *I Love Lucy, The Honeymooners*) and concentrated on the placid, impeccably groomed moms of *Leave It to Beaver* (June), *Ozzie and Harriet* (Harriet), *Father Knows Best* (Margaret), and *The Donna Reed Show* (Donna) (Douglas, 1994, pp. 50-51). Some shows left women out altogether (e.g., *Bonanza*).

Some of these shows have been cited so often as examples of certain kinds of families and family roles that they have become cliche (e.g., Oprah can refer to "that Donna Reed sort of thing" and her audience smiles in easy recognition). Still, it is important to examine some of the particulars of such programs to understand what practices constituted normality at that time, which ones persist, and with what significance. It could go without saying that June, Harriet, Margaret, and Donna were white, slender, and almost always in dresses. All were attractive without being striking. None worked outside the home or showed any signs of ever having serious career aspirations. None spoke about having gone to college. Each was centered in her ordered, clean, and comfortably appointed (but not ostentatious or elegant) suburban home, and each was very concerned with the emotional well-being of her children (no less than two, no more than three) and husband. None of the wives or husbands discussed anything related to political issues, nor did the husbands' jobs (in some cases, unknown to viewers) seem to have much impact on the family. It was as though reality centered around the individual home, with occasional forays into largely generic schools, stores, churches, and (for husbands) jobs. Among the messages sent by these shows was that home life was important, but there was virtually one kind of home life that was acceptable, and it was largely up to women to create it. It is important to note that the men in these programs were as narrowly defined as the women with one important distinction: They had lives, however ambiguous, outside the house. Americans who watched a broad spectrum of TV in the 1950s had access to those lives through programs that centered on work or public affairs. Thus, although both mothers and fathers in TV land were seen largely at home, men had identities beyond fatherhood.

Strong, capable women were largely absent from film as well. What intelligence they were allowed was used to get a husband. This was, after all, the era of the popular film *How to Marry a Millionaire* (1953). As Haskell documents, strong and complex female leads gave way to fairly one-dimensional beauties epitomized by "good girls" such as Doris Day, "bad girls" such as Elizabeth Taylor, and "innocent sex symbols" such as Marilyn Monroe. Haskell argues that the emergence of these character types after World War II was no accident because they left plenty of room for white men to resume their accustomed public and private positions without fear of competition or, even more alarming, challenge to the entire social system.

Ironically, at the same time that these constructions of sex symbol, wife, and mom were being promoted by virtually every segment of U.S. society, women were under attack from some psychologists, sociologists, and other social commentators for being neurotic, overprotective, and even domineering (Evans, 1989; Johnston, 1992). It's certainly possible that some women reacted to the restrictions of the postwar years in destructive ways. Indeed, Friedan (1963) draws on women's testimony to that effect to document the oppressive nature of 1950s society. Unlike Friedan, however, the vast majority of public voices did not raise fundamental questions about gender-based spheres of activity or coordinated media campaigns. Instead, they asked, "What's wrong with women?" "What could women be doing better?" "What product could women buy that would seem to address these 'needs?' "

Who benefited from such a system? The easy answer is men. Men didn't have to choose between family and career, independence and virtue, intellect and sexuality. Yet some realized that such benefits came at a price. They were physically and emotionally separated from their families. They were often stuck in dull, unfulfilling jobs. Broadway lore has it that when *Death of a Salesman* debuted, men sat in the audience stunned or weeping, unable to leave after the final curtain fell. Some working-class men, industrial workers such as coal miners and steelworkers, felt trapped by dangerous and underpaid work to which they could see no alternative. Conversely, some women felt they benefited from male dominant hegemonic relations. As in the late 19th century, they had a clear sense not only of being needed but of being put on a pedestal as well. Working-class women, many of whom *did* work outside the home, saw staying at home as a privilege in light of the tedious and often demeaning work world available to them (Johnston, 1992, pp. 11-14).

> Although they were bombarded with propaganda about happy housewives, most middle-class women did not feel manipulated. They felt they were choosing the best of all possible worlds. Instead of the feminist hope of the 1920s of combining marriage and careers, their hope was for affluence, sexual fulfillment, and a house full of children. Only when they achieved their dreams and lived within the confines of the feminine mystique did many of them feel trapped. (Johnston, 1992, p. 208)

More obvious beneficiaries are those who benefited from profits secured from discriminatory pay scales and the support that women gave to the entire apparatus of single-family responsibility for child care, laundry, housing, food preparation, and emotional support. Capitalism benefits from patriarchy. When assumptions about female inferiority and domesticity are blended with the tenets of capitalism, a hierarchy is constructed that consists not only of gender privilege but of economic privilege as well. Add race, and the picture becomes even more complicated. What emerges most clearly, however, is a situation in which public and private life is separated and public life is reduced to working life, which is more valued. The home conforms to the workplace, and the workplace conforms to the drive for private corporate profit. Women's willingness (albeit reluctant in some cases) to take care of all unpaid duties, including community work, and many low-paying jobs such as grade school teaching allowed corporate white middle- and upper-class men to dominate decision making in critical areas such as health care, law, religion, politics, and the economy. Women's willingness to be ornamental allowed a proliferation of products directed toward their need to "improve on nature." And their subservient acceptance as primary consumers ensured that the 20th-century notion of planned obsolescence would endure (Ewen & Ewen, 1982).

Feminism per se was not a major issue in the 1950s and early 1960s, so there was little call for overtly antifeminist efforts. Moreover, many professional women of the time rejected organized political struggle, believing "that such ideological loyalties led to mass conformity and emphasized irrationalism. They often believed that feminism . . . minimized the differences between men and women, especially the consequences of women's reproductive role" (Johnston, 1992, p. 239).

*Third Wave: The Counterculture and Beyond*

The 1960s is often seen as a time of seamless counterculture movements. Conservative commentators of the 1980s and 1990s often lump together antiwar protest, women's liberation, "free love," and drug use (emphasis on the latter two) as if they emerged from a single, unprecedented impetus and concerned exactly the same people. The civil rights movement—hotly contested by conservatives at the time and the one strong ideological link between the antiwar and women's movements—is almost never mentioned except to acknowledge it as the one "good" cause. As Marilyn Quayle ("Marilyn Defends," 1992) said in her speech to the 1992 Republican National Convention,

> I came of age in a time of turbulent social change. Some of it was good, such as civil rights, much of it was questionable. But remember, not everyone joined the counterculture. Not everyone demonstrated, dropped out, took drugs, joined in the sexual revolution, or dodged the draft. . . . Not everyone believed that the family was so oppressive that women could only thrive apart from it. (p. 1).

Many people during the 1960s, hundreds of thousands in fact, began to see connections between racism and sexism. It's likely that some of these people questioned sexual double standards and the necessity to marry before engaging in sex. Some may also have experimented with drugs. But to equate serious political activists with "dropouts" and chronic drug users is simply false. In fact, a hallmark of early civil rights and antiwar organizers was their high educational level, their refusal to take drugs, and their disdain for "flower children" whom they saw as frivolous and self-indulgent. Quayle contrasts "the counterculture" with "most of us" who "went to school, to church and to work." In fact, school and at least some churches were focal points of political protest. It's true that opposition to significant social change was often expressed by educational and church leadership. On the other hand, the antiwar movement as well as the civil rights movement was full of clergy and people who expressed deep spiritual faith. University hierarchies may have been deeply committed to government policies and "old boy networks." But students' attitudes against sexism, racism, and the war in Vietnam were heavily influenced by university-based activities such as teach-ins. So there's no simple line between those who "went to school, to church, and to work" and those who didn't.

Why, then, do people like Marilyn Quayle blur these distinctions? Is such sloppy history a conscious distortion on the part of people who should know better? Perhaps. More likely, it's a way of seeing the world that protects those who benefit the most from the status quo. One result is to reduce political critique to accusations of solipsistic fashion trend. Another is to taint any noble motivations that might be associated with opposing war and sexism by implying that participants were morally depraved (again, it should be noted that in the late 1950s and early 1960s, it was antiracism that was portrayed by conservatives as morally depraved). If the deep, widespread, and complex challenge to the U.S. dominant culture that took place in the 1960s can be dismissed as one big, unfortunate aberration—like platform shoes, only more dangerous—then those who benefit from that culture can continue essentially unchanged. As Quayle stated in the same speech, "We had a stake in the future, and though we knew some changes needed to be made, we did not believe in destroying America to save it" ("Marilyn Defends," p. 1). The root of these changes is never specified, but it seems clear that the root—Gramsci's (1988) "kernel" of capitalism—is not to be addressed because that would "destroy America."

Marilyn Quayle's particular target in this speech seemed to be feminists, although they are never named as such. Instead, there are references to women who want to live outside "the family" and be "liberated from their essential natures as women." These radicals are contrasted with reasonable women, such as herself, who are open to "new choices and challenges" but who believe we must "go back to the future."

Particularly ironic about putting the women's movement into what Quayle and others considered the same unholy vat as all other political radicals and moral libertines is that the women's liberation movement that emerged in the 1970s was formed, in part, as a reaction against the sexism of the political left and contemporary youth culture. By the early 1970s, numerous women who had been active in civil rights and antiwar efforts decided that there was something wrong about the fact they were still relegated to the "back rooms" of social change. Just like their nonleftist sisters in corporate America, they were making coffee, running the copier, and smiling supportively at male speeches that they'd heard before. Just like their married sisters, they were supposed to be available for emotional support and sexual comfort (Davis, 1981; Ewen & Ewen, 1982; Johnston, 1992).

However, the women's liberation movement that came of age in the 1970s wasn't primarily concerned with left-wing sexism. In the most immediate sense, it emerged in reaction to the stifling domesticity of the postwar years. Women who had experienced independence and satisfaction in public spheres realized that they weren't content with being helpmates again. They wanted more for themselves and for their daughters (Douglas, 1994, pp. 45-59; Evans, 1989, p. 195). They made Friedan's (1963) *Feminine Mystique* an immediate best-seller. But modern feminism was also a continuation of the critique of fundamental aspects of U.S. society that had started centuries earlier.

From what did many women still want to be liberated? One list would be include the following:

- Restrictions against educational and employment opportunities
- Laws that put them economically, physically, and socially under the control of husbands
- Laws and practices that ignored their health needs
- Almost total responsibility for housekeeping and child care
- Moral double standards
- Narrow standards of beauty that were often difficult, if not dangerous, to obtain
- An overall sense of being regarded as less than fully human (As seen on a T-shirt, "Feminism is the radical idea that women are human"; attributed to scholar Cheris Kramarae)

What was the nature of the opposition? As in the past, it took many forms, some of which even looked like agreement. Why was there opposition? One answer is that there was honest disagreement. Another is that liberation would undermine some of the most essential ideological pillars of patriarchy and capitalism. If sex-based inequities were eliminated in a male-dominated society, then by definition, men would lose privilege. For example, if social mores shifted to the point where working fathers took as much re-

### Hair Dye . . . I Mean, Color

Hair color has been an important marker to women. The terms *blonde, brunette,* and *redhead* so closely identify females that stories can be told about women without ever referring to more than their hair color. The correlation between hair color and identity doesn't apply to men: Blonde jokes aren't about blond men. Hair dye—I mean, color—is marketed to women with the promise of changing their life experience. Clairol asks, "Is it true that blondes have more fun?" and even promises that the right color will let a woman capture her true identity. So ingrained is the belief that men's and women's hair color signifies different things that "dye" is marketed to men with the product name, "For Men Only."

sponsibility for domestic duties as working mothers, many men would lose the career edge they currently hold (Schwartz, 1993). If women's worth became more a matter of ability than artificially manufactured looks and material possessions, then by definition, corporations and their advertisers would lose obsessive consumers. For example, if aging were considered a natural and even ennobling process for women, the sales of items such as hair dye and wrinkle cream would diminish.

As will be discussed, change with regard to these issues has occurred, some of it dramatic, since the 1960s. However, it should also be noted that *after* each major change, some of the fiercest opponents to that change argued that the change was only logical and served to prove the flexibility and strength of the status quo. Marilyn Quayle can sound quite reasonable in 1992 when she speaks of women's "new choices and challenges" without having to admit the bases of those changes. And she can allude to the destruction of America without having to articulate ideological assumptions because patriarchy and consumerism are still assumed by many to be central to "the American Way."

## Strategies of Opposition

In his study of the Students for a Democratic Society and their opposition to the Vietnam War, sociologist Todd Gitlin (1980) uses constructs of hegemony to analyze why the serious, thoughtful, and sincere aspects of the antiwar movement were then and are now routinely dismissed. Gitlin concludes that it was more than a matter of Nixon's "dirty tricks" and outright harassment. The legitimate press effectively buried the Left through omission, marginalization, trivialization, and when all else failed, demonization and polarization (pp. 27-28). Gitlin doesn't claim that such resistance efforts were always self-conscious. Rather, they seemed to their practitioners and many mainstream observers to be "natural" and "inevitable" reactions to clear threats.

Hegemony responds to challenges against patriarchy and women's inequality in similar ways. In addition to the five hegemonic responses identified by Gitlin, we note that co-optation has been important to the maintenance of capitalist hegemony in regard to gender relations.

Opposition to women's equality in the late 20th century has been pervasive, multifaceted, and intense, but it has not been the result of a conscious, organized conspiracy; rather, leaders of hegemonic institutions are simply enforcing the requirements of dominant relations. And some of the key agents for capitalist hegemony have been women (Faludi, 1991, pp. xxi-xxii).

### Omission

Some of the earliest feminist studies focused on language and how even something as seemingly benign as vocabulary can reinforce patriarchal assumptions (Lakoff, 1975). One of the clearest and yet most hotly contested examples is the use of the same term as a masculine referent and a human one. *Mankind, man,* and *he* have been claimed by many to be universal terms, embracing both sexes. And yet the terms obviously specify a particular sex as well. Moreover, female terms are not assumed to be inclusive. In other words, the English language makes it possible for us to speak of humanity ("mankind") without acknowledging women at all.

### The Politics of the Personal

Feminists contend that the root of female oppression occurs in the division between public and private and the devaluation of the latter. It isn't just that women have been excluded from public life but that what are considered private issues— the family, health, pregnancy, housework, sexual practices— are not worth examining. Women's attempts to reveal the connections between public and private are crystallized in the adage, "The personal is the political."

Consider the question, "Who wears the pants in this family?" It refers to the person in control. It implies that there should only be one per family. And it clearly indicates that such a role is normally masculine. That it has sometimes been humorously applied to a woman indicates how abnormal such a so-called power reversal has been considered.

What are we to do when Sally Gray, who has been Sally Gray for 35 years, marries Frank Russell and becomes Mrs. Frank Russell, and what of the many benefactor lists for organizations such as charities, arts endeavors, and civic groups that continue to be dominated by couples listed as Mr. and Mrs. His Name? What about all those wedding invitations and reception place cards that do the

**Looking Good = Capitalism**

Susan Douglas (1994) contended that popular culture's fascination with depicting Soviet women as scowling, hairy, muscular creatures corresponded to the dominant culture's need to counter the fact that Soviet women were becoming doctors and engineers (p. 22). Being strong and intelligent doesn't count if you don't look "feminine." Pre-Soviet women look like Julie Christie in *Dr. Zhivago*. Communist women must look like linebackers in drag.

same. Where did the women's names go? Where did the women go?

Omission has not been the dominant response to the contemporary women's movement. In fact, at least since the late 1960s, women's issues have been given substantial, albeit not always accurate, coverage by mainstream news media (Davis, 1981). In contrast, in grade school and high school, social studies are largely silent about early suffrage and contemporary issues. Many Americans, both female and male, are completely ignorant of the over 70-year conflict that women went through to get the vote. Nor are they aware of the fact that the vote was not extended to women until after the First World War, decades after it had been extended to black men. One result of this ignorance is a common belief—given voice by Marilyn Quayle, among others—that attaining equality for women is simply a matter of time, that social progress is a steady, benign process of updating knowledge rather than a political struggle. Moreover, the scant treatment given the women's movement that reignited in the 1970s gives some the impression that all the battles worth fighting have been won, that any further challenge to the status quo is obviously out of bounds.

## Marginalization

Marginalization of subordinate groups has long been a primary operation of cultural hegemony. Grade school texts have often set the tone for years of education and reading to follow. For example, *Faraway Ports* (Hildreth, 1940), a widely used primary reader in the United States and Britain during the 1940s, presents stories on a wide range of topics: personalities, places, and cultures. Young animals learn skills and have adventures. Children discover cultures with different types of dwellings, toys, and pets. Ironically, despite the fact that all authors and editors of the text are women, none of the protagonists (including the animals!) are female. Women and girls appear, but they are always relegated to minor or supporting roles. Unfortunately, modern textbooks have not made much progress. And marginalization in grade school texts is repeated in adult political conversations.

Since the first murmurs of women's liberation in the 1960s, opponents have dismissed it as irrelevant. American women were commonly portrayed in the media as the most advantaged in the world; how could they possibly think they were oppressed? If anything, critics argued, it is men who suffer because they have to deal with the irrationality of "the opposite sex" (Douglas, 1994).

Inequalities between men and women in the United States are avoided by focusing on the relative advantages that middle-class white women in the United States have compared with working-class women or women in nonindustrial countries. In a typically hegemonic construction, restrictions on women's opportunities were presented as advantages: Oppression was designed to look chivalrous or cute. Of course, being the "queen of the house" or "the girls in the office" didn't protect women from long hours of low-paying hard work. But the image of well-off American women obscures inequality and detracts from efforts toward economic independence and access to decision making. In 1970, women were legally restricted in most states from working overtime on a paying job, but few legislators were concerned with women's "double shift" of housecleaning and child care. Women were prevented from holding paying jobs that required lifting weights as low as 15 pounds, although they routinely lifted much heavier children. Women were encouraged to shop, ridiculed as spendthrifts, and yet precluded from getting credit cards and mortgages in their own names (Joreen, 1970). Finally, women's experience of oppression (or almost anything else for that matter) was simply not the same as men's and, thus, was ignored. Being able to vote, an important hegemonic practice in the United States, does not resolve women's extreme cultural, social, and economic marginality.

Forced economic dependence, vocational barriers and lack of acceptance as public voices were very much in place for women at the onset of the modern women's liberation movement, yet many political, intellectual, and cultural leaders kept asking, "liberation from what?" ABC national news anchor Howard K. Smith voiced particular outrage that women would compare their situation with that of "truly oppressed" minorities such as African Americans (Douglas, 1994). Many male New Left leaders expressed the same sentiment (Morgan, 1992). News reporters seemed eager to cast women's liberation protesters as "a wacky, self-seeking, publicity-hungry fringe of unrepresentative women" (Douglas, 1994, p. 159).

Hollywood and independent filmmakers reacted by shutting women out of films more than ever before. The period between 1962 and 1973 was

> the most disheartening in screen history. . . . The growing strength and demands of women in real life, spearheaded by women's liberation, obviously provoked a backlash in commercial film; a redoubling of Godfather-like machismo to beef up man's eroding virility or, alternatively, an escape into the all-male world of the buddy films like *Easy Rider* or *Scarecrow.* (Haskell, 1974, p. 323)

In short, feminism was simply a nonissue to the defenders of capitalist hegemony. It wasn't central to their notion of politics, economics, or culture, and therefore, it didn't need to exist.

*Trivialization*

Stuart Ewen (Ewen & Ewen, 1982), among others, has observed that 19th- and 20th-century attire tends to encourage the perception of men as responsible, no-nonsense leaders and women as decoration. Great insight is not needed to notice how women's fashion undercuts women's mobility and credibility. High heels with open toes, "big hair," tight short skirts, huge cumbersome shawls, and clingy sheer blouses have all been heavily marketed— not just to fashion mavens who live for style but to female professionals who must argue cases, negotiate fees, present competitive campaigns, and preside over complicated decision making. When fashion designers decree "a return to femininity," they inevitably mean a return to clothing and grooming that signals fragility, emotion, sexual availability, and frivolity (Faludi, 1991).

Opponents characterize feminism as a joke. Although measurable discrepancies such as salary differentials and job restrictions are too apparent, other criticisms are trivialized as minor or silly. Labels such as "women's libbers," "libbers," and "bra burners" prevent any engagement on the substance of capitalist cultural hegemony. It seems of little relevance to such name-calling that no bras were ever burned at any women's equality demonstrations, including the famous Miss America protest of 1968, which supposedly inspired the label (Faludi, 1991, p. 75).

Whereas films chose largely to ignore the issue, TV sitcoms had a field day putting out-of-context feminist jargon in the mouths of characters who clearly had no idea what they were talking about. Ellie May of *The Beverly Hillbillies*, Lisa of *Green Acres*, Gloria of *All in the Family*, among others, spouted superficial rhetoric that was clearly contradicted by the "realities" presented in their respective shows. In true sitcom fashion, an irritating but ultimately trivial problem is created and resolved in 30 minutes (minus time for commercials). In these cases, the problem posed is that a slightly daffy but otherwise perfectly fine woman is foolish enough to believe that she is part of an oppressed group. She is led astray by some trend-driven agitator or book, and the solution is for the other characters, usually her husband or boyfriend, to gently allow her to see the error of her ways (Douglas, 1994, pp. 196-198).

## Demonization

One historical indication that women's challenges to patriarchy were making significant inroads was that their issues were no longer ignored, put in the margins, or trivialized. Quite the contrary. Elizabeth Cady Stanton observed as early as 1848 that one sign of real progress was when you were portrayed by your opponents as sinister. A 1913 *Life* cartoon titled "Militants," commenting on the suffrage movement, depicts four women in three different ways. One row shows faces that are unattractive—harsh, dour, and heavy—captioned, "As They Are." A second row shows faces that are saintly and heroic, with radiant lines, halo, and laurel wreath— above is the caption, "As They Think They Are." The last row is titled "As They Appear To the Police and Shopkeepers"; faces here are demonic with glinting eyes, pointed ears, bared teeth, and horns (Banta, 1987, p. 17). When a movement becomes too threatening to dominant relations, hegemony responds by reinforcing its ideological pillars, portraying the challengers in the most vicious light possible.

In 1992, Pat Robertson told the National Republican Convention that contemporary feminism encourages women to leave their husbands, kill their children, practice witchcraft, and become lesbians. Robertson was only articulating a crude defense of patriarchy and capitalist cultural hegemony. Any hegemony seeks first to bolster existing relations, so organized backlash to social movements historically coincides with the first indicators that real change is being made (Faludi, 1991, pp. xviii-xx). Just as depictions of blacks shifted as they gained political power (from comedic pickaninnies and nurturing mammies to violent criminals; Bogle, 1994; Riggs, 1987, 1991), so when the women's movement gained momentum, dominant representations and media images of a confused but essentially likable girl give way to the homely man-hater with no fashion sense and hairy legs who could think of nothing better to do than attack the system for which she was unfit.

Much was made of the general perception that outspoken feminists Betty Friedan and Bella Abzug were not conventionally attractive (contrast this with the lack of such observation with regard to Phyllis Schafley, a leading opponent of an Equal Rights Amendment for women). Much was made of the fact that some women associated with women's liberation didn't shave their legs or wear makeup or smile a lot. Of course, one of the defining elements of feminists was—and continues to be—the rejection of women as essentially ornamental and the correlating rejection of the idea that women must alter themselves drastically to achieve that ornamental worth. Proponents of such a position would quite naturally eschew what they believed to be feminine conventions imposed by fashion and cosmetic advertisers and patriarchal needs.

The issue for many women is twofold. Why should physical attractiveness to men be my primary goal? And why must I go to extreme lengths to achieve it while men are more or less taken as they are? Thus, 1970s feminists faced a quandary. If they wore blue eye shadow, curled their lashes, wore 3-inch heels, and elaborately arranged their hair, they would fit the standard definitions of beauty and thus be qualified to speak as women, consenting to their subordination within capitalist hegemony. Conversely, if they didn't believe such consumerist fashions were necessary, they wouldn't subscribe to them and would risk being dismissed as insufficiently female—"mannish" (Buechler, 1990, p. 200). In a truly dramatic social construction, looking natural was equated with being unnatural.

A common form of hegemonic retrenchment equates feminists with lesbians, a tactic that discredits feminists to many "average Americans" and even turned feminists against each other, disrupting their efforts to forge counterhegemonic alliances. Like the 19th-century suffragists who were willing to abandon black women to gain middle-of-the road political support, so too do some liberal feminists shun the "taint" of homosexuality to gain acceptance. Evans (1989) observes that "like red-baiting, the charge that women who challenge traditional gender boundaries were lesbians (and that lesbians were somehow 'unnatural') [has] been used to contain feminist insurgency throughout the twentieth century" (p. 294).

### Being Female Versus Looking Feminine

As their 1996 Mother's Day storefront display, a funky resale shop dressed their female mannequins in waist-cinching dresses, 3-inch high heels, and ruffled organdy aprons. Interspersed among them were 1950s-era appliances. A young boy passing by with his mother asked, "Why are they wearing such silly clothes to do housework?" His mother explained that in the 1950s, when such attire was popular, people thought that women should look feminine no matter what they were doing. Truly confused, the boy responded, "I don't get it. If they're women, how could they not look feminine?" Good question.

A particularly disturbing but commonly made accusation was that feminism was not just an attack on patriarchy and its practices but a visceral attack on men. Critics used words such as *castrate* and *emasculate* to describe the consequences of women's liberation. From this perspective, to be equal with a man meant to deny him his masculinity because privilege was apparently integral to that identity. To deny advantage was to deny meaningful existence.

Feminists could not possibly be "real women" because real women could not possibly want things to change in any significant way. And if some real women were momentarily swayed, it was because they had been infected by "outside influences" (Douglas, 1994, p. 180). It is a strategy that has been used against labor unions, the civil rights movement, and the 1960s antiwar protest as well: the argument that insidious outside agitators must be responsible for disturbing the peace because critiques of the system could not possibly rise organically.

## Polarization

Demonization encourages another practice—polarization. To call some women "impersonators" means that other women are "real." To call only some women feminine meant that others were "unfeminine." This disjunctive perspective has been identified by chroniclers of women's higher education who noted 18th-century critics' contentions that women would have to choose between advanced education and childbearing because their delicate systems couldn't tolerate the strain of both. Such a viewpoint appears again in the tendency of 1950s Hollywood movies to juxtapose beauty and brains, virginity and depravity, ambition and domesticity. Actresses such as Thelma Ritter, Celeste Holm, and Joan Blondel were apparently deemed not attractive enough to be love interests (the only central role allowed women in that era) but often played sidekicks who could be smarter and tougher than the leading ladies.

Such polarization allowed opponents to do several things that undermined the effort to achieve gender parity. They claimed to be supportive of "real women" while dismissing feminists. They used any women's opposition as proof that there was no systemic inequity due to patriarchy—just some malcontents seeking attention. They spoke as though there was an inexorable barrier between working women and mothers that prevented the former from having any nurturing qualities or domestic interests.

One of the linguistic developments most disappointing to supporters of the contemporary women's movement is the growing popularity of the disclaimer "I'm not a feminist, but . . .," a phrase invariably followed by statements that support feminist ideology. What is the speaker pushing away when she disavows that title? Is she truly critiquing central tenets and practices, or has she come to accept the narrow definition of feminism proffered by those who fear an identity that has the power to unite a large number of peo-

### Secretaries' Day

Secretaries' Day was invented in 1952 and quickly endorsed by florists, card shops, and other retailers. One way to view this manufactured tribute is as a formal recognition of an essential but often underrecognized sector of our workforce. If this is the primary justification, one wonders why there aren't similar days to honor people such as miners, slaughterhouse employees, sanitation workers, house cleaners, migrant farmers, grade school teachers, and postal workers. From the perspective of hegemony, Secretaries' Day functions to encourage secretaries (still a predominantly female group) to accept their often underpaid and overextended positions because they are "really appreciated," as evidenced by the once-a-year lunch or bouquet of flowers.

Executive bosses (still predominantly male) routinely make much more money than the people they praise as "making them look good," while asking them to attend to personal errands and other jobs well outside the job description. Such inequities prompted some workers' advocacy groups to use Secretaries' Day as a time to demand "Raises, Not Roses" (Evans, 1989, p. 300).

ple? Culturally speaking, demonization in image coerces subordinate group members to accept or at least tolerate hegemonic relations. Thus coerced, hegemony advances with "consent" against subordinate demands.

## Co-optation

As Gramsci said, hegemony is coercion wearing the velvet glove of consent. Faced with demonization, the contrasting comfort that hegemony seems to provide attracts subordinate members. Fleeing coercion, subordinates are recruited to superficial change (as if it were substantive) in the name of reason and progress. For hegemony, bringing in subordinate supporters doesn't challenge or disrupt dominant power but reinforces it. Like the martial arts practitioner who seems to yield only to throw the opponent off balance, capitalist hegemony seems to incorporate feminism, simultaneously diffusing substantive threat and bolstering the status quo.

In tandem with coercion, then, co-optation is instrumental in renegotiating subordinate consent. Subordinate representatives play off their identities as subordinate group members to better sell dominant relations as beneficial to all. Hegemonic institutions mask advances as significant change and grant small favors to selected subordinates as evidence of the magnanimity of their leadership. Thus, by the 1930s, women had entered the professional workforce in unprecedented numbers and popular discourse was full of references to "the modern woman." But with few exceptions, the jobs were markedly lower in pay, power, and status than those of men. Women were nurses but not doctors, secretaries but not executives, nuns but not priests, primary teachers but not university professors or even public school principals.

The other variation of co-optation was and is the reduction of feminism to individual choice; primarily in the social arena of "style." Being a "modern" or "liberated" women was no more difficult than finding the right clothing and hairstyle. Freedom from oppression as a class of people was conflated with individual freedom to make minor choices.

From the 1920s into present times, advertising provides clear examples of this latter approach. Products ranging from perfume to cars have been marketed to the "new woman," although few had anything to do with enhancing her actual and economic strength or independence. In fact many products, such as cigarettes, are actually harmful, and others, such as cosmetics, reinforced the very cultural practices that the women's movement challenged.

Two of the most infamous advertising campaigns were for Virginia Slims cigarettes and Enjolie perfume because the ads were so blatant in their evocation of "feminism" and the products so far removed from actual feminist values. The Virginia Slims print campaign that ran for several years used sepia-tinted photographs of ostensibly late 19th-/early 20th-century women (thus trading on early suffragist images) who had been "oppressed" because they weren't allowed to smoke. These were juxtaposed with photos of tall, slender models who were very fashionably dressed, radiantly happy, and holding Virginia Slims cigarettes. The slogan read, "You've come a long way, baby" and clearly implied that smoking was an achievement of equality. Enjolie's television and print ads featured triptychs of a glamorous female model swinging a briefcase, cooking, and swaying in a seductive negligee. The copy read, "I can bring home the bacon, cook it up in a pan, and never, ever, let you forget you're a man." On television, this was sung to a sexy blues beat. These were not depictions of moral courage, intellectual achievement, or freedom from the real political and economic constraints of the past. These were sex symbols who used briefcases as props and kept the goal of individual pleasure foremost. As was (and still is) the case with hundreds of ads, women's liberation was used as something that could be purchased. Moreover, it was portrayed as a matter of individual will; either you had the nerve to wear Enjolie and smoke Virginia Slims or you didn't. There was no collective action required. There was nothing substantive about the political or economic system that needed to be changed. There was nothing that men needed to do differently. In Gramscian terms, emergent opposition to capitalist cultural hegemony was co-opted as an alternative practice within dominant relations.

Women's liberation was reduced to mass-produced, consumer-based "individual " style.

In the late 1960s, when many young women resisted the fashion industry's appeal, mass media tried representing working women as secretaries, receptionists, models, nurses, and flight attendants, often depicting them as sexy helpers (Wolf, 1991, p. 31). This was, after all, a time when flight attendants were invariably female and could be hired on the basis of age (young), appearance (beautiful), and marital status (single) (Davis, 1981, pp. 16-25). It was a time when Southwest Airlines put stewardesses in hot pants and ran ad campaigns that read, "Hi! I'm Susie! Fly Me!!" and the best-selling book about working women was *Sex and the Single Girl* (Brown, 1962). Corporate America could support careers for women as long as those careers made no demands on male privilege either in terms of men's control of professional power or women's dual functions as helpmate and sex object.

The fashion industry was challenged again in 1972 when John Molloy created the "dress for success" guide for corporate women. Although initial profits could be made on the dark suits and accessories he recommended, designers, manufacturers, and stores quickly realized that this approach would not provide the kind of sales volume to which they were accustomed. Molloy's whole point had been to provide a "uniform" for white-collar women similar to that worn by white-collar men, arguing that women needed fewer articles of clothing and that sexuality as well as nonessential differences between male and female colleagues would be de-emphasized.

> Eventually, *The New York Times Magazine* ran a piece declaring that Molloy's strategy was passé, and that women were so confident now that they could abandon the suit and express their "femininity" once more. Many media for which the fashion industry provided a sizable portion of their ad budget quickly followed suit. (Wolf, 1991, p. 44)

Traditional forces proclaimed victory for women's rights, reduced the argument for desexualized clothing to women's insecurity, and promoted new rounds of fashion in the name of reclaiming femininity. Implicit in this stance is the belief that neutral business uniforms are somehow natural for men.

Co-optation is particularly important to understand when examining hegemony with regard to women because, as noted at the beginning of this chapter, women are usually integral parts of men's public and private lives; the gender-privileged group can-

**What Are Little Boys Made of?**

Gender scholar Sandra Bem tells the story of a young boy who had long admired his older sister's colorful barrettes and asked his mother if he could wear some to school. "Of course," the mother replied. However, when the boy arrived, his best friend (also male) approached him with genuine confusion. "I thought you were a boy!" "I am!" answered the first child. "You can't be," replied the second, "you're wearing barrettes, and only girls wear barrettes." "No," responded the first, and to prove his point, he pulled down his pants. "See, I'm a boy!" According to the teacher who observed this exchange, the second boy just kept looking at his friend's hair and said solemnly, "You can't be a boy; you're wearing barrettes."

not effectively distance themselves in the same ways as those privileged by race and class.

## The More Things Change . . .

The "kernel" of capitalist cultural hegemony remains, especially in the consumerization of women as objects and as shoppers, but it would be a big mistake to argue that significant change has not occurred with regard to women's political, cultural, and material positions in the United States. Major hegemonic institutions have recruited women to renegotiated dominant arrangements, especially in terms of politics. Women not only vote but have, on occasion, constituted a significant voting block. A substantive theme of the 1996 Republican Presidential Convention was openness to women in an effort to close the often-cited "gender gap" between Dole and Clinton. Women hold powerful elected and appointed positions in record numbers. They also have a much greater presence in other traditionally male occupations. As the last century ended, it is not unusual to see female medical doctors, police officers, accountants, corporate managers, military officers, news reporters, business consultants, lawyers, and university professors. In a speech to a Chicago women's group, columnist Anna Quindlen summed it up with an anecdote about her 1995 visit to a primary school class in which a young boy began his question to her with, "Look, I know that girls can be anything they want"—a phrase that would not have been uttered by a grade-schooler 20 years earlier.

Numerous, more positive and more varied representations of women and girls now appear in popular and "high" culture. Warner Brothers and Disney cartoons have featured more female characters. The Bugs Bunny et al. characters had been virtually all male (even Tweety!). The creation of Tiny Toons (1990) and Animaniacs (1993) brought some interesting female characters center stage. Disney's animated full-length features, long criticized for their long-suffering but beautiful heroines who had to be rescued by heroes (*Snow White, Cinderella, Peter Pan, Sleeping Beauty*) began to produce more independent and capable female protagonists (Miss Bianca, Ariel, Belle, Pochahantas, and Mulan)—albeit in the end they never challenge male supremacy. Alternatives to Barbies and baby dolls now exist, most strikingly in The American Girl collection. Magazines directed at children (e.g., *Cricket*) have shown both boys and girls in a wider range of activities as well as more ethnic and religious diversity. Magazines directed at girls (e.g., *Full Moon*) minimize fashion in favor of articles on ecology, health, books, music, sports, and social issues. Fashion layouts in catalogs and magazines feature more girls' clothing suitable for physical activity. Toy catalogs present more things as gender neutral. The explosion in children's publishing that occurred in the late 1980s (baby boomers having babies) included dozens of books about strong, talented females. Similarly, there was a significant rise in feature films with young girls at the center of the action.

Cultural images of adult women have changed as well. After a spate of TV series with men as heroes and women as victims, the mainstream television networks produced *Cagney and Lacy, Roseanne, Murphy Brown, Designing Women, Kate & Allie, China Beach, Golden Girls, Sisters, My So Called Life, Dr. Quinn, Medicine Woman* and, more recently, *Cybill, Buffy the Vampire Slayer, Ellen,* and *Judging Amy.* Several acclaimed dramatic series that featured strong character ensembles—*Hill Street Blues, L.A. Law, Star Trek: The Next Generation, Chicago Hope, Law & Order,* and *Family Law*—portrayed women as competent, complex professionals. Roseanne Barr and Oprah Winfrey became two of the most powerful people in television production. Mainstream films at least occasionally put women in unexpected roles, as in *Aliens.* And there were a few overtly feminist films, such as *Thelma & Louise, Making Mr. Right, She-Devil,* and *A League of Their Own.* By the mid-1980s, the fastest-growing segment of one of the best-selling book genres was the one featuring female sleuths. And female comedians were allowed to make jokes about things other than their appearance and husbands. Some advertisers went beyond the Virginia Slims approach of exploitative images to cash in on deeper social changes: oppositional images and messages now appear regularly in advertisements for consumption. One of the most striking examples of this hegemonic adjustment was the Nike campaign that ran funny/lyrical/tough copy with depictions of women as self-reliant, wholly worthwhile human beings.

Increasingly, print and video advertisers have included women in ads that depict life outside the home and men in ads that feature housework and child care. Women's magazines have expanded to acknowledge working women, working mothers, and older women who saw themselves as more than grandmothers. Arguing that advertising made them compromise content, *Ms. Magazine* became ad-free in 1990 and flourished.

Change occurred at the level of "high culture" as well. Although women had long been prominent as performers in certain areas (e.g., ballet and opera), they took on more roles as primary creative forces—artistic directors, choreographers, playwrights, curators, composers, novelists, directors, conductors. During President Bill Clinton's first term in office, two women served a poet laureates. Moreover, the work of these people as well as their artistic foremothers was increasingly promulgated and valued through the efforts of feminist scholars. Departments and programs of "women's studies" exist in practically every major university and college. Feminist cultural criticism has become more common-place in such bastions of cultural anointment as *The New York Review of Books*.

Since 1970, the basic tenets of patriarchy have also been questioned by an increasingly visible homosexual culture. Occasional television series and advertisements have depicted same-sex couples, giving the appearance that lesbian and gay life are part of mainstream culture. Of course, such images also spur arguments that the United States is in the throes of self-destruction. Thus, as TV viewers witnessed Mariel Hemingway kissing Roseanne and anticipated Ellen's "coming out," support grew for the Defense of Marriage Act, which stipulated that marriage can be legally sanctioned only between women and men. In short, dominant gender roles have bent but not broken.

As in most hegemonic relations, the substantial material, political, and cultural changes described here have been contradictory and difficult to secure. For every strong female TV character and gender-neutral toy and women's studies class, there were countless rejections of the same as well as numerous examples of the oppositional strategies already discussed.

What these examples do signify, at least for the purposes of this book, is that gender-based definitions and boundaries and power relationships are being contested more openly than before. What had appeared as the seamless and exclusive normality of postwar masculinity and femininity can no longer be taken for granted.

In other words, despite the surface appearance of tranquil relations and the crass engineering of historic records, hegemony always faces challenges, always renegotiates its relations. Even growing up female in the 1950s was more contradictory than popular myth proclaims. Douglas (1994) cites the familiar examples of media messages to be dumb, beautiful, pliant, large-breasted helpmates to men. But she also remembers hearing post-Sputnik exhortations to study hard and serve your country and believing that they included her (p. 22). She remembers listening to the Shirelles and other "girl groups" acknowledge sexual tension and believing that they validated her own confusion (pp. 83-98). She even found solace in the relative competence and independence of TV's Samantha (*Bewitched*), Cricket (*Hawaiian Eye*), and Gidget. She concludes that "much of what we saw was porous, allowing us to accept *and* rebel against what we saw and how it was presented" (p. 9).

> The mass consumption of that culture, the ways in which the shards got reassembled, actually encouraged many of us to embrace feminism in some form. For throughout this process, we have found ourselves pinioned between two voices, one insisting that we were equal, the other insisting that we were subordinate. After a while, the tension became unbearable, and millions of women found they were no longer willing to tolerate the gap between the promises of equality and the reality of inequality.... Here's the contradiction we confront: the news media, TV shows, magazines and films of the past four decades may have turned *feminism* into a dirty word, but they also made feminism inevitable." (Douglas, 1994, pp. 9-10)

Douglas's analysis evokes the theoretical tenets of hegemony— that the dominant culture asserts and protects itself through consent whenever possible but is open to negotiation when that consent becomes too strained. One of the biggest contributors to that strain is the tension between experience, your life as actually lived, and the messages about that life that you see manufactured around you.

The many messages that undermine absolute patriarchy signal that the cultural, material, and political terms of consent are being renegotiated. Transparently patriarchal messages have been successfully modified by highly individualized consumer-oriented messages. Crude biases and practices against women in education and employment have been mitigated by selectively recruiting a significant number of individual women into leading hegemonic institutions.

Overall, the current condition of women in the United States clearly indicates the persistence of capitalist cultural hegemony. Oppositional themes have been creatively incorporated into dominant hegemonic representations and relations, and for now, the ongoing social contradictions of gendered inequality have been papered over by rewarding some of those who consent to the established order.

## . . . The More They Stay the Same

Although women in the United States have indeed made gains, they continue, as a whole, to encounter significant disadvantages in terms of attaining socioeconomic security, job fulfillment, home and work balance, and political representation (Schwartz, 1993). Moreover, the gains they have made are commonly exaggerated in attempts to stem what is characterized as a tidal wave of powerful women. Faludi (1991) reports case after case of headlines blaring the triumphant "arrival of women" in male occupations while the actual figures remain in single digits and, in some cases, decline (pp. 363-378). Men in corporations whose top management is only 6% female talk readily about the imminence of "reverse discrimination," although most admit that they have no real examples (Murphy, 1995). College campuses are characterized as havens of feminist intolerance and other forms of "politically correct" oppression, although the examples cited by the *Dartmouth Review* and similar journals seem confined to a handful of schools and a very small percentage of faculty.

Women have indeed increased their presence in the strongholds of societal power but remain significantly underrepresented in most nondomestic areas. Hegemonic institutions make the minimal adjustment necessary to reassure subordinate groups that the social arrangements are beneficial. In 1999, although women made up over 50% of the population, less than 10% of the U.S. Senate and approximately 13% of members of the House were women. There were three female governors. Two of nine Supreme Court justices were women. Although an increasing part of the workforce, women composed less than 10% of top corporate management and approximately 17% of college and university leadership.

The recruitment of representatives of subordinate groups to hegemonic institutions parallels the continued subordination of the overwhelming majority. Thus, women are significantly more likely than men to be poor, to be the head of a single-parent household, and to be severely harmed or killed by domestic violence. Adolescent girls are much more likely than their male peers to suffer from chronically low self-esteem and eating disorders. Studies indicate that around half of American girls report being on a diet on any given day and most dislike their bodies (Pipher, 1994).

Such skewed numbers indicate that, despite cultural hegemony's claims of equal opportunity, outcomes differ substantially by sex and that the difference is not due to chance. But percentages are only part of the story. More important considerations are why these lopsided situations persist after decades of efforts to end sexism and why so many people are willing to believe that the need for such efforts is over.

The mass media (so long accused of perpetuating narrow stereotypes) has created a false sense of egalitarian workplaces. Television programs, movies, and ads that purport to depict professional settings such as hospitals, law firms, newspapers, police departments, and research labs routinely show more ethnic and gender diversity in higher places than actually exists (hooks, 1995). And although some advocates of change might approve, believing that role models encourage diversity, hooks and others voice apprehension that the images invite complacency and even backlash.

Another perspective can be provided by the phenomenon of "cultural space." Katha Pollitt (Media Foundation, 1994) talks about the willingness of mainstream media to hear and report different voices. She observes that although a good deal of media coverage was given to feminists during the late 1970s and early 1980s, that space has shrunk considerably, and so has the space allotted traditional critics of feminism—men, religious conservatives, even right-wing women such as Phyllis Shafley. What there *is* space for, according to Pollitt, are young, presumably hip women who eschew certain feminist positions.

Pollitt looks at the initial flurry of sympathetic media attention to the research and reportage of date rape and then the almost total rejection of it based on one young woman's testimony. Although the very idea of date rape long had been questioned in the conservative press, the fact that such criticism was predictable made it unremarkable. But when Katie Rophie, a very contemporary-looking and -sounding Harvard undergrad, questioned the seriousness and widespread occurrence of date rape, the story became a national sensation despite the fact that her skepticism was based primarily on personal observation ("no one I know has been raped on a date") and earlier critiques of date rape studies published in the conservative press. The real story, then, is about an educated and ambitious young woman's rejection of feminism—a story that many editors apparently wanted to report.

Understanding hegemony suggests that resistance to gender equity lies in the enormity of the change that feminism poses. The challenge to patriarchal-centered society is as fundamental and far-reaching as Galileo's challenge to an earth-centered universe. This is not merely a question of objective data but political, economic, and social privilege. Unfortunately, most men benefit from capitalist hegemony—insofar as they identify with patriarchal representations—and identify its existence with their own condition. As one man said during a gender awareness workshop, "I'm all for equality, but I don't see why I should give up my advantages as a man—I mean, that makes me feel like I'm being put at a disadvantage."

This sentiment indicates how thoroughly capitalism has incorporated patriarchy in its defense. Gerda Lerner (1986), among others, has observed that women's ultimate responsibility for "the human aspects of life-nurturance, caring for the helpless, the young, the old, and the creation of a livable environment—and men's ultimate evasion of that responsibility—structures inequality between the sexes into every institution of society " (pp. 140-141). Capitalism compounds the situation by measuring value by income and making domestic work the least valuable. Changing this, Lerner concludes "will demand the transforming and restructuring of all institutions of society and the creation of new forms of community" (p. 144).

In Gramscian terms, women's liberation needs to be part of a counterhegemonic movement. An urgent historic task for feminists and their allies is the gathering of a new historic bloc with a political and cultural program that speaks to the needs of diverse subordinate classes and groups. Demands for women's equality have concrete aspects: child care, equal pay, opportunity for female participation in science and politics—all issues that benefit working- and middle-class *men*. Women's liberation requires the end of capitalist hegemony and any counterhegemony to capitalism must include women in its leadership and the demands of women in its program.

Business, education, government, medical care, law, the arts—all—are more or less structured on assumptions of divisions between public and private life, with women taking care of the home in unpaid or very low-paid capacities. What allows practices now considered integral in these professions (e.g., long hours at work, frequent and prolonged travel, intense focus on task) has been that "someone else" has been tending the children, buying and cooking the food, cleaning the house, washing the clothes, running the errands, maintaining family ties, and volunteering in the community.

Many professions have developed around an essentially two-tiered system with women almost always in the poorly compensated support positions—secretaries, nurses, clerks, assistants, grade school teachers. The mere *call* for shifts in this allocation of responsibility and compensation is seen as monumental—pitting advances of women to the disadvantage of men. The shift is certainly monumental but more directly to the disadvantage of corporate greed and hegemonic structures serving capitalism. Thus, capitalist hegemonic institutions always attempt to confuse the beginning of change with actual change; even the slightest movement is seen as significant and sufficient. The fear of fundamental change, abetted by images of "progress," encourages the perception that no further change need occur.

Some opponents of feminism acknowledge the continued difference between men's and women's lives but justify that difference by invoking the supposedly neutral phenomenon of "personal choice." According to this position, no one is "preventing" women from pursuing professions; no one is "making" women choose between children and career; no one is "forcing" women to go on endless diets and have cosmetic surgery; no one is "stopping" women from being athletes, no one is "requiring" women to put their husbands' careers first. It just happens. These are simply the choices that individuals make. And following this logic, that so many individuals are making these choices indicates that there is something natural and reasonable about these arrangements. Anyone who says otherwise must believe in politically naive conspiracy theories or that women are too stupid to make up their own minds (Sommers, 1994).

However, as we have tried to point out in this text and as numerous critics using the tenets of hegemony have illustrated, it does not take a conspiracy theorist to see patterns of cultural rewards and messages. It is not a matter of conscious conspiracy or individual intelligence when a person believes that her or his social identity is affected by these rewards and messages. The patterns endure because they "make sense" to those who benefit most and offer rewards to those who cooperate. An individual risks a great deal when he or she ignores these patterns, although some succeed.

Gender is one of the most primary aspects of our self-knowledge and self-esteem. Unlike biological sex, which is largely defined by inborn characteristics, gender is socially constructed. By definition, gender is dependent on what other people think—what other people agree is masculine and feminine. And as Ewen (1989) observes, it's not enough for most of us to realize that the argument can be falsely constructed. To know that something is artificial does not necessarily diminish its force. And contemporary popular culture forcefully promotes images and practices that communicate appropriate gender roles and expectations—images and practices useful to a U.S. hegemony of consumerism and capitalism.

### Just for Kids

The mail-order catalog "Just For Kids" might lead children to believe that boys and girls engage in a few similar activities (such as art) but are divided by interests and abilities. According to photographs and descriptions in the catalog, here's what boys and girls are and what they "do":

| Girls | Boys |
| --- | --- |
| Are cheerleaders | Are firefighters |
| Talk on the phone while they cook | Drive race cars |
| Are brides | Are superheroes |
| Sing | Play the guitar |
| Are ballerinas | Are doctors |
| Have fantasies | Have adventures |
| Are princesses | Are knights |
| Are ladies-in-waiting | Are construction workers |
| Are Southern belles | Are astronauts |
| Are mommies | Are martial arts experts |

Throughout, little girls are apparently absorbed in fantasy and appearance, eagerly working at fashion, makeup, and hairstyle. Little boys are more energetic and extroverted in their activities.

*Little girls are supposed to be "beauties in training."* Despite the success of American Girl dolls, Barbie still reigns supreme. There are currently over 50 varieties of Barbie on the market, most of which clearly indicate that being terribly thin and fashionable is their raison d'être. Even when Barbie is being "athletic," she is being attractive. Promotions for the "Sporting Life" series contain statements such as "Cycling—pedaling pretty!" "Ice-skating—pretty gliding!" "Aerobics—great workout look!" Some Barbies are even formally dedicated to high fashion shopping (e.g., Madison Avenue Barbie, Bloomingdale's Donna Karan Barbie). Attempts to give Barbie serious pursuits are undercut by the need to keep her glamorous (Dr. Barbie wears a pink sheath and spike heels under her lab coat). Attempts to acknowledge other standards of beauty are also largely compromised. Although Barbie is now available in versions that signify different ethnic groups, they all look like . . . well, they all look like Barbie! The only difference is skin tone and costume. The same is true of Barbie's "historical figures." The ever present smile, the big hair, the permanent eye makeup, and the impossible figure are still there. The message seems clear. You can be whatever you want, but remember that your constant obligation is to look good according to seemingly universal criteria.

Toy stores and catalogs are still full of beauty products and costumes that emphasize this "vocation." A 1990 Lillian Vernon catalog (over 120 million mailed according to company figures) had the following items for girls, promoted in the catalog's text and photography: personalized vanity table, heart-shaped makeup mirror, jewelry box with twirling ballerina, full-length mirror, and dress-up items/Halloween costumes fixated on beauty rather than activity. Even an ice-skating outfit emphasized what Barbie might call "pretty gliding!"

Some undoubtedly would argue that all of this is "just fun"; it's fun to ornament yourself and human beings have done it for centuries. True. But if self-decoration is a fun-filled human impulse, why are there no boys putting on lipstick and striking poses with feather boas? Beauty is clearly signaled as a female pursuit; indeed an occupation. Furthermore, the feminization of masculinity does not mark the "softening" of partriarchy as much as it portends the increasing consumerization of male identity. Representations of femininity are chained to market-driven images, whereas men are being seduced by Madison Avenue's portrayal of masculinity (Willis, 1991).

*Little girls are junior caretakers.* These catalogs, as well as a walk down the aisles of any Toys R Us store, also indicate that girls are supposed to be interested in homemaking and child care. Toy appliances are often coded in "girl colors" of pink and lavender. Television ads and toy packaging routinely show little girls cuddling dolls and stuffed animals while saying "I love you" in sweet tones.

Being a pretty and caring girl may be all that is necessary to have an identity. Consider, as Katha Pollitt (1994, pp. 152-156) did, the case of Smurfette (a character in a cartoon series still broadcast daily on cable television). There are, apparently, 100 Smurfs, each with a distinctive personality trait or talent. Jokey plays practical jokes, Painter is an artist, Brainy is smart, Baker is a gourmet, Papa is wise, and Grouchy is grouchy. But Smurfette is simply a smurfette. Her identity is being female, which, according to her behavior patterns, consists of smelling flowers, worrying about her appearance, and taking care of the boys.

Girls are also supposed to *be* loved. A study of greeting cards designed to be sent to children (Murphy, 1994a) revealed that girls (and young female animals) depicted on the cards were overwhelmingly passive; their primary functions were to look pretty and to receive affection. Only girls were addressed with words such as *dear, darling, adorable, charming,* and *precious.* "Sweet girls" outnumbered "sweet boys" by almost 7 to 1. And boys only got to be *lovable, cute,* and *huggable* during their first year (e.g., "To a sweet baby boy on his first Easter"). In fact, some cards designed for boys went out of their way to dismiss emotion. For example, one card featured a wrestler cat (kittens, of course, were reserved for girls) who growled, "get out of my face." Another depicts a detective rabbit who tells the card's recipient that he has a secret—that the recipient is loved. "But don't let it get around," the rabbit warns. This juxtaposition in greeting card design illustrates the most significant point of this section. It's not just that girls are supposed to be loving and lovable but that boys are not.

*It's OK for little girls to expand their horizons, but not for little boys.* A survey of several mass-produced artifacts directed at children —films, television shows, books, greeting cards, toys, and after-school activities—indicates that girls have more options than boys in some respects. Although still expected to be pretty, loving, and lovable, girls are now encouraged to be more athletic, career minded, and daring. Disney's Belle (*Beauty and the Beast*) reads incessantly and has the courage to take her father's place as hostage of the Beast. Warner Brothers' Dot is as wild and wacky as her male playmates. And despite the lack of attention from the toy catalogs mentioned earlier, no self-respecting superheroes team is without a female member. Soccer teams and science clubs are full of girls. Such changes signal challenges to patriarchy in that they fundamentally alter certain ways of thinking about girls.

But if the essential structure of patriarchy is to be confronted, one would expect perceptions of boys to be shifting as well. Sexism is not eliminated when girls become imitation boys but when assumptions about male superiority (and the necessarily corresponding female inferiority) are undermined. But catalogs that depict girls playing with chemistry sets do not show boys with dolls or making pretend meals. The Beast still needs Beauty to tame him. Ballet is still the province of little ballerinas, and boys' choirs are maintained not just for their distinctive sound but because a separate identity must be maintained to get most boys to join (R. Webster, choirmaster, personal communication, September 23, 1995). Moreover, boys are rarely depicted on teams or in groups of girls: Dot has two brothers with whom she has escapades, the six standard Muppet Babies have Miss Piggy, Superfriends allows two females to join the gang of numerous superheroes, but there is no cartoon configuration that has the odds reversed. Is this just a happenstance or does it simultaneously reflect and convey our lingering belief that boys are the model and girls are the variation? A tomboy is cute. A sissy is to be abhorred. To aspire to be masculine is normal. To aspire to be feminine is OK only if you are female.

*Women should still aspire to be "feminine."* Although the messages directed at children may be the most blatant, clear and pervasive messages are aimed at older females as well. Wolf (1991) gives compelling evidence that a commercially defined beauty continues to be promoted as an essential aspect of womanhood. No matter what else a women aspires to be, her vocation must include a certain kind of beauty, preferably one for which she must buy many products. Wolf contends that the terms used by magazines and advertisers have changed in response to the women's movement: the beauty myth has replaced the *Feminine Mystique;* in the 1950s, Friedan (1963) lamented that "there is no other way for a woman to be a heroine" than to "keep on having babies"; today, a heroine must "keep on being beautiful" (pp. 66-67).

Wolf's (1991) point is not so much that there is a conscious conspiracy against women as that the powerful economic interests of the fashion, cosmetic, and advertising industries have a great deal to gain in convincing women that they must aspire to a certain standard of beauty; to be beautiful (within the cultural hegemony of U.S. capitalism) is to be a consumer. So great is the corporate fear that women might abandon their products that beauty industry advertisers routinely refuse to support magazines and other outlets that allow questioning of these standards. Gloria Steinem, first editor of *Ms. Magazine*, tells stories of how advertisers rejected placement in editions that carried stories about medical hazards of makeup and plastic surgery. Thus, in 1990, *Ms.* decided to eschew all ads in an effort to obtain the journalistic freedom to print articles and photographs that questioned commercial norms.

The difference between *Ms.* and other "women's magazines" can be startling. A 1991 survey of both traditional and self-styled alternative women's magazines (none of them "beauty" or fashion magazines *per se*) revealed that all but *Ms.* put a heavy emphasis on a very narrow standard of appearance and the products to achieve that appearance. In fact, the "alternative" magazines' concentration on young, thin, Caucasian, high-fashion models made their insistence that they spoke to working women (*Working Woman*), older women (*Lear's*), and contemporary women (*New Woman*) all the more disingenuous (Murphy, 1994b). The real message seemed to be that although it is good to have careers and inevitable that one grow older, a woman should make every effort to look attractive while doing so.

Such messages support certain economic interests, but how do they support patriarchy? For one thing, they perpetuate the belief that one of a woman's primary functions is to be decorative. And according to popular culture, being decorative is usually incompatible with being smart, competent, and powerful (unless you're evil or looking for an even more powerful man). Countless female professionals have been told, "But you're too cute to be a lawyer" (doctor, accountant, Ph.D., etc.). According to this logic, looking pretty makes a woman less threatening—hence, the attempt (albeit ill-fated) on the part of the Price Waterhouse accounting firm to prevent an extremely successful woman from becoming a partner on the grounds that she didn't look feminine enough. Although she sued and won, her case provided a revealing glimpse at the kind of assumption that continue to guide such choices as which women get to be news anchors (Wolf, 1991, pp. 34-40).

*Women should still aspire to be mothers (which really means primary parent).* Consider the numerous and widespread messages that tell women, men, and children that women should be the primary nurturers in families. The term *working mother* simultaneously implies that mothers who stay home don't work and that there's no need for the phrase *working father. Parents Magazine* (1998 circulation 1,925,000) indicates through picture and text that mothers are the real parents. Fathers appear only in "special features." Talk shows and advertising regularly convey the impression that there are two distinct and opposing camps: working mothers and stay-at-home mothers. Magazine stories and newspaper articles often decry the ill effects of "latchkey children," day care horrors, and the decline in "family values." The villain in such features is always the mother who would rather pursue a career or escape an unhappy marriage than take care of her family. Ironically, villainy disappears when the mother in question has no career to pursue but is dependent on welfare. In this case, she is expected to take any job she can get and find day care wherever she can.

Magazines and newspapers applaud high-profile women who leave their careers because they realize "what is really important." The March 1994 issue of *Barron's* featured a cover story titled "Working Women: Goin' Home," complete with a 1940s-style, apron-clad mom holding an apple pie. The front page of the May 18, 1995, *Chicago Tribune* contained a large color photo of a female physician carrying her 15-month-old son and holding the hand of her 3-year-old (Stein, 1995). The photo and the story convey the impression that mothers "make life" and are more satisfied than working women. Stories about extended leave, alternative career paths, flexible scheduling, flextime, job sharing, and telecommuting invariably assume that job equity plans are for working mothers; men rarely feel that they need to consider such options. Of course, such reforms help women balance their "double shift" as mother and worker, but they do little for diminishing the expectation that to be a parent is to be a mother or that it is primarily a woman's responsibility to be a parent.

Corporate workshops on "glass ceiling" issues frequently erupt in frustration over women's "unfair" expectation that such "private matters" as family issues should be any concern of business. Of course, family issues have a relationship to the workplace. No parent of preschool children could work outside the home unless he or she had someone to take care of those children during certain hours of the day. Captialist hegemony organizes discourse and institutional practices with the assumption that care of children is the female parent's duty, developing a large and complex system of work that depends on wives to take care of "private matters." But working women don't have wives. If women are to work outside of the home either the nature of the workplace or the nature of child care will have to be renegotiated. This is not to say that individuals don't make their own decisions. It is to acknowledge that those decisions take place within economic, material, and social structures built around assumptions of power and value.

Distributed through and by hegemonic institutions such as media, legislatures, and business groups, contemporary messages and cultural practices prevent substantive discussion of important issues such as the well-being of children, the vitality of communities, and the sanity of our workplaces. Capitalist hegemony poses false polarizations, distracting women and men from the positive benefits of structural change. If children suffer from lack of parental contact and care, why shouldn't working fathers participate more? Why don't companies that demand 60 hours a week and frequent travel reexamine their policies? If "family values" are what's "really important," why does capitalist cultural hegemony stress the need for material possession? Where are the articles praising fathers for quitting work? Why can't mothers and fathers split equitable household, child care, and career obligations? Why aren't life choices discussed in terms of ranges of possibilities? Why can't day care involve good and competent people who might enrich people's lives rather than endanger them?

The most obvious answer is that thoughtful discussion of these questions would overturn fundamental assumptions and practices of existing hegemony, not simply about gender but about work and success and happiness. It would require that "successful women" as well as "successful men" reconsider the configuration of success away from individual consumerism. It would truly question the relationship between material possession and happiness. It would probe the division between private life and public life. It would require that men define masculinity in ways that didn't simply oppose femininity. In sum, thoughtful discussion would challenge the basic tenets of consumer society and American capitalism.

## The Negotiation Continues

In their groundbreaking, albeit controversial books, Susan Faludi (1991) and Naomi Wolf (1991) argue that the contemporary women's movement has triggered a significant backlash, ranging from denial and verbal hostility to co-optation. Anna Quindlen (1993) and Susan Douglas (1994) observe that substantive change has occurred. Understanding hegemony gives credence to both of these claims. Patriarchy has fundamentally changed and patriarchy has essentially remained.

This paradox is apparent throughout popular culture. Four sites illustrate particularly well how hegemony has renegotiated subordinate consent without disrupting dominant control: romance novels, daytime dramas, women-centered sitcoms, and the coverage of women's sports.

### Romance Novels

Romance novels have often been seen as a barometer of female conformity to patriarchal structure. The genre is popularly characterized by voluptuous and emotional women whose success is marked by their ability to attract handsome and powerful men.

Moreover, the supposedly minimum literary value of these books supports assumptions about the minimum intellect of the readers. Janice Radway (1984, 1993) offers some compelling alternative analysis. She observes that romance novels privilege *romance*, the emotional connection between women and men, rather than explicit sex or economic dependence. Moreover, the tension in the story is often provided by the female protagonist's resistance to what she fears will be the smothering effect of traditional marriage. Radway (1984) claims that romance novels often present attractive portraits of strong, self-reliant "heroines" who are capable of defying the "hero" as well as changing him so that he values her "female perspective" of loving and caring for another (p. 54). They offer a vision of relationship (usually marriage) that can accommodate the independence and identity of both partners rather than a paternalistic or patriarchal relationship (pp. 78-79, 102).

Radway (1993) does not defend these books as a whole in terms of serious literary merit, but she does claim positive functions for the reading activity itself. Reading romance provides a source of guiltless self-interest and pleasure for many women who are otherwise devoted to pleasing others (Radway, 1984, p. 95). It also gives a variety of women a loose sense of community across socioeconomic lines. Radway (1984) concludes that the popularity of this genre both sustains and subverts traditional values, including those of patriarchy, although she acknowledges the passive nature of both the reading activity and the typical heroine's primary activity (being loved) (p. 118).

Understanding hegemony, however, casts Radway's optimistic read in a different light. Reading romance provides an escape from hegemony, not a replacement for it. By relying on romance reading for satisfaction and fulfillment, women tolerate their limited real-life roles and are diverted from pursuing actual potential and social activity outside the highly individualized act of reading a book. Incorporating more progressive images and alternative, albeit idealistic, representations of male-female relations, romance novels sell well but do little to change the social conditions of women who must read before, during, or after they complete their chores as wife, mother, and discriminated-against worker.

*Daytime Dramas*

Targeted primarily at women, daytime dramas, or "soap operas," emphasize emotional relationships between people, usually featuring heterosexual romance. Although being with a man is often a daytime drama heroine's main goal, she is also portrayed as self-reliant and assertive. Her need for sexual fulfillment is seen as normal, often laudatory.

John Fiske (1995) offers an appraisal of soaps that echoes Radway's read of romance: The typical female character's ability to understand, facilitate, and even control relationships makes her powerful, an attribute seen as good as well as evil. Men are often deficient in this arena, needing to be taught by women or easily manipulated. In addition to being good-looking, "heroes" are usually sensitive and articulate. Private rather than public (e.g., work) lives are the focus of attention and energy. However, stable and traditionally nuclear (hierarchical) families are not. Thus, according to Fiske, "soaps" invert some of patriarchy's values (physical power, cool logic, external achievement, male supremacy). He concludes that "women and men on daytime soaps are probably more equal than in any other form of art or drama or in any other form of real life" (p. 345).

As with romance novels, the point here is not that soap operas are models of feminism. Desirable women invariably conform to traditional standards of beauty and nurturance, and their success as women is measured by their abilities to attract men. Moreover, the widespread denigration of soaps and romance novels indicates that whatever alternate vision they present has limited influence.

Deborah Rogers (1995) gives a sober antidote to Fiske's cultural study. Rogers observes that, invariably, successful businesswomen on soaps are unhappy, manipulative, and evil. Through character representation, dialogue, and narrative, the "moral" of soaps tells stay-at-home women that happiness comes only to those who have husbands and children; women are capable in all venues, but the home is their haven—if they have a good husband.

Popular cultural genres like romance novels and soap operas are sites where dominant hegemony incorporates subordinate concerns—articulated according to dominant frames. Such negotiation rests largely in the hands of writers, producers, and advertisers —"intellectuals" of hegemonic institutions servicing U.S. capitalism. Hegemony continually changes, constantly working to answer the needs of subordinate groups, issuing new images, organizing new practices, but always with the caveat that alternative practices emerging from subordinate concerns must be revised to serve capitalist cultural hegemony. Ironically, Fiske, Radway, and other critics who find subordinate resistance in hegemonic practices are obliquely reinforcing consent to existing material, political, and cultural relations.

## *Sitcoms*

After several years of relegating strong, funny women to roles as sidekicks, major television networks released a host of women-centered sitcoms in the mid-1990s. Several have already been mentioned and others should be added to the list: *Roseanne, Murphy Brown, Grace Under Fire, Ellen, Hope and Gloria, The Nanny, Cybill, Caroline in the City, Pearl, Suddenly Susan, Sabrina,* and *Clueless.* Several (e.g., *Cybill, Ellen, Hope and Gloria*) featured women whose lives revolve around work and friends rather than boyfriend, husband, or family. Some (e.g., *Murphy Brown, Grace Under Fire*) featured single mothers. Some (*Roseanne, Murphy Brown*) showed moments of intersection between work and family and attempted to address the struggle of "balancing." Some (e.g., *Roseanne, Pearl*) had female leads that did not conform to traditional standards of beauty. And some (especially *Roseanne* and *Murphy Brown*) proved that they could attract and sustain a wide and loyal following despite attacks from political and religious critics. Thus, in terms of both quantity and variety, there seems to be more cultural acceptance of women operating outside the parameters of traditional patriarchy. As Douglas (1994) observes, "Here is our fantasy about, dare I say it, speaking truth to the patriarchy. . . . It's the women who rule here, and these shows wink knowingly at their female audience, flattering our sense that without our shrewdness, persistence, and, yes, anger, the world and the men in it would fall apart" (p. 28).

Hegemonically speaking, the knowledge that Douglas applauds disempowers women because it has no political expression, no collective organization. The quiescent resistance rises only as far as the arm of the couch to reach for the TV remote. Such "rebels" are easily sold off to advertisers as audience share: female, 16 to 45, independent, middle-class, socially progressive, culturally radical, good consumer.

In her analysis of *The Mary Tyler Moore Show* and *Murphy Brown*, Bonnie Dow (1995) uses the construct of hegemony to support her argument that mainstream television adapted feminism to support rather than challenge fundamental beliefs about "the public/ private dichotomy that separates the roles and responsibilities of men and women in a patriarchal culture, and . . . conventional cultural valuations of masculine and feminine behavior" (p. 201). Dow contends that these programs illustrate how television adapts to social change. In the 1970s, Mary Richards was a comforting example of how women's liberation could be accommodated without really challenging conventional relations between the sexes. By the late 1980s, when Murphy Brown appeared, the cultural mood had changed and so had prime-time feminism. Murphy is as much a symbol of the *costs* of feminism as she is a symbol of the *benefits* of feminism (Dow, 1995, p. 213).

In many 1990s shows there seems to be an "even allotment" of women's roles that question the traditional system of gender relations and women's roles that support it. Ellen could wear pants and eschew makeup, but she was "balanced" by Paige who is marked by her sexy clothes and stupid remarks. Murphy was balanced by Corky. Roseanne's iconoclastic daughter Darlene was balanced by aspiring princess Becky. Although Grace was supposedly a pioneer in an all-male workplace, her private life defines her and takes most of her (and our) attention. Cybill and Maryann were smart and self-reliant but consistently console themselves with shopping, eating, and romantic fantasies. Are these sitcoms challenging certain aspects of patriarchy? Yes. But character representations are portrayed as individual qualities rather than political analysis. What is "normal" has expanded but not fundamentally shifted. Television, like all hegemonic institutions, absorbs impulses toward social change by turning them into forms compatible with dominant interests (Gitlin, 1980, pp. 242-282). Women can change but only within the context of consumer society.

In most programming and reruns, television series (drama or sitcom) still present a "man's world" with a few (very possibly one) female(s) as complement. It is the "Smurfette Principle" writ large: *Taxi, NYPD Blue, Seinfeld, Law and Order* (and lest we forget—*Hogan's Heroes, F-Troop, Welcome Back, Kotter,* and *I Dream of Jeannie* —still live in reruns. There have been exceptions—*China Beach, Designing Women, Family Law*—but the increase in quantity of female leads does not change their character nor the overarching narrative.

## Women's Sports

The growth in participation and patronage of women's sports, both school based and professional, has increased exponentially since the early 1970s. Some of this expansion can be attributed to the activism of particular female athletes, especially in the realms of professional tennis and golf. Some is ascribed to Title IX of the 1964 Civil Rights Act. The amendment, passed in 1972, decrees that no one will be excluded from participation or discrimination in any federally funded educational programs (Feminist Majority, 1995). Since its enactment, girls' participation in high school sports, for example, rose nearly 1,000% (Rohwer, 1994). According to the Feminist Majority Foundation (1995), only 15.6% of college athletes were female in 1972, but by 1993, they were estimated to be 34.8%. At the 1996 Summer Olympics, women were "the go-to guys (sic!) of these Games—the stars in a pinch" according to one *Newsday* journalist who went on to observe that television and marketing interests have responded to surveys of TV viewers to make women's gymnastics the "centerpiece sport in the Summer Games . . . just as women's figure skating is the main attraction in the Winter Games (Jeansonne, 1996). Buoyed by sharply increased public interest in women's NCAA and U.S. Olympic basketball, a women's professional basketball league was formed in 1998. And the U.S. women's soccer team garnered enormous support as they made their way to the 1998 World Cup Championship.

But women are still on the sidelines. Although there was an explosion of new high school female athletes in the early 1970s, the percentage has grown very slowly since 1978. According to the Department of Education, participation of female high school sophomores actually declined between 1980 and 1990 (from 46% of all 10th-grade girls to 41%) while the percentage of 10th-grade boys involved in athletics remained at 63% (Feminist Majority, 1995). The Feminist Majority Foundation also reports disparities at other levels:

> Men coach 50% of women's college teams; women coach 2% of men's teams.
> Men administer 79% of college women's athletic programs.
> 80% of high school athletic directors are men.

These numbers per se do not evidence overt discrimination. But they do indicate familiar patterns of social perception and material consequence. In almost any given profession, men are more likely than women to hold the highest-ranking and the highest-paid jobs (the exceptions being fashion modeling and acting in pornographic movies). Moreover, there continues to be a widely held perception that female athletes are not feminine, whereas male athletes are almost the personification of masculinity. One study concluded that "the overriding standard against which [both male and female] athletes are eventually evaluated is the gender schema where the women athletes tend to be rated significantly less positive. Females are perceived as either "good at being an athlete or good at being a woman but not both" (Martin & Martin, 1996, p. 296).

Title IX, acknowledged by many to have boosted women's athletic opportunities, is criticized by some for not doing enough and derided by others for ruining sports, especially at the college level (Marcus, 1996). Olympic coverage is credited for expanding appreciation of female athletes. It is disparaged by others—either for ignoring the "less feminine" sports such as softball and soccer in favor of the glamour of gymnastics (doll-like girls with glitter in their hair) or for turning the entire event "into a soap opera" to appeal to women viewers (Remnick, 1996).

## Conclusion

The challenge to patriarchy in U.S. society continues but only as consumerism is further entrenched in politics and culture. Although a large number of women as well as men will say that the fight for gender equality (or equity) has been won, few would actually contend that patriarchy itself no longer prevails. Instead, they would probably claim—as defenders of the status quo have done for years—that enough women benefit from the system as it is. Although disagreeing with the premise, many feminists would concede that this shared perception is indeed as powerful a roadblock to systematic change as any overt opposition. Enough women have thought they could win if they "played by the rules" that they did not and do not question the rules. Of course, the few who are recruited to hegemonic institutions (e.g., Carleton Fiorina, CEO at Hewlett-Packard; Mary Mahoney at Howard Johnson; Jill Barad at Mattel; Janet Reno, Department of U.S. Justice) argue that there is no "glass ceiling anymore," no discrimination, and all are equal. For these few individuals, this has some validity. Thus, promoted by government, corporations, and media as proof of big change, these spokesmodels for capitalist hegemony provide important cultural, material, and ideological evidence for securing consent from the other 63 million working women who still suffer from discrimination (Glasheen & Crowley, 1999, pp. 3, 24).

Yes, rules do change. Change may occur in spurts—goaded by moments of organized militancy around particular issues such as voting or shifts in economic necessity such as World War II. When such spurts disrupt the hegemonic order, dominant-class forces respond with organized resistance and orchestrated backlash. Hegemony tolerates gradual change more readily, as challenges can be tamed or neutered. Yet although capitalist cultural hegemony may appreciate acceptance by critics such as Mansbridge (1986) who find solace in the "negotiation" of personal relationships through daily conversation, such daily communication may also become part of a larger social movement, if politically organized.

As noted at the onset of this chapter, gender relations are somewhat different from those involving race and class because they are necessarily intimate on the personal level. For women isolated in the home, there is less recourse to organized, collective action because of the material and emotional interdependence of most women and men (hence the chuckles that greet the rare story of a housewife who "goes on strike"). And there are tangible benefits to consent (e.g., the material rewards of being a "trophy wife"). Challenges to capitalist patriarchy are most likely to occur outside the home, in sites where women (and men) collectively interact.

As we note the systematic and coercive discrimination against women in education, on the job, in the legal system, and in the marketplace, we recognize capitalist hegemony's crucial dependence on mutual assent. The contradictions in the social existence and daily life of women accentuate the usefulness of hegemony as a construct for understanding the situation of women. The unique social position of women should not obscure the similarities that women have with other subordinate groups. One of the most striking is the array of strategies that hegemonic institutions have used to make inequities seem "normal." Another is how hegemony seduces women to trade opportunities for collective progress for modest individual gain.

Diverted by hegemonic institutional and ideological accommodation, feminism heightens class differences between women. Educated, middle-class, professional women have made dramatic advances: In the last 20 years, the percentage of females in business, medical, and law school went from less than 10% to more than 40%. But

> Gains made by women in the professions added to the growing economic gap between the working class and the professional-managerial class . . . [there have been] no comparable gains for young women who cannot afford higher degrees, and most of these women remain in the same low-paid occupations . . . feminism has had little impact on the status or pay of traditional female jobs like clerical,

retail, health care, and light assembly line work. (Ehrenreich, 1999, p. 11)

Recruiting professional women to hegemonic institutions helps shield capitalism (and patriarchy) from more serious challenges by women interested in building a counterhegemonic social movement.

Can feminism survive such class polarization? If it doesn't, women's issues and women's rights will simply be absorbed into a "kinder, gentler" patriarchy that magnanimously no longer calls women "girls" or "honey" but continues to marginalize fundamental challenges. The women's movement sorely needs an infusion of radical working class feminism that resurrects an incisive feminist project addressing welfare rights, child care, health care, working conditions, equal pay, and other economic and political issues. As women congregate at universities, factories, and offices, they must transcend their immediate condition by sharing their experiences with other women, collectively analyzing the condition of all women, and uniting in a campaign for equality at work, school, and home. As an integral part of capitalist society, women may be recruited to represent capitalist hegemony. But because they are integral, they are central to the construction of a new counterhegemony that can replace patriarchy, consumerism, and sexual oppression.

Women remain women even when they enter the "man's world" and continue to live and work under the terms of existing hegemonic social relations. As examples cited in this chapter have suggested, ultimately, women (or any subordinate group) can wrench concessions or renegotiate their social relations only to the extent that they foster *collective* solidarity and politically organize their social power in action with others. The next chapter investigates further the social power of working women and men, without whose consent capitalist cultural hegemony in the United States could not exist.

# 4

# Class Contradictions and Antagonisms

> Hegemony begins in the factory.
> —Antonio Gramsci (1947/1971, p. 285)

Discussing class in a communication text is a risky business. The concepts and relations are complex and unfamiliar. Moreover, many communication scholars (e.g., King, 1987) accept the prevalent academic belief that power in the United States is the result of some combination of merit, skill, and persuasion (Dahl, 1967). References to social class are either summarily dismissed as being too simplistic for our modern mass society or they are thoroughly contested. Studies in the humanities have no interest in empirical studies of class, and "there is little agreement among social scientists . . . on the exact meaning of class or the explanatory power of the word itself" (McNall, Levine, & Fantasia, 1991, p. 1). Ironically, contemporary communication studies accept the inherent social dimensions of communication practices, but—reflecting the ideological hegemony of capitalist America—the concept of *class* has been frequently rejected, avoided, or ignored.

Early rhetoricians, however, had a different appreciation of social relations. They not only recognized social position as a primary ingredient of power, they took sides in political battles. In claiming that "man is the measure of all things," Protagoras was advocating the rights of common citizens to judge truth and make policy against the absolutists and the social elite. In contrast, Plato envisioned philosopher-kings directing all of public and private life, all communication, and all decision making. Plato recognized how social position affects political interest and social behavior. He fretted that democracy was "rule by the mob" and in *The Republic* favored a hierarchical class structure with the social elite ruling under a strict moral order. Aristotle's theory of power was less prescriptive, more insightful, and just as aware of social class. In *Politics*, Aristotle described different political systems such as monarchy, oligarchy, aristocracy, and democracy and analyzed their social bases of power, including sex, age, education, and social class. Isocrates sought to inculcate elite Greek youth with a sense of civic duty, patriotism, and tradition. G. E. M. de Ste. Croix (1981) and Ellen and Neal Wood (Wood & Wood, 1984) have explained that many of the ongoing rhetorical disputes in early Greece were actually debates over class interest.

Contemporary communication theorists are more circumspect in their identification of power in communication. Andrew King's (1987) survey of theories of power is hopelessly equivocal. Vernon Cronen and Barnett Pearce (1982) position "speech episodes" within their larger culture, indicating the influence of social position and social organization on communication. Yet they show little interest in social structures and class relations. Symbolic interactionists likewise generally avoid class questions, although they insist that neither the self nor the society can function without symbols derived from social interaction—interaction that inevitably reflects and reconstructs particular social orders. Some media critics (Carey, 1989; Fiske, 1987, 1989, 1991; Nelson & Grossberg, 1988) and many postmodern rhetorical theorists (Derrida, 1976; Laclau & Mouffe, 1985; Lyotard, 1984) have either been disinterested or downright hostile to class perspectives in their studies, preferring to idealize the "power" of the reader and viewer to decode messages for their own purposes. Fiske (1989) celebrates the pleasure of young Australian Aborigines who watch old U.S. TV westerns and cheer for the Indians against the white soldiers

(p. 25). But like all who wave aside material conditions, Fiske (1989) confuses vicarious triumph with actual life conditions: Cheering TV shows, no matter how loudly, does not bring self-determination, independence, or equality to the Aborigines.

James Lull (1995) and John Thompson (1990) have been more balanced in their presentations, recognizing different "forms of power," including economic, political, symbolic, and cultural. Nonetheless, they contend that cultural power can overcome environments structured by political and military authorities (Lull, 1995, p. 71). Ultimately, for Lull, corporate-run mass media can be liberating (p. 167). Despite his fairly nuanced rendering of communication, culture, and power, he effectively erases social class from social relations and cultural contexts, concluding that social forces cannot control people's lives anyway (p. 175).

Sociological discussions of class have been more extensive and contentious. Theoretical followers of Max Weber and Emile Durkheim have staked out positions that over the years have vehemently challenged Marxist conceptions of class. Weber (1946) proposed a multidimensional view of social stratification that redefines social class in terms of occupational skill, privileging status as a determinant (rather than an attribute) of social power. Durkheim (1964) saw social inequality as the result of individual ability or merit, dismissing class and class conflict as unnatural. Most sociological theories since Marx (1859/1970), Weber (1946), and Durkheim (1964) (Aronowitz, 1974; Dahrendorf, 1959; Mills, 1956) have been developed with one or more of these approaches in mind.

Sociology in Europe followed a different trajectory that cannot be fully related here.

Louis Althusser (1969, 1972) gave us the concept "ideological state apparatuses," which he saw as organizing class interests throughout civil society. Roland Barthes's (1972, 1977) semiotic dissection of advertising, fashion, and the media interpreted the ideological influence of dominant social groups. In *Image, Music, Text* Barthes (1977) argued that the construction of popular myths in mass culture disguises the social construction of a class-biased society. Through repeated and pervasive use, manufactured popular culture infiltrates common sense as social practices and relations become "naturalized." Similarly, Pierre Bourdieu (1977, 1984) outlined the role of economic, cultural, and *symbolic* capital in the production and reproduction of social class and social structures. Others worked from different perspectives, of course, but these three theorists have had some influence on American sociology and communication, especially in terms of drawing our attention to social class as a crucial dimension of communication and culture.

Recognizing the controversy over social class in communication studies and sociology (and its pervasive absence from much of social science and the humanities) prompts us to provide some working definition of social class in the United States, because it is decisive to understanding Gramsci's conception of hegemony in capitalist society. Here we rely on work that has already been done (Domhoff, 1967, 1986; Kerbo, 1983; McNall et al., 1991; Wright, 1985). Feature articles in *Time, Newsweek,* and daily newspapers on the disappearing "middle class" suggest that such awareness increasingly enters popular discourse. Michael Lind's (1991) article in *Harper's* even has intimations of Althusser, Barthes, and Bourdieu, when he describes the wealthy as people who walk, talk, eat, dress, and think the same.

Who are *they*? In Lind's (1991) terms, they are the "overclass," approximately 5% of the American population who own the corporations and the news media, control elections, use affirmative action to relieve social pressure, and live in affluent "gated" suburbs. Lind's overzealous journalistic license in describing class society reads well but obscures the workings of class relations. Our interest in hegemony, communication, and culture requires a more systematic unpacking of social class and class interactions.

In this chapter, we depart from our focus on the culture industry that organized the previous two chapters, although previous observations illuminate the rough outline given in this chapter. We begin with the importance of class in analyzing ideology and cultural practice. We follow with an outline of the material, political, and cultural ingredients of contemporary class relations and end with a few observations about class culture in the United States.

**Building Blocks**

To make the distinction between structure and formation more graphic, imagine a set of children's building blocks. The blocks are "structured" in specific ways, with different sizes and shapes, such as cylinders, cones, squares, rectangles, and so on. The blocks may be stacked in many different "formations." Some formations are more stable, some are precarious, and some are impossible, given the structure of the blocks. For instance, various squares and rectangles will support a number of different shapes, but a large square or rectangle cannot be stacked on top of a single small cone. Metaphorically speaking, the material shape of the components of a social structure provides the building blocks for possible class formations.

## Social Structures

Metal, wood, and other raw materials are useful to humanity, but as long as they remain underground or standing in the forest, they are useless. It takes human labor to transform natural resources into useful items for human survival. A variety of techniques and practices have been employed over the centuries that have helped secure and improve human existence. In the process of production, men and women produce social relations that define and organize their activities. Societies are formed through the combination of productive practices and their accompanying social relations. Of course, there are many ways for humans to inter-act with nature and many ways for them to interact with each other. Thus, there have been many different forms of society: bar-barism, communalism, slavery, feudalism, capitalism, and social-ism, to name a few.

Every society can be characterized by how the necessities of life are produced from nature—by the social relations that organize production, distribution, and consumption of necessities among groups and individuals in society. Capitalist society is character-ized by highly industrialized productive forces producing goods *collectively* with stratified social relations that distribute benefits, rights, and responsibilities *hierarchically*. By productive forces, we mean the "whole range of means available to human beings for mastering nature and producing material goods to satisfy their needs," encompassing the means of production, labor power, and advanced technology (Jalée, 1977, p. 10). The *means of production* in-clude natural resources (coal, oil, wood, water, etc.) and the instru-ments of production (tools, machinery, transportation, etc.).

Capitalism is an economic system in which the means of produc-tion are privately owned and operated for individual corporate profit. *Labor power* is the human capacity to work, without which no transformation of natural resources to useful things could oc-cur. Capitalism organizes labor power as wage labor. *Technology* and the skill and experience embodied in technology through sci-ence, invention, and knowledge improves the efficient use of labor power acting on nature by employing technical innovation to the productive process. Contemporary American capitalism combines the immense power of collective American labor with the latest technology and most advanced equipment available to produce commodities for corporate sale.

The social relations of American capitalism are not as advanced, progressive, or socially egalitarian as the productive forces might allow. Production is highly socialized; the labor process is collec-tively organized according to an extensive division of labor. Pro-ducers no longer individually create their own clothing, grow their own food, or construct their own furniture (excepting, e.g., Amish communities). Instead, to meet the needs of society as a whole, bread, cereal, cars, televisions, computers, building supplies, and most other socially useful items are mass produced in enterprises or a series of enterprises that involve thousands, if not hundreds of thousands of people. Individuals perform many tasks, employ many different skills: extraction, design, transport, manual labor, skilled machining, packaging, quality control, and so on. Producers "are not simply individual workers, side-by-side in a given enterprise" but workers who "have been made into a real 'collective' worker by the division and organization of labor" (Jalée, 1977, p. 12) and by the production of goods for society as a whole. In capitalist America, a highly socialized, coordinated group effort is required for the production of even the smallest item destined for mass consumption.

In contrast to the highly socialized production process, neither the producers of goods nor society as a whole directs, controls, or decides the goals of social production. Instead, the means of production—from factories to railroads, from oil wells to banks—are privately owned, operated, and directed for individual profit. Mineral deposits, forests, water, and even the air may be ostensibly "owned" by the public while thousands of citizens participate in transforming nature's bounty into items for human consumption, but the legal exploitation and profit from these resources are held privately. In short, production is socialized, but the decisions over production are authoritarian and bureaucratic. Moreover, the benefits and profits from social production are unevenly distributed among social groups and individuals.

The combination of advanced productive forces and monopoly ownership of the means of production creates social relations that require millions of Americans, who own no productive resources beyond their own labor, to sell their labor power to capitalist owners in order to live. Thus, on one side, we have workers, without whom no production would be possible, striving to maximize their wages and salaries. On the other side, there are capitalists, who own the means of production, without which no production would be possible, seeking maximum profits from their machinery and property. Importantly, these antagonistic relations of production are not relations between individuals per se but are social relations between classes of individuals linked to each other by an insurmountable contradiction. "The contradiction between the private ownership of the means of production and the social nature of production is the fundamental contradiction of the social system" (Jalée, 1977, p. 13), providing the material backdrop for the production and negotiation of other social and cultural practices.

## Class Defined

The primary social contradiction of capitalism is structurally expressed as an antagonism within productive relations, relations that are not simply between individuals but social relations between classes. Hence, we define social class as *a group of people who relate to production in similar ways and share a common location in the relations of production* (Therborn, 1983, p. 39). The capitalist class owns the means of production but rarely works there. The working class does not own the means of production but sets them in motion by physically using tools, machinery, and labor power on raw materials and their products. In terms of production, the working class owns only its labor power, which must be sold to the capitalist for a wage, whereas the capitalist depends on the worker to create goods, which must be sold for a profit. Other classes can be similarly defined according to their relationship to the means of production. For example, the managerial middle class is economically excluded from ownership of the means of production and is also generally excluded from actually using the means of production. Instead, the manager's relation to the means of production is administrative and supervisory, organizing the labor process and holding a monopoly of knowledge about the productive process (Poulanzas, 1978).

Note that these broad class categories are very rough sketches. In each case, we could delineate class groupings within a class and in relation to the overarching social structure (Wright, 1985). Finance capitalists have a different relationship to the means of production than do industrial capitalists or small business entrepreneurs. Likewise, industrial workers have a different relationship to the means of production than do teachers, retail clerks, or service workers. For the upcoming discussion on class and culture, however, we do not need to empirically identify all the relational nuances between social class positions in the United States. It should suffice to say that classes can be generally defined in terms of their relationship to the means of production in any given society.

## The Significance of Social Class

Defining social class in terms of its relationship to the means of production provides only analytical concepts for explaining the social *structure*. But structures don't act; people do. Moreover, the production of things coincides with the production of social relations. Having defined social class, we must also identify the practical consequence and the social significance of that abstract structural condition. This is necessary and possible because social class has a "subjective component, is a process, is defined in relation to other classes and is historically contingent" (McNall et al., 1991, p. 4).

Practically speaking, the importance of any class depends on its relation to the means of production *and* on its relationship to other classes and society as a whole—relationships that change over time. For instance, under feudalism, peasant production of food was crucial to the survival of the social order, but as capitalism developed, the peasantry was freed from serfdom, and its social significance declined. Those peasants who maintained their connection to the land (their means of production) gradually found their relationships to other classes altered as they became tenant farmers, sharecroppers, and eventually independent farmers. More important, such individualized agricultural production ceased to be economically crucial to the capitalist production of food in industrialized countries. Other classes, defined as relative to the means of production, have evolved differently relative to other classes and society as a whole. For example, since the capitalist class established its ownership of manufacturing, its relationship to the means of production has been fairly constant, but its relationship to the church, the nobility, independent artisans, and society in general has changed dramatically over the centuries.

By the mid-17th century, capitalists began manufacturing commodities for the market, eventually providing the objective basis for economically and politically challenging the existing social relations of feudalism. As capitalism became the predominant productive system in the mid-18th century, society as a whole (with the exception of the church and nobility, of course) felt constrained by feudalism. The capitalist class became the leading class once it could challenge the feudal nobility for the right to economically, politically, and ideologically organize society and culture. Throughout Europe, revolutions for liberty and a free market forced a restructuring of social relations between the classes. Once the capitalist class had established its political predominance in newly organized "nation-states," its economic and cultural influence expanded rapidly. The social power of all other classes was altered as well: The nobility, which still exists in Europe, lost its feudal privilege; the peasantry slowly declined in number and economic importance; first the working classes and later the middle classes of entrepreneurs and managers grew rapidly. The social structure of feudalism positioned classes in relationship to the land, the major means of production of that historic era. As another means of production developed—the capitalist manufacture of commodities—other classes emerged and challenged existing social relations. The social significance and social power of each class was a combination of its structural relationship to the means of production (either feudal or capital) and its political relationship to other classes (both feudal and capitalist).

We realize that this dense narrative introduces many unfamiliar concepts and a whole new way of looking at the world. A much longer explanation is necessary to clarify and defend many of the claims advanced here. But for now, we offer three observations based on the above account:

1. Structural conditions of production provide a useful compass for identifying social class.
2. Based on their relationship to the major means of production, social classes have varying degrees of power.

3. The political power and social impact of each class depends on the battles and interactions with other classes.

These conclusions lead to some important questions for our discussion of class hegemony. What is the relationship between the social structure of class society and the specific *political* formation of classes? How does the social structure affect the capacity for subordinate class political action? How do individuals and groups experience the social structure and their class positions?

*Class Formations*

Erik Olin Wright (1985, 1991) argues that class structures do not determine class formations but determine only their probabilities; classes are actively formed from social relations within and between classes. Structured social relations *limit* possible class formations, such that "one cannot group anyone with anyone while ignoring fundamental differences, particularly economic and cultural ones. But this never entirely excludes the possibility of organizing agents in accordance with other principles of division" (Bourdieu, 1987, p. 8). Other factors such as gender, race, ideology, culture, and government action shape the actual political formation of classes.

In this view, class structure is simply the context for other social processes (Wright, 1991, p. 19). Such a perspective is important for hegemony, because class structures set real limits on the material and political resources available for building subordinate consent. For example, feudal peasants outnumbered the nobility but individually had scant material resources and no political perspective with which to build social alliances and reorganize society; hence, the peasantry did not, and could not, hegemonically lead a bloc of artisans, traders, merchants, craftsmen, and other urban groups. The emergent European capitalist classes provided socially useful goods and a libertarian political ideology that appealed to broad class sectors, although the actual class alignments, the battles against feudalism, and the subsequent political institutions varied from country to country.

**Confronting Poverty**

Average Net Worth for U.S. Families (adjusted for inflation)

|              | 1985      | 1999      | Change (by percentage) |
|--------------|-----------|-----------|------------------------|
| Wealthiest 1% | $7.5m     | $10.2m    | +35                    |
| Top 20%       | $865,000  | $1.1m     | +19                    |
| Middle 20%    | $55,500   | $52,000   | –5                     |
| Bottom 40%    | $4,600    | $2,800    | –36                    |

Considering a poverty level of $20,000 for a family of four, more than 17% of Americans are poor. The 1999 Center on Budget and Policy Priorities found that the gap between rich and poor in the United States is larger than at any time since the Great Depression: The richest 1% have as much after-tax income as the poorest 100 million (38% of the population). Under such conditions, capitalist hegemony increasingly loses the material basis for consent, and social unrest is likely.

We can conclude that similar class structures allow for different class formations (Cohen, 1990; Levine, 1988; Poulanzas, 1978). John Stephens (1979) found that differences in organized working-class strength and activity led to differences in the class formations of 17 Western capitalist nations after World War II (see also, Esping-Anderson, 1978; Valocchi, 1991). Or as Wright (1991) says, class formations are "created through the strategies of actors attempting to build collective organizations capable of realizing class interests" (p. 19). As actors become aware of their lived experience, they choose strategies based in large part on their class position and activity. A bridge must be built between the structure (which is how relations are organized and normalized) and actual human action, a bridge that is constructed symbolically, ideologically, and politically (Wacquant, 1991, p. 56). The more closely that human action is connected to the existing social structure, the more likely it is that such action will successfully constitute certain class formations.

Within the contemporary United States, certain formations are likely, easy, and stable: Managers are convenient hegemonic allies of corporate owners (Domhoff, 1967); skilled workers, engineers, and skilled planners are likely hegemonic allies of skilled supervisors; production workers, unskilled workers, skilled workers, and family farmers are also possible hegemonic allies (Preis, 1964). Other formations are not likely: capitalist owners joining union organizing drives or supporting worker demands for shorter hours and higher wages, for instance. Of course, race, gender, nationality, and religion affect class formation, as well, but the structure still sets limits. It is more likely that black professionals and even black workers would join hegemonic institutions on dominant terms than it is that white CEOs would challenge corporate practices on behalf of black workers and the unemployed. Why? Because structural parameters subject individual class members to a set of mechanisms that impinge directly on their lives as they think, choose, and act in the world (Wright, 1991, p. 23).

The *current class structure* provides more material and political resources to the dominant capitalist classes than it does to the subordinate working classes; consequently, hegemonic representatives can offer tangible rewards to subordinate individuals and groups who sign on to capitalist hegemony. In comparison, what do subordinate classes and groups have to offer dominant capitalist classes? An appeal to their humanity and ethics? Yes, but at what price? An end to their dominant social position? *Individuals* from dominant classes may be converted to a new way of life like Saul on the road to Damascus, but never in history has a dominant *class* or group willingly given up its power.

Today, the class structure of the U.S. makes possible the formation of capitalist hegemony because the socioeconomic system can still provide for the material well-being of a majority of the working population. Until now, capitalist control over vast material resources has been sufficient to diffuse, diminish, or crush challenges to capitalist hegemony. Although social movements and class struggles have successfully modified the American political landscape, hegemony has survived mostly by the judicial dispensing of structurally available social and economic benefits to oppositional classes and groups. Any explanation of why and how workers, blacks, or women consent to their own subordination would be incomplete without reference to the contemporary class structure. Likewise, any conjectures about counterhegemonic movements would be naive without consideration of the strengths and contradictions of that class structure. Finally, although dominant classes and their political representatives have more economic, political, media, and other organizational resources and skills than subordinate groups, the particular class formation and the specific hegemonic relationship will change as their material resources are depleted and as subordinate classes organize and mobilize their own independent social and political power.

## The Capacity for Class Action

The strength of one class is not directly proportional to the weakness of other classes; each class has its own strengths and weaknesses. Lembcke (1991) argues that working-class power increases as capitalism develops (p. 85). Classes are interconnected, but they relate to production, each other, and society as a whole in distinct ways. They have concrete and unique capacities for political and cultural action. Prevalent and emergent cultural practices develop out of the contradictory political relations that dominant and subordinate classes negotiate and battle over. These relations are the outcome of challenges, responses, and adjustments to resource allocations and social responsibilities. In other words, class formation affects class capacity; social links must be organizationally established within and between classes.

In the long run, each class fights to improve its social position and quality of life relative to other classes and material possibilities. Each class fights from its position in the social structure with the social and political resources available and accessible. Bourdieu (1978, 1987) speaks of common properties that members of the same social class share as economic, cultural, informational, social, and symbolic "capital." Organizational expertise and historical experience will also influence a class's capacity for action. Each class consequently has actual and potential material, political, and cultural capacities for action.

Goran Therborn (1983) sees class capacity to act in two parts. First, each class possesses an *intrinsic* strength based on its "power" resources, roughly what we have been calling material, political, and cultural resources. Second, class capacity to act depends on the *hegemonic* capacity to use available power resources to isolate, divide, intimidate, and strike against oppositional classes (p. 39). We would add that hegemonic capacity also includes the ability to lead and represent existing and potential class allies by using material, political, and cultural resources, including symbolic resources that can be mobilized to "impose a [new] vision which is grounded in reality" (Bourdieu, 1987, p. 14). Therborn (1983) identifies the fundamental resource of the capitalist class as the *expanding market* and its ability to satisfy other classes. The main resource of the middle class of small-business people is its *autonomy* or independence from employers, workers, and landowners. The fundamental resource available to the working class in Therborn's taxonomy is its *collectivity*. He argues that each class formation effectively depends on the varying degrees of capitalist market expansion, middle-class autonomy, and working-class collectivity. Therborn argues that hegemonic capacity thus depends on the ability of a class to deploy its intrinsic capacity to or against other classes.

The intrinsic capacity of individual power continues to shrink in corporate America (Deetz, 1992; Lembcke, 1991) and so does the power of small business and farming. On the other hand, the collective power resources of the U.S. working class are immense. The class is numerically large, geographically widespread yet concentrated in urban areas, highly skilled, well educated, and socially necessary for the functioning and recreation of this society. If hegemonic capacity is dependent on class strength, the working class has the necessary economic and social power: Try to imagine an office, factory, school, restaurant, train, or department store without workers.

Although capacity depends on strength, strength does not equal hegemony. The transfer of intrinsic strength into hegemonic strength depends on the conscious intent of the class and its form of organization. In this regard, the potentially powerful American working class has been stunted. The political and social power of the American working class has generated social reforms and economic rewards only *within the context of capitalist hegemony*. Despite some notable exceptions, the working class has yet to mobilize its intrinsic strength against the capitalist class in any concerted manner.

In political terms, a class exists only when there are leaders authorized to speak and act for people who recognize themselves as a class. McNall (1988) even argues that it is "in mobilizing, in trying to actually change the economic and political system, [that] people create themselves as a class" (p. 10). In this sense, the American working class has failed to become a *political* class because it has not mobilized its ranks or led its own culturally diverse membership. Without organizing its intrinsic strength, the working class has nothing to offer politically or culturally to the broad middle classes. In contrast, capitalist institutions and practices have repeatedly and continuously obstructed and derailed all counter-hegemonic organization of the working class by, in part, preventing it from recognizing itself as a class.

*Living Class Relations*

Although class is structured by productive social relations, the lived experience is not and cannot be felt in that way. Indeed, "no amount of knowledge of the inseparable connection between the structure of the relations of production and the lived experience of those relations can alter that experience, just as no amount of science can affect the fact that the sun *appears* to move around the earth or that a stick *appears* to bend when it is placed in water [italics added]" (Burawoy, 1979, p. 17). Detached from the conditions that produce it, the lived experience is the "material" from which classes are constituted (Gutman, 1977). This class experience develops in many ways, ways that are distinct and observable in language, stories, and ideas of community and solidarity that help politically and culturally construct social class. One might say that the closer individuals are in social class, the greater their probable shared lived experiences. "Similar dispositions and interests are likely to reproduce practices and representations of a similar kind," including the "sense of one's place and adjustments in perception to understanding one's position" (Bourdieu, 1987, p. 5).

Bourdieu (1987) discerns the "homogenizing effect of homogeneous conditions" (p. 6). Consequently, he suggests that we can predict and observe that individuals who share similar positions in society—who share an identifiable set of conditions of work and community, for example—will likely share similar social practices, relations, behaviors, beliefs, and symbols. Logically, then, we can anticipate that a concept of social class would help account for variations in cultural practices, such as Pierre Bourdieu (1978, 1984), John Kasson (1990), David Halle (1991), Diana Crane (1992), Angela Partington (1993), and Joan Kron (1994) have demonstrated about sport, social etiquette, living room art, public culture, fashion, and home decor, for example.

The key to capitalist power is profit—profit resulting from the sale of commodities produced by workers who are paid less than the value of the goods they produce. The key to capitalist hegemony, however, is in the *lived experience* of that commodified social relationship. All Americans have experienced the "homogenizing effects" of their class position under capitalism, and all Americans—whether corporate owner, manager, farmer, or worker— have also experienced the "homogenizing effects" of commodity production and popular culture.

*The Use and Exchange of Commodities*

How do we experience commodity production? In the past, goods were produced primarily for individual self-use. Peasants produced bread for their own use, for instance. Under capitalism, however, bread is not produced for the baker to eat, but to sell. Wonder Bread has a *use value* (it can be eaten); it also has an *exchange value* (it can be sold). Exchange value is expressed in money. Money is an exchange value "through which different use values are exchanged" (Jalée, 1977, p. 16). A loaf of Wonder Bread may be "worth" $1, the same exchange value as a Bic pen or Gillette razor, for instance. When the bread or pen or razor is sold, it keeps its use value, but because it is produced for exchange, it is a *commodity*. Although all commodities have both a use value and an exchange value, a commodity is anything that has been produced specifically for sale or trade. In the contemporary United States, almost everything is a commodity. Commodities may be consumer goods made for individual use, or they may be capital goods, which are goods used for other production, such as raw materials, machinery, or semiprocessed goods (Jalée, 1977, p. 16).

Commodities have use value only because human labor has transformed natural raw materials into products that can be used by humans. Land is a commodity, depending on its location and its mineral resources. Ores are useless in the ground; they must be dug up, melted, and cast to make screws, bolts, or fixtures. Trees aren't lumber or pulp; they must be cut down, chopped up, and processed to make wood and paper. In other words, natural resources have only *potential* use value until human labor turns them into socially useful products, explaining in part why underdeveloped countries can be resource rich but materially poor: They do not have the necessary human resources contained in machinery, technology, and labor skills for turning natural resources into products.

Natural resources become raw materials through human labor, but in our culture in particular, raw materials themselves undergo extensive processing to become consumer or capital goods: Intermediate products go from one factory to another, where a small group of engineers and a large number of manual workers transform semifinished goods into industrial machinery or consumer goods. All down the line, one finds labor. The effectiveness of a worker's labor is increased by machinery, but even this is only the result of *earlier* human labor. "All human products are manufactured, and are the product of human labor—the only source of value. . . *the only common content of all commodities is the labor which has produced them"* (Jalée, 1977, pp. 18-19).

Commodities thus have exchange value because they have in common the human labor that produced them. As described above, modern capitalism depends on the collective, socialized labor of masses of workers. This labor process is quite complex. Some products require less labor than others, but each product is the result of a specific amount of human labor for its production. The product of any corporation is the product of the labor of its workers, its machinery (which is the product of earlier human labor), raw materials (which have also been acquired through human labor), and scientific knowledge (which is the historic result of human labor expressed in inventions, discoveries, and knowledge about nature). "One may conclude that *the value of a commodity is determined by the amount of labor socially necessary to produce it,* 'socially' being taken in the widest sense to mean the general [cultural] conditions in a particular society" (Jalée, 1977, p. 20). Of course, the value of each commodity cannot be measured precisely but only through a relationship of rough equivalence. With money as the means of exchange, the medium for human labor as it were, the monetary expression of the exchange value of a commodity is *price.* Money is a reification, an abstract thing that represents actual human relations of production.

This summary of commodity production should suggest its importance for social relations and cultural practices. Commodity production, presented as "consumerism" in popular parlance, is a defining characteristic of contemporary American capitalism. Under capitalism, even human relations are stamped with a price tag (Willis, 1991).

Human labor now is a commodity that has use value and exchange value and that requires human labor for its reproduction. The cost of the production and reproduction of human labor includes the cost of meeting the physical and cultural needs of workers—food, clothing, shelter, and the minimum existing cultural necessities such as transportation, entertainment, leisure time, recreation, and so on.

If the value of each commodity is the amount of labor necessary for its production, where do capitalists get their wealth? Workers give the entire product of their labor to the capitalist in return for wages. By paying workers less than the value of the goods produced, the actual value of their labor, capitalists keep the *surplus value* of the goods and call it *profit*. Capitalists thus always try to purchase necessary labor power at the lowest wage possible—explaining why corporations try to avoid unions (which may demand higher wages), accept and promote race discrimination in hiring and income (which keeps wages down), and often seek out production in underdeveloped countries (where labor can be produced and employed more cheaply).

If the value of a commodity depends on the labor power necessary to produce it, it follows that a smart capitalist seeks to increase workers' labor without increasing their wages. This can be done in several ways. One way is through "speed-up," getting workers to work harder or faster for the same hourly pay. Another way is through the introduction of technique or technology so that expended labor is more efficient. Strip mining coal, for instance, extracts more coal than shaft mining and replaces thousands of workers. Capitalists in general can reduce the cost of labor in general by reducing the cost of reproducing labor power. For example, increasing the productivity of subsistence goods (food, clothing) permits workers to live on less money by purchasing cheaper mass-produced goods and relieves some of the pressure for higher wages. In a more paradoxical example, a culture that advocates or accepts two-income families disguises the decline in real wages for all workers, making low incomes for both men and women more tolerable because the economic burden for the production and reproduction of the family and future workers is shared. At any rate, capitalism depends on workers producing value worth more than their wage. Such economic practices require political securities and cultural justifications; hence, capitalist classes strive for hegemony.

Most people would not consent to the inequities of productive relations if it were obvious that they were getting less than the value of their work, but capitalist socioeconomic relations appear natural and logical when mediated by the consumer market. Unlike peasants or family farmers, workers cannot live on the goods they produce. They must purchase their necessities and luxuries as consumers in the marketplace. Capitalists cannot live off the products of their corporations, either. They must be sellers in the marketplace to realize their profits. Thus, as Lukács (1923/1971) argued, human relations necessary for capitalism appear in the marketplace, reified as relations between things. The production of profit appears as a production of things. Workers do not attribute profit to the difference between their wages and the selling price of the goods they produce. They believe profit is an earned reward for clever venture capitalists or the result of the manipulation of prices in the marketplace (Burawoy, 1979, p. 29).

The lived experience of commodity production increasingly homogenizes American culture. Filtered by ownership, advertising, and ideology, the major media produce cultural products that "manufacture consent" for existing hegemonic relations based on commodity production (Herman & Chomsky, 1988). If Bourdieu (1987) is right about similar social positions producing similar dispositions and behaviors, then we should expect that millions of American consumers "positioned" in front of the television set and subjected to similar conditions of existence under commodity capitalism might develop similar dispositions, especially on many national and international issues that are experienced almost solely through the media. U.S. capitalist classes meet important *material* needs through the production and distribution of commodities; *politically* organize laws, institutions, and relations that defend commodity production and property rights; and through the media *culturally* direct the daily lives of most Americans as consumers. And significantly, all social classes are similarly constrained by dominant representations of the commodified world (Bourdieu, 1987, p. 9).

Although we can discard the postmodern contention that all is "flux" and completely indeterminate, this is not to say that our social reality is predetermined. Rather, the interpretations and spins we put on social reality are chosen from an existing set of visions and relations based on commodity production. The contradictions and inequities of commodity capitalism are not understood as structural defects, however, but experienced in hegemonically ideological terms as individual or group inadequacies. We cannot predict how individuals will respond to the existing social world, but we can say with some certainty that the lived experience of commodity production atomizes and isolates individuals from each other (Mattelart, 1979). Human beings may respond differently, but they are all generally treated as nameless, faceless "consumers" and "target audiences" for the realization of corporate profits. Moreover, commodity production and exchange *does determine* that many people will have to work at less-than-satisfying jobs out of sheer necessity. Ninety-seven thousand college graduates are janitors, not from "free choice" but because existing social relations require people to work in order to eat (Longworth & Stein, 1995, p. 6).

Filtered through the language of the "free" market, social problems appear as individual misfortunes or inadequacies. Thousands of children go hungry, hundreds of families go homeless, and millions are without jobs, education, or health care, but in a commodity-driven society, these concerns are questions for the marketplace. Schools are closed and social services cut because an inanimate budget can't be "balanced." Under capitalism, private profits come before human needs.

In the United States, human relations are reified and objectified by the market relations of commodities. Human values become commodities; housing, health care, education, and transportation go to the highest bidder. The production of exchange value undercuts production of use values. Capitalist social relations are culturally ingrained and ideologically rationalized in the United States as everyone undergoes the "homogenizing effect" of commodity production that creates a "hegemonizing effect" for social relations necessary for commodity production. Social inequality and social problems can be explained as race, nationality, or gender deficiencies; as the apathy or meanness of individual employers or government officials; as a misfortune; as unfair trading practices by other countries; as God's will; as a problem caused by illegal immigrants, welfare cheats, and so on; and by other familiar rationalizations and scapegoating explanations. These discursive constructions

### All Aboard?

When the Broadway Limited ended its run from Chicago to New York in 1995, a spokeswoman said, "It's a sad day at Amtrak when we lose a passenger train, but at the same time, we have to keep in mind that the changes we're making will restore the corporation's health" ("Another Legend," 1995, p. 14). Only by focusing on exchange value can *ending* a passenger service make a rail company that exists to provide passenger service appear stronger.

have material consequences. Both the actual conditions and the appearance of conditions are real and affect our daily lives. Just as a stick appears to bend when placed in water, our understanding of capitalism is similarly distorted by its everyday appearance.

Materially, we recognize capitalism in money, consumer goods, and commodities; politically, in institutions from the legal system to the two-party electoral system; and culturally, in dominant ideologies as expressed in news and entertainment. Imposed on everyday life by the class structure, organized by dominant political formations, and inculcated through everyday cultural experiences, these expressions appear natural because they are universally prevalent for all individuals in all classes from cradle to grave. These appearances are just as important to our understanding as the underlying social relations that they represent because the actual relations and their everyday appearances are constrained and potentially liberated by our daily practices.

## Living in the American Dream World

American hegemony *and* its oppositions are constrained by the material, political, and cultural practices of capitalism that are ideologically expressed in beliefs such as individualism, democratic pluralism, and consumerism. Over the years, these beliefs have been neatly codified into the tenets of the American Dream: hard work, fair play, individual freedom, economic security, progress, and so on. This symbolic representation of American capitalism is not primarily manipulative or propagandistic, however— although elements of agenda setting can be found in media constructions of social events (Gans, 1972; McCombs & Shaw, 1972; Rachlin, 1988) and instances of propaganda by corporate interests can be discovered (Jowett & O'Donnell, 1992).

The material resources for capitalism have long been plentiful in the United States, especially in land and natural resources that until recently seemed to spread out forever over the Western horizon. Laurence Shames (1994) has argued that America's hunger for more, which was satisfied during the frontier era when there seemed no limit to American desire, has become an essential part of our history and character. Indeed, there has been a presumption, driven by the frontier experience and later the industrial revolution, that the U.S. would keep on booming. Obviously, American class relations have developed in tandem with both the growth and the ideology of growth.

Early on, the frontier provided raw materials for economic booms, laying the material basis for capitalist hegemony. Even as immigrants came from Europe, settlers and prospectors moved further west into the land of plenty. Emergent working-class mobilizations in the latter half of the 19th century were countered and partially offset by the continuous opening of new frontiers, which relieved the pressure of unemployment, supplied more raw materials, and eventually created markets for consumer goods (Shames, 1994). The industrial revolution followed, providing a new frontier of opportunity—creating thousands of jobs and churning out goods for millions. When the system stumbled in the 1930s, established social relations broke apart and industrial unions captured a little power, but their victories were soon offset by the postwar shift of capital to new economic "frontiers" in the south and the west. And at least since the late 1970s, U.S. capital has undertaken a wholesale movement to the economic "frontiers" of Latin America and Asia, where raw materials and labor are plentiful and cheap (Lembcke, 1991, p. 87). This is not to imply that working-class mobilizations haven't occurred or that they haven't affected class formations in the United States. On the contrary, workers have periodically acted on their hegemonic capacity. Still, until recently, the capitalist class has usually had sufficient material resources to weather any working-class storm.

American capitalism also benefited from the ethnic diversity of the American working class, which allowed a divided labor market. The rapid industrialization of the United States, compared with Europe, also fostered the growth of a large white-collar management class (McNall et al., 1991, p. 5), which helps cushion the antagonisms between workers and owners. Cross-class political forms developed before industrialization, blunting the development of independent working-class activity. As Therborn (1983) suggests, class relations and their specific formations have changed under the contradictory impact of working-class mobilization and an expanding capitalist market (displacing independent small-business and farming operations with monopoly production).

In the last century, independent working-class action has won the 8-hour day, Social Security, unemployment insurance, some environmental protection, and other important changes in social relations. At the same time, the needs of capitalist production resulted in free public education, mass transportation, and other social services, such as telephones, sewer systems, and public libraries. Capitalist expansion has destroyed the family farm, organized and trained a massive working class, displaced small business with corporate chains, relied on small business to fill the gaps in production and service, created a large managerial middle class, "downsized" managers out of their jobs, encouraged immigration, organized opposition to immigration, organized cultural diversity in the workplace, fomented racial animosity, and carried out other contradictorily progressive changes.

Capitalist hegemony has survived by providing the working classes relative economic security and social progress. As Werner Sombart once said, "Socialism in America came to grief on roast beef and apple pie" (Orr & McNall, 1991, p. 101). Capitalism has delivered "a chicken in every pot, a car in every garage" for a large number of Americans. The opportunity for advancement based on economic booms, coupled with a burgeoning consumer society that manufactures cheap goods for all, has given some reality to the Dream. The United States has been an international trendsetter in marketing the consumer-oriented quality of life.

## The Reality of Dream Politics

Not all has been wine and roses for leading hegemonic powers in the United States, however. To secure ownership and control over vast American resources, J. P. Morgan, Andrew Carnegie, John D. Rockefeller, Cornelius Vanderbilt, and their fellow "class"mates had to get down and dirty; bribery, deceit, and terror were liberally used during the prime of capitalist industrialization (Lundberg, 1937). Matthew Josephson (1934) told of "robber baron" Carnegie's "rapacity," Rockefeller's "terrorism" in monopolizing oil, and Morgan's iron rule of the "money trust" in capturing industrial and railway combinations. The carving up of America by the rich and the superrich frequently encountered resistance from workers and farmers. Although the stories are absent from most high school textbooks, historically, capitalist owners have relied on the police, the army, and private militias to enforce social relations objected to by workers and farmers. Hegemony of today has been built on the coercion of the past.

Police beat, shot, and killed workers advocating an 8-hour work-day (1886); armed Pinkerton detectives invaded the steelworkers' town of Homestead, Pennsylvania (1892); 14,000 federal troops occupied Chicago during the American Railway Union's boycott of Pullman, and a federal grand jury jailed union leaders, including

Eugene Debs (1894); city police and hired gang members beat women and children during the Lawrence textile strike (1912) (Lindsey, 1942; Meltzer, 1967; Yellin, 1974). When Greek, Italian, Slav, and Mexican miners struck for better working and living conditions in Ludlow, Colorado, in 1913, Rockefeller's security guards fired on them with machine guns and set fire to their tents, killing at least 51 people (Yellin, 1974, p. 236). The coercive triumph of the American industrialists temporarily reduced working-class opposition, but once the economic boom of the 1920s had passed, workers again sought adjustments to industrial relations and owners again resorted to violence.

In the late 1930s, private business and government officials regularly used hired guards, vigilantes, local police, and federal troops to defend corporate industrial practices. In many cases, men, women and children were killed. Businessmen organized "citizen's councils" to attack strikers in Minneapolis (Walker, 1971), policemen clubbed longshoremen in San Francisco (Quin, 1979), and county deputies and National Guardsmen fired teargas at autoworkers in Toledo. In 1937, Chicago police opened fire on a Memorial Day union picnic outside Republic Steel in Chicago, killing 10 and wounding 88; National Guardsmen in Youngstown, Ohio, killed 18 strikers and arrested 200 that same year (Preis, 1964). When his social reforms failed to quell worker unrest, even the president intervened on behalf of private industry: In 1940, FDR sent 3,500 federal troops armed with bayonets, machine guns, and mortars against union picket lines at an aviation plant in Inglewood, California (Preis, 1964). Evaluating the full account of labor's battles for social reform since the industrial revolution reveals that capitalist hegemony has been difficult to secure, repeatedly needing the armor of coercion.

Since World War II, corporate owners and their lawyers have relied more heavily on court injunctions and fines to break union campaigns for better working conditions, although when milder coercive practices falter, legal and vigilante violence is still employed. In recent years, police have teargassed, assaulted, and jailed meat packers in Austin, Minnesota; miners in West Virginia; and corn-processing workers in Decatur, Illinois, for example. Although not everyone would absolve unions for forcing confrontations with corporate owners, the point is that as long as hegemony is the preferred class formation of the dominant capitalist classes, armed and deadly coercion against the working class seems as close as a phone call to private guards, local police, or federal troops.

## The Preferred Choice

The use of coercion may secure dominant control over subordinate groups, but relying on coercion too often can upset the delicate balance of the status quo. Armed intervention or even court injunctions are economically and politically costly. Worst of all, for the capitalist classes, the legitimacy of the government, the media, and existing social practices may be challenged. For example, as a pattern of violence against union families unfolded during the 1980 strike against Standard Brands in Clinton, Iowa, the "neutrality of civic, media, legal and religious institutions was called into question"; "trust in the larger society was considerably shaken" (Fantasia, 1988, pp. 205-206), and radical populism became the dominant ideology for most of the 1,300 workers and their families. The "realization that the corporation could mobilize the resources of the police, the courts, the city council, and the National Labor Relations Board on its behalf was a sobering one" (p. 206), and the "collective definition that emerged characterized community institutions [including the local media] as agents of the corporation" (p. 218). In response, union workers and their supporters created their own community institutions: They published their own newspaper, established their own security force, attended a liberation theology Methodist church, and frequented only union-friendly taverns and stores. Through their organizational forms and political and social activities, the striking workers and their allies "created an alternative cultural form in many respects distinct from, and in opposition to, the dominant society. In the course of the conflict, the hegemonic fabric of their world—its practices, expectations, and perceptions"—was ruptured (Fantasia, 1988, p. 217). The working class was forced to "mobilize previously untapped resources" in its own defense (p. 218). Only with the complicity of the news media and the union's own national bureaucracy, was Standard Brands able to contain the conflict within Clinton, Iowa. Still, the strike illustrated how precarious dominant ideology and accepted social practices can be when the material and political conditions for hegemony are disrupted. Marc Cooper (1996) provides a more recent example in his "Socialism in Decatur" essay.

All corporate attempts to renegotiate the terms of the relations of production are potentially just as disruptive to class relations as the Clinton Corn strike. On the other hand, if capitalist classes and their representatives can secure and maintain working- and middle-class consent, daily life is more peaceful and the social order is more stable. Consequently, dominant classes avoid serious confrontations with the subordinate classes (unless material conditions force them to break the social peace for their own survival or perhaps if they see a politically and organizationally weak subordinate group). As discussed throughout this book, dominant groups prefer to lead with the consent of the subordinate, consent that must be constantly renewed.

Bourdieu (1991) has argued that hegemonic consent is constructed through representations of the world that organize and orient both dominant and subordinate groups according to an existing set of political and symbolic visions. Because the existing set of political and symbolic representations are the fruit of past battles, dominant groups have a decided advantage over subordinate challengers. Hegemonic leaders legitimately get to name social relations as right or wrong, preferable or not, possible or not. Indeed, if society were not filled with social and political contradictions flowing from structural antagonisms, hegemony once established would be almost automatic. However, because capitalist hegemony rests on recurring and increasing material inequalities, dominant leaderships will be repeatedly questioned by subordinate classes and groups. Successful hegemonic leaderships must mount political strategies that can buffer material inadequacies.

Therborn (1983) identifies three strategies for containing counterhegemonic challenges. One of the most effective strategies is *displacement*. Dominant classes try to displace class antagonisms to other social characteristics such as ethnic, religious, or national differences. For instance, Henry Ford avoided unionization of his auto plants for many years through a conscious campaign of ethnic division (Widick, 1972). As long as whites opposed black member-ship in the UAW, Ford was able to persuade black workers that un-ions were undesirable, thereby avoiding unionization. Another strategy that dominant classes count on is *submission*. Subordinate groups that become resigned to the weakness of their position or that have been politically or physically defeated are more apt to "consent" to domination. Following dramatic defeats such as those at Homestead, Ludlow, and Republic Steel, for example, the labor movement largely submitted to corporate demands for many years. Finally, the capitalist class can better secure consent if alter-native visions for social relations are hidden. Through the *isolation* of subordinate class segments (white-collar, service, ethnic group, black, and female workers, etc.) from the class as a whole and from their potential cross-class allies (shopkeepers, farmers, profession-als, etc.), the intrinsic social power of the working class is weak-ened and diffused. In many respects, the history of labor-capital re-lations in the United States can be read as a journey marked by these hegemonic strategies.

Although these strategies simultaneously build consent and ob-struct opposition, they do not *prevent* subordinate groups and indi-viduals from participating in or organizing other cultural practices because consciousness of the social world is structured and frac-tured by multiple and frequently conflicting everyday life experi-ences. In Gramsci's (1947/1971, 1988) view, knowledge and thought depend on that contradictory material existence. Accord-ingly, if the different spheres of our material existence (family, work, community, etc.) are consistent and complementary, hege-mony will be coordinated. On the other hand, if these spheres are contradictory, some practices will be at odds with some attitudes and ideas. Too much inconsistency may even lead to ruptures in the social order. Hence, hegemony must construct social practices that bring consent and must limit practices and processes that con-flict with dominant legitimacy and leadership.

Researchers in history and sociology generally agree that the rise of large corporations was the decisive economic development in this nation's history (Roy, 1991). At first, capitalist classes built institutions contributing to their own class cohesiveness. "But over time, members of the class increasingly penetrated into institutions that spanned across classes, thereby broadening their hegemony" (Roy, 1991, p. 144). Once the capitalist class organized itself as a political class, it turned to cultural practices that displaced class identities and disguised class power.

## Cross-Class Hegemonic Organizations

Historically, structural contradictions have been cushioned and hegemony has been bolstered by cross-class organizations to the extent that their practices and languages have inhibited class association and "conservatized" the working class. In the early 20th century, multiclass fraternal organizations such as the Masons, the Odd Fellows, the Knights of Pythias, and over 600 other orders institutionalized displacement of class through the language of brotherhood. Fraternal orders attracted almost half of the American population, including millions of workers. Membership in these cross-class fraternal orders obstructed class action and class consciousness through the promotion of pro-capitalist ideologies.

The fraternal lodge was a place where workers rubbed shoulders with bankers, merchants, and politicians in an elaborate hierarchical system that used rituals, oaths of secrecy, and pledges of fraternity and material assistance. The "rhetoric of the fraternal brotherhood acted to suppress the real and meaningful differences" (Orr & McNall, 1991, p. 104) in class power and class interest. Fraternal orders led by upper-class members claimed there were no differences between social economic classes. The language of fraternal brotherhood (individual responsibility, labor-business harmony, capitalist progress) produced different responses to labor's material conditions than the language of unionism or radical politics (collectivity, solidarity, community, equality, socialism) might have produced. Fraternities bolstered the language of cross-class commonality with organized material benefits. Through the fraternal order, members were eligible for health and unemployment insurance and sick pay, could count on employment references and business referrals, and gained the social prestige of middle-class respectability. Fraternal orders, whose members outnumbered union membership 6 to 1 in the 1920s, removed some of the incentive for working-class self-organization by displacing social antagonisms from class issues to cross-class fraternities having a rhetoric of capitalist progress.

Religious groups, ethnic organizations, and multiclass political parties have also displaced class through practices and ideologies that emphasize other explanations for social and personal problems. Constrained by religious, ethnic, populist, or nationalist rhetoric and practices, such organizations have undercut the formation of conscious working-class organization. And class organization is "one of the ways people have learned about the nature of their oppression and about how to articulate the values they wish to protect" (McNall, 1988, p. 10). Without independent organizations with clear ideologies, the working class has been politically handicapped, and consequent class formations have generally favored dominant capitalist classes. Capitalist hegemony has been strengthened by cross-class organizations that emphasize and mobilize other social identities for workers, interfering with the growth and development of independent working-class political organization.

## Two Parties, One Hegemony

Today, the rhetoric and ideology of the two-party electoral system may be the paramount means for diffusing and displacing working-class politics in the United States. The official version of democracy says that (a) all of us are free and equal; (b) nobody can shove us around; (c) public opinion is independent and unconstrained, and all people can know the facts so as to make up their own minds on all the issues; (d) we go to the polls as citizens and register our will there; and (e) the will of the majority will be carried out by elected officials. The hegemonically preferred view of electoral politics promoted by the media and mainstream political scientists (Polsby & Wildavsky, 1967) holds that Democratic and Republican politicians act as "transmission belts" for the public's policy preferences (p. 269). If such a view is true, then how can we explain Lyndon Johnson's escalation of the U.S. war in Vietnam after he was elected with a clear public mandate for peace? Or Jimmy Carter and the Democratic-majority Congress failing to pass a single piece of pro-labor legislation despite the nearly unanimous support of trade union members? Or Bill Clinton's backtracking on the environment despite overwhelming public support for protection and regulation?

A more critical read (Domhoff, 1967, 1986; Kerbo, 1983) asserts that assumptions about representative pluralist democracy are incorrect. Dominant capitalist interests effectively control and direct both parties, although popular mythology has cast the Democrats as more "liberal" and more responsive to blacks, women, and labor (Domhoff, 1986). Actually, the Democrats and Republicans do not really compete but, rather, collude against the public; as institutional representatives of hegemony, they share dominant ideologies, such as patriotism, deregulation, cuts in social services, and support of individualism and consumerism. Both parties in their majority supported the invasion of Grenada and Panama and the war against Iraq. Representatives from both parties backed the North American Free Trade Agreement (NAFTA) and the General Agreement on Tariffs and Trade (GATT) economic treaty between the major industrial nations. Both parties have championed reductions in funding for housing, education, unemployment, welfare. In short, as public opinion polls have shown over the last three decades, political parties will not always reflect the policy preferences of the majority of citizens. It may even be that the American two-party system "discourages policy discussion, political education, and majority preference" (Domhoff, 1986, p. 120). Meanwhile, campaign laws and media coverage obstruct independent working-class political activity. Mainstream public discourse is inundated with coverage of "horse-race" elections where there are few issues beyond personality: Gerry Ford falls down a lot; Jimmy Carter lusts in his heart; Ronald Reagan forgets things; Bill Clinton has affairs. Most high school student government elections offer as much substance as contemporary national elections dedicated to image building and issue avoiding.

In a class society, such ritual electoral practices are crucial. Capitalist hegemony justifies inequality with its ideology of equal opportunity. Citizens freely voting for the candidate of their choice is an important symbolic ritual for this mythology. Indeed, hegemonic institutions expend a great deal of energy, expense, and expertise in creating this spectacle of democracy. Campaigns are run year-round with enthusiastic support and coverage by the news media. As the primary means of registering one's political opinion, elections take on a seeming urgency and importance. Wearing buttons for candidates, following the campaign in the news, arguing about issues, and especially actively campaigning as a volunteer for the candidate of choice behaviorally integrates individuals into their "citizen" identities as Democrat or Republican. Just as the language of fraternal "brotherhood" without regard to social position obstructs awareness of class, so too, the language of two-party politics replaces class interest with classless American values. Former Speaker of the House Newt Gingrich (1995) lists among American values "the ethic of individual responsibility" and "the spirit of entrepreneurial free enterprise" (p. 33). Accordingly, individual freedom and capitalist opportunity are the main supports of democracy. The language of two-party politics not only promotes democracy as the twin sister of capitalism but instills the expectation that each voter has an unencumbered influence on American politics.

Campaigning and voting for Democrats and Republicans obstructs subordinate group political independence and organization, and involvement in hegemonic institutions does not translate to subordinate power. Moreover, at no point will dominant representatives allow subordinate-group decision making to affect the economic/material "kernel" of capitalist social relations, in

Gramsci's (1988) terms. To ensure hegemonic control of government agencies, the Democratic and Republican parties must always be led by representatives of dominant-class interests who hold similar hegemonic ideologies and act to maintain established social relations. At the same time, and in a slightly contradictory manner, to be hegemonically effective, these representatives must also campaign in popular terms to provide subordinate groups and individuals with a symbolic, yet material, demonstration of equal opportunity in politics.

Each election year, the media showers us with much concern, anxiety, and enthusiasm for elections as the key to American democracy, but despite the banners, bells, and whistles, voters don't really make any policy decisions when they vote for candidates. Citizens may go into their private voting booths once every couple of years and vote for the candidate of their choice, but whatever promises were made or implied, the elected official has no legal or institutional responsibility to pursue any particular policy at all. Ultimately, a successful politician's concern for constituency is always mitigated with a concern for corporate and party sponsorship. As long as the two-party structure sets the rules for the game, even the measured public response to "throw the bum out" can at best replace him or her with another of similar ilk. "The more often this country goes through particular campaign rituals, the more natural those rituals seem to be ... [as] the processes of presidential campaigning justify themselves through sheer repetition" (Gronbeck, 1984, p. 493), legitimizing the process and creating acquiescence and quiescence among the public. In short, elections function less as a means of decision making and more as a means for convincing citizens that participation in the ritual is what really matters.

In an attempt to coordinate economic and political conditions, the language of American hegemony drenches political discourse with the claim that democracy and capitalism are two sides of the same valuable coin, and the myth of popular democracy portrays political power as unconnected to economic power. Studies targeting the candidate selection process upset that narrative, however.

Researchers have consistently found that running for national office means having to obtain the backing of at least a part of the corporate elite. Indeed, over two thirds of all campaign contributions come from a handful of corporate owners and directors (Domhoff, 1979; Dye, 1979; Kerbo, 1983)—with 34% of all contributions donated by a mere .1% of the population (Lind, 1991, p. 43). With rare exception, congressional representatives are lawyers or businessmen before coming to Washington. Most members increase their financial investments after election to Congress. The large percentage of lawyers in the American political system, about 40%, is highly atypical compared with other countries, suggesting to Domhoff (1986) that "the classless nature of American political parties" creates a climate and need for hegemonic representatives who "have the skills to balance the relationship between the corporate community that finances them on the one hand and the citizens who vote for them on the other" (p. 128). Publicly, most of these representatives may rail against "special interests" and "big government" on behalf of the "average American," but given their social background and shared lived experiences we should not be surprised that congressional members share political perspectives and ideological views that support capitalist social relations.

More important for actually running the country, corporate owners wield considerable influence in the policy-forming process of government. Kerbo (1983) explains that capitalists supply money and personnel to fund university and foundation research for capitalist-sponsored planning groups that make recommendations to the government and the media to influence the public and their elected "representatives" (Kerbo, 1983, pp. 215-216). Top funding foundations have a majority of capitalist class members (Dye, 1979). Even the Corporation for Public Broadcasting, ostensibly dedicated to public information, is heavily dominated by corporate-serving conservatives (Jackson, 1993). The leading policy-planning forums, the Council on Foreign Relations (CFR) and the Committee on Economic Development (CED), are clearly capitalist class institutions (Domhoff, 1986). Formed by leading capitalists during World War II, the CFR has the stated intent of influencing government to act in best interests of business (Shoup, 1975).

## The Power to Decide

Capitalist hegemony does not concern itself solely, or primarily, with building consent. Hegemony's ultimate function is to secure and serve dominant interests. Thus, in the late 1990s, U.S. Treasury Secretary Robert Rubin brokered the deregulation that cleared Citibank's merger with Traveler's Insurance. ("Teflon Bob" also negotiated his own reward: A few days after the merger, Citigroup announced that Rubin was its new cochairman.) U.S. Treasury/Citigroup Rubin is only one example of "the overrepresentation of members of the corporate community . . . at the highest levels of the executive branch, especially State, Defense, and Treasury Departments," which are "interlocked constantly with the corporate community" (Domhoff, 1986, p. 143), ensuring that the "kernel" of capitalism is politically well protected.

Beth Mintz (1975) found that 90% of all cabinet members from 1879 to 1973 were members of the upper class or associated with major corporations before their appointments, with little difference between Democratic and Republican administrations. G. William Domhoff (1986) believes that corporate-funded organizations, such as the Rockefeller Foundation, Carnegie Foundation, RAND Corporation, Trilateral Commission, Brookings Institute, Council on Foreign Relations (CFR), and Committee on Economic Development (CED) "determine the outcome of any policy struggle" (p. 144). During the late 1970s, for example, all of the recommendations of the CFR and CED were adopted by the Carter administration (Dye, 1979), which promoted their corporate-friendly policies "for the public good."

Henry Kissinger rose to cabinet member via the CFR as did Jimmy Carter's national security adviser, Zbigniew Brzezinski (Dye, 1979).

## Labor Solidarity
## Challenges Hegemony

In 1934, Teamster's Local 574 struck for union recognition of drivers and coal yard workers in Minneapolis, challenging the political hegemony of an anti-union employer's association called the "Citizen's Alliance" (Walker, 1971). Influenced by the conscious political leadership of socialist trade unionists, Local 574 did not limit its campaign to narrow union tactics or concerns and immediately reached out to hegemonically lead the entire working class of Minneapolis by organizing its intrinsic social strength—collective solidarity.

Local 574 held mass meetings nightly, published a newspaper, set up its own hospital and commissary, formed a "women's auxiliary" that staffed picket lines and strike kitchens, and organized "flying picket squadrons" to monitor 50 roads into the city, turning nonunion trucks away. "The entire labor community was awakened and mobilized to support the strike, the Central Labor Council voted its support, and thousands of union and non-union workers joined street battles against strike breakers and police" (Fantasia, 1988, p. 21). Unemployed workers were mobilized to support the strike, and cross-class alliances were formed with supportive farmers and shopkeepers to distribute food and other supplies.

Although support for democratic pluralism still predominates in high school texts, the "amount of empirical evidence slowly building on the nature and existence of powerful elites in this country" (Kerbo, 1983, p. 257) has made it difficult for academic researchers to deny the power of corporate class power in the United States. This position should not be reduced to some conspiracy theory of elite control, nor should it be interpreted to mean that capitalist forces will ultimately win any social, political, or economic struggle. Rather, the evidence shows that the mechanisms of dominant-class rule are complex, encompassing economic relations that

Having lost its political legitimacy, the capitalist class turned to coercion: Martial law was declared, and the National Guard was sent in. But the collective power of the working class was too strong: Protest rallies of 40,000 were held, the working class physically defended itself, and its unity and alliances held. The strike was victorious.

An emergent oppositional hegemony had appeared. Along with the Toledo Auto-Lite strike and the San Francisco longshoremen strikes, the Minneapolis Teamsters inspired workers across the country and helped pave the way for the massive social movement of labor in the 1930s and 1940s (Dobbs, 1972). For the next decade, the working class began assembling a new hegemony that threatened many of the social institutions and cultural practices of capitalist society. Large sections of the working class placed little confidence in corporations or government agencies, relying instead on mass picket lines and class action against employers. Business and government made significant structural adjustments to refurbish capitalist hegemony and ultimately displaced union solidarity with American patriotism during World War II. Still, labor had gained legitimacy, and social welfare programs, such as unemployment insurance and Social Security, were established.

include monopoly ownership of international corporations and political relations between these corporate institutions and government agencies and representatives. Indeed, capitalist hegemony could not be constructed without the massive and constant intervention by corporate interests in government policy making. To lead society, dominant groups must direct economic, political, and cultural resources. In a mass society such as the United States, the political administration of those resources falls largely to government institutions.

The task for hegemonic leaderships is to attract, involve, and incorporate subordinate groups and individuals in political projects that cement subordinate interests to dominant relations—a task outside the purpose of capitalist-led policy groups but almost seamlessly accomplished by the two-party electoral system. In the United States, millions of individuals from the working and middle classes devote millions of hours promoting candidates from the Democratic and Republican parties in the belief that they are participating in an important political process. Besides detracting from the time and energy that could be devoted to oppositional politics and culture, two-party politics creates a language that isolates class identities as un-American "special interests." Battles between "liberals" and "conservatives" are confined to hegemonically acceptable disagreements: Whichever "side" wins the debate, dominant-class interests are secure. Chomsky (1989) has argued that Democrat and Republican "hawks" and "doves" debate tactics, never strategy; whatever the geopolitical "hot spots," from Vietnam or Nicaragua to the Persian Gulf, both sides unequivocally agree that the United States has the right to intervene. Likewise on domestic issues, Democrats and Republicans alike agree that the interests of private enterprise outweigh social responsibility; regulations on industrial health and safety, food and drugs, environmental protections, and public media, for instance, are regularly set aside (Cohen & Solomon, 1993; Kellner, 1990) unless social movements are able to mobilize enough political pressure to threaten the legitimacy of the policy-making process. Whenever there is a lull in subordinate social protest, indicating a lack of counterhegemonic capacity, the big question becomes, How far can dominant forces go in realigning political conditions before subordinate groups resist?

As we have reiterated throughout this book, hegemony breaks down as belief in the legitimacy of social relations and practices dissipates. One manifestation of that breakdown may well be the continued decline in voter registration and voter turnout. Fewer and fewer Americans participating in the two-party elections threatens to disrupt the symbolic importance of that ritual process.

Significantly (with the possible exception of African Americans), this increasing nonparticipation is not a sign of resignation or submission; rather, it has to do with a general distaste for the electoral process. For example, voters in the 1992 New Hampshire primary opted overwhelmingly for "none of the above" in a preelection opinion poll. Given the needs of hegemony to head off further erosion, more motivational and educational appeals to participation will be forthcoming from the media, led by subordinate spokesmodels (e.g., rap singers encouraging voter registration). Sections of the capitalist class will resort to supporting various "independent" or "third-party" candidates to generate some interest and controversy in an attempt to seduce more citizens back to the ritual process. Without widespread working-class participation, elections would fail to legitimately represent subordinate-class interests; respect for the authority of officials and their actions would slip. Although hegemony can tolerate apathy and what Chomsky (1987) calls quiescent opposition, withdrawal from hegemonic practices is potentially the first step toward counterhegemonic practices. Much more could be written about electoral politics à la the Democrats and Republicans and the policy-making process, but this brief account should at least demonstrate the political importance of the ritual for recruiting participants to hegemonic relations.

## Working Toward Hegemony

By now, the contradictory connections between social structure and class formation in a commodity-driven capitalist society should make some sense. We have argued that institutions are part of the social structure and reproduce class relations because classes struggle over and within institutions (or control their own). Of all places where practices, languages, and relations are lived and shared by individual class members, of all places where consent is important to dominant-subordinate relations, of all places where hegemony is constructed, the most important place must be at work. As Antonio Gramsci wrote (1947/1971), hegemony is "born in the factory" (p. 285). The factory—or shop, field, office, store, and anywhere else commodities are produced or distributed—is where coercion and consent coordinate class relations into hegemony.

The workplace is the site where classes are formed, interact, and struggle over their relations. The culture of work is not simply the physical actions of production but a total experience objectively located in social relations, practices, and institutions. The workplace culture provides a distinctive way of life organized with meanings, values, practices, languages, and social relations. This is a class culture in that the workplace is where value is created, where goods necessary for society are produced, where relationships between the classes are hammered out. In terms of personal development, "The challenge of work, or the lack thereof, measurably affects the development of the worker's physical, cognitive, emotional, and other capacities. Indeed, the content of work, its prestige and social contribution are the basic elements of self-esteem" (Bowles & Gintis, 1977, p. 71). For most Americans, work is the principal site of daily activity and the substance of personal identity. Whether they will have a class identity or some other identity depends greatly on how working relations unfold. In the pages that follow, we consider some of the components that affect hegemony at work.

The habits of a nation took years to develop and have needed constant reinforcement as successive waves of artisans, farmers, and immigrants entered American factories. Creating a pliant workforce has not been easy. Contrary to popular belief, "The Protestant work ethic was not deeply ingrained in the nation's social fabric" (Gutman, 1977, p. 4). Men and women who entered the factory brought more than their labor power. They also brought the knowledge, values, and experiences of their prior cultural existence. Between 1850 and 1890, capitalism industrialized culture as workers collectively experienced the introduction of machinery and the unbridled drive of capitalist owners for profits. The early industrial workplace in America placed class identities at the center of each person's material existence as capitalist managers struggled to inculcate "good" work habits in their employees: to educate, persuade, and finally coerce workers to punctuality, efficiency, subservience, and diligent work habits.

Following the violent class battles at the turn of the century, industrialists turned to "scientific management" as a means of efficiency and control, which they hoped would eradicate class conflict (Howard, 1985). Howard cites efficiency expert Frederick Taylor in the claim that "rationality" would eliminate all possibility of dispute between employers and workers. Under scientific management, Taylor argued, "the men who were formerly called bosses . . . become the servants of the workmen." In exchange for ceding the control of work to these impartial experts, workers would share in enormous productivity gains that scientific management made possible (Howard, 1985, p. 96). In industry, government, and media, efficiency and control became the universal value for human progress, concealing the commodity relationship based on profits made from value withheld from wages. Increased productivity meant harder work, less worker reward. Recurrent "downsizing," such as the loss of 12,000 jobs with the 1995 "downsizing" merger of Citibank and Chemical Bank in New York, illustrates that corporate efficiency and control will continue to have the same consequences for workers.

Taylor's approach to productivity requires a pliant, docile, and disciplined workforce, but that poses a problem. When an owner (generally a man) buys a lathe, he gets one with certain specifications and capacities for a certain price, but when he "buys" a worker, he gets only potential. He faces the problem of how to get the most work for the wage. In the 1920s and 1930s, Ford had a sociology department of 40 men looking for an answer. Ford's investigators visited workers to determine their eligibility for employment in his auto plants. Workers were questioned about their marital status, diet, recreation, and religion; interviewers reported on each worker's general habits, home conditions, and neighborhood. Only those with acceptable financial, moral, and cultural habits—read: pliant, docile, disciplined—were allowed to be "associates" at Ford (Fantasia, 1988, p. 28). Of course, neither Ford nor any other industrialist could screen all employees for work. Consent to productive social relations had to be built "on-the-job," so to speak. Hence, under a plan for the "Americanization of Aliens," leading corporations such as Ford and International Harvester initiated paternalistic company programs to socialize immigrants to attitudes more in line with industrial work.

## Welfare Capitalism

Following the strikes of 1919, major corporations developed "welfare capitalism" as a means to boost worker productivity and loyalty. U.S. Steel, International Harvester, Swift, Armour, and Western Electric "all assembled comprehensive welfare capitalist plans involving five kinds of activity: restructuring interpersonal relations at the plant, rewarding workers through wages and promotions, experimenting with industrial democracy, instituting welfare programs, and assuming community responsibilities" (Cohen, 1990, p. 163).

Employers undercut ethnic subcultures by integrating work groups and sponsoring classes in American civics and English. Separating workers from their ethnic peers left workers isolated in their relations with bosses, who were given "special training programs designed to improve their skills in handling workers on the shop floor," telling them to "teach, don't boss" and that "the modern supervision of labor is a psychological problem" (Cohen, 1990, p. 168).

Welfare capitalists complemented improved interpersonal relations with wage incentive programs to maximize worker efficiency and restrict worker collectivity. Individual workers were rewarded with a "bonus" wage for producing above a standard rate set by the company. As one manufacturer put it bluntly, "When each worker is paid according to his record there is not the same community of interest" (Cohen, 1990, p. 170).

The most "progressive" companies also instituted employee representation programs, including work councils and company unions, which made proposals on working conditions, ran sports programs, administered group insurance plans, and were used to more easily fire workers and reduce wages. Similar employee representation plans reappeared in the 1980s as quality circles and the "team concept."

Western Electric skipped the representation gimmick and took a "human relations" approach in collaboration with Harvard professor Elton Mayo. Experts determined that by talking privately with every hourly worker at least once a year "they could keep employee grievances individual and nourish an alliance between laborer and top management" (Cohen, 1990, p. 174).

Changed corporate communications were augmented by improving worker benefits. Harvester and others granted sick pay, pensions, paid vacations, and employee stock option programs to "remove the argument of class distinction" when workers compared themselves with salaried staff.

Finally, these welfare capitalists extended their largesse to the greater community in an effort to displace other identities and practices that would compete with company authority and legitimacy. Western Electric's sports program, which sponsored 14 organized sports for workers became a model for other companies nationwide. Industrial leagues were organized so teams could compete against neighboring factories and plants, with the explicit purpose of building company morale. " 'When you start this,' said the Chicago Association of Commerce, 'your employees will begin to work six days a week and not five . . . the ball club will be something they can rally around' as players as well as spectators" (Cohen, 1990, p. 177). Nonethnic social events were sponsored, featuring dance and music from mass popular culture as companies sought to "reconstitute community" into a "happy family" of corporate workers sharing a common culture and respect for authority. Radio clubs, family bowling teams, big band dances, and company magazines devoted to employee personal events were sponsored. U.S. Steel, Western Electric, Harvester, and others funded the YMCA, the Boy Scouts, neighborhood parks, libraries, and schools. Companies provided fuel for local churches and hosted contests in gardening—everywhere reaching out to persuade citizens that the corporation was the most responsible institution in society (Cohen, 1990, p. 181).

The experiment in corporate-led worker welfare fits Therborn's (1983) typology for capitalist hegemonic strategies. Early 20th-century welfare capitalists implemented strategies of *displacement* by promoting the company as the primary worker identity, of *submission* by hiring cooperative workers and firing uncooperative ones, and of *isolation* by obstructing opportunities for worker collectivity. The hegemonic relationships of welfare capitalism were precarious at best, and the programs themselves failed to operate the way employers intended. As Cohen (1990) notes, "Manufacturers found it easier to sweeten the icing than to enrich the cake," and they would pay a price for "promising a treat and then leaving their workers' appetites unsatisfied" (p. 187). The benefits of welfare capitalism pleased workers, but it also raised their expectations about what work should provide.

When the productive capacity of American workers outstripped their purchasing power, the American market faced an "overproduction" of goods that brought the Great Depression and destroyed the material preconditions for welfare capitalism.

> When there were orders, employers prized dependable, trained workers. But in more difficult times, managers expected employees, not the company, to absorb the loss. With eyes glued to the bottom line of the balance sheet, employers in the end showed more commitment to stabilizing production than their work force. (Cohen, 1990, p. 186)

As we have noted throughout this text, when material conditions don't meet subordinate expectations, hegemony may be threatened—as it was by industrial workers in the 1930s and 1940s.

Ultimately, all hegemonic relationships are unstable because even entrenched behaviors are challenged as individuals have new experiences that affect their outlooks and attitudes of yesterday and today. Hegemonic strategies aimed at winning consent come up against the contradictions within the social structure and the political interests of individuals who share class experiences. Practices, actions, choices, and political goals of the subordinate groups may be postponed but can never be fully deterred. Such is the case with work. If it is a site of hegemony, it is also a place where class counterhegemony can be constructed.

## Counterhegemony at Work

The roots of counterhegemony exist in the capacity of the working class for collective, political organization and activity. Under existing social relations, working-class counterhegemony seems unlikely, almost surreal. Echoing Marcuse (1964), some researchers have claimed that monopoly capitalism has "de-skilled" the working class and rendered it incapable of independent action (Aronowitz, 1983; Braverman, 1974). Much of this research focuses on the *individual* job and accepted capitalist hegemony as the norm. However, if working-class capacity resides in working-class collectivity as Therborn (1983) believes, then individual job positions are the wrong unit of analysis. In addition, capitalist hegemony is the norm only so long as the material, political, and cultural needs of the subordinate working class are met. If history is any guide, we should anticipate challenges in one or more of those areas. If the reality of everyday life tells us anything, we should realize that even our most serene moments are ripe with contradictions. Periodically, these contradictions rupture the social order, revealing the underlying interests of social relations. Certainly, "the best of all possible moments to achieve insight into the life of a human being is during a fundamental crisis. . . . It is when all hell breaks loose that the powerful forces which organize and control human society are revealed" (Fantasia, 1988, p. 16). Lacking ruptures, we must look to the contradictions within the practices of everyday life, which, if not resolved or buffered, will explode the relative tranquility of the status quo. We should be able to find within any hegemony ingredients that could be turned to counterhegemonic purposes.

The most important element of working-class counterhegemony has already been discussed. It is that which constitutes political class action for the working class—collectivity, organized consciously and politically. A primary goal of capitalist hegemony is to prevent the creation of a politically independent working class.

When workers associate as workers, they create new bonds and links, and

> whether or not a future society is consciously envisioned, whether or not a "correct" image of the class structure is maintained, the building of solidarity in the form, and in the process, of mutual association can represent a practical attempt to restructure, or reorder, human relations. (Fantasia, 1988, p. 11)

Gramsci (1988) recognized such a nascent new society in the emerging culture of the factory councils in Turin and promoted those formations in his paper, *Ordine Nuovo.* He later argued that political organization was essential to ensure that oppositional cultural practices would lead to a counterhegemonic social movement.

Following Gramsci, we must look for evidence and instances of collective activity by workers, however elementary, that might lead to more developed political action. In identifying sources for counterhegemony, we should recognize what Raymond Williams (1977/1989) extrapolated from Gramsci: Emergent cultural practices can be oppositional only if they are not crushed or incorporated into dominant culture. Thus, we also look for evidence and instances of corporate practices that obstruct working-class solidarity or direct working-class cultural practices toward individualism rather than collectivity. Collective practices as well as tendencies toward community can, in the course of a struggle, be transformed with surprising speed into full-fledged counterhegemonic activities—as illustrated by "cultures of solidarity" in revolutionary upsurges in Nicaragua (Rothschuh, 1986) and Chile (Mattelart, 1980), in past labor struggles such as the Teamster rebellion in Minneapolis (Dobbs, 1972) and other union organizing drives and strikes (Burawoy, 1979; Fantasia, 1988; Preis, 1964), and in contemporary working-class battles such the Staley fight in Decatur, Illinois, or the union organizing drive at Tultex in Virginia.

The collectivity of the working class appears in different forms today than it did in the past. Assembly lines, garment factories,

### Paradise at 111

In the 1970s, Citibank's internal operating costs were increasing, motivation and morale were low, 36,000 customer inquiries were backlogged. The first response was to automate the process like an auto assembly line, but operating officer Richard Matteis had a better idea. He created a "humanized," decentralized, flexible work center so a variety of tasks could be performed by the same "self-motivated" computer worker. Selected workers were trained in the new technology and given more personal responsibility. The new center at 111 Wall Street was soon touted as "Paradise" by the *Harvard Business Review*, the *New York Times*, and technology magazines. Production increased, labor costs dropped dramatically, and the work environment improved.

Unfortunately, all the changes and new technology didn't create a paradise for everyone who used to work at 111. By the time all of the equipment was installed, two thirds of the employees had been laid off, and the remaining third were "promoted" to "workstation professionals." No workers were involved in designing technology or its use, although they did help choose the furniture and color schemes. As one manager recalled, "A lot of money was spent on window dressing." All computer work was now monitored for productivity; fewer management positions were needed, but management's traditional authority remained. One technician called it "a great leap sideways." Technology was humanized, and humans were programmed for better motivation, attitude, behavior. Matteis and Citibank succeeded in creating an atmosphere of change without changing the corporate hierarchy—a paradise for profits if not for participation (Howard, 1985, pp. 110-117).

"sweat shops," and farm labor are still managed in much the same authoritarian manner as 40 or 50 years ago, but the political terrain has been leveled and reforested as employers expend tremendous resources to weaken and break working-class solidarity. Most significantly, with the Taft-Hartley labor bill of 1947, written "line by line and paragraph by paragraph by the National Association of Manufacturers" (Fantasia, 1988, p. 56), employers and government can more easily interfere with and obstruct the formation of collectivity and solidarity. Although unions were recognized as "legal," Taft-Hartley made most solidarity activity *illegal*, including boycotts, secondary strikes, and mass picketing. Now, under the cover of law, the government systematically intervenes in defense of the economic hegemony of capitalism through court injunctions and the National Labor Relations Board. Corporations have also turned to anti-union lawyers and public relations campaigns to maintain their advantage on the shop floor. Where they have learned from past conflicts, large corporations have also created a new culture of work—with or without unions. This "new, improved" culture cushions employee submission with the attraction of membership in the "corporate family" through various employee-participation programs such as quality circles or quality of work life committees. Under these conditions, worker collectivity has been diffused.

Even during the era of unions, worker collectivity was undercut. The restructuring of relations in the plants and offices that were unionized gave some power to the workers, but this relationship was structured to manufacture consent, not rebellion (Burawoy, 1979; Fantasia, 1988). Union recognition and the mandate to negotiate contracts gave more power to the working class, but the bureaucratic system imposed on the workforce channeled conflict into drawn-out arbitration procedures and sharply limited solidarity. When the International Longshore and Warehouse Union gave up control over working conditions in exchange for no layoffs, a guaranteed minimum workweek, and early retirement funds, companies hired workers at lower wages with fewer benefits. Senior workers were protected at the expense of younger workers, and worker unity was lost (Howard, 1985, p. 183).

Acceptance of "management rights" made the union into the primary enforcer of the contract among the workers. The steady process of co-optation onto government boards and later joint management-labor councils added a certain legitimacy to union leaders but served as a brake on labor activity. Forty years of schooling in the social contract between labor and management has housebroken most labor leaders, who have "diluted, deflected, and bartered away mutual solidarity" (Fantasia, 1988, p. 27). In 1995, when incoming United Autoworkers Union president William Yoder said his main interest was to avoid strikes, he was publicly distancing himself and the UAW from the primary source of collective power by union members.

The time when unions won 94% of the votes for union recognition are gone. Unions have failed to mobilize worker solidarity within and between workplaces, and companies have constructed scenarios that obscure the aims and character of union-organizing drives (Levitt, 1993). Today, the lack of aggressive union activity coupled with an intensified employer resistance retards labor solidarity and collectivity, leaving the playing field open to corporate takeover.

## The Corporate Culture

Entering the 21st century, many social theorists and critics find that the corporation has become the dominant institution in American society (Deetz, 1992; Howard, 1985; Schiller, 1989). Herbert Schiller (1989) relates a vision of corporate feudalism where a handful of corporate lords are at war in takeovers and mergers of American businesses. Globalization according to the U.S. "New World Order" turns employees from citizens into resources, where obedience to the company is more important than loyalty to church, family, or community. The lines of command of this new feudalism are strictly hierarchical and authoritarian, although the benevolent corporate lords provide pleasant work environments, salaries, and corporate cultures of togetherness. This corporate form delivers commodities as consumer goods, and a pro-growth ideology sustains more consumption. Transnational companies own magazines, newspapers, and entertainment industries that distribute the bulk of news and information to society (Mosco, 1998). Stanley Deetz (1992) believes that corporations have "colonized" our world, overshadowing the government, family, community, education, and the mass media. The government subsidizes corporate growth, but the market regulates social policy. According to Deetz, democracy is threatened as the government defends the power of corporations and the marketplace (1992, p. 21).

Corporate domination in America has brought "a corresponding decline of social identity based on small, local communities," loosening traditional bonds (Howard, 1985, p. 121). Relationships are no longer provided by home and family, which has been "dismantled" by experts in health care, childbirth, nutrition, education, fashion, morality, elder care, shelter, leisure, and funeral services who have "expropriated these functions from the family where they had been provided as use value to return them in exchange as commodified goods and services" (Luke, 1989, p. 108). Support from friends can be replaced by a therapist; child rearing can take place in day care; community value sharing can be replaced by exercises in schools; meals can be purchased at the drive-through. In all, consumer services meet crass individual needs, substituting for family, community, and other social collectives. We have been Disneyfied and McDonaldized (Ritzer, 2000).

The family and community are now structured around the demands of work: "moving, choice of living community, and timing of children are increasingly tied to work rather than to kinship and community ties" (Deetz, 1992, p. 24). Today, 85% of all households have working mothers. The average workweek has increased from 40 to 50 hours in the last 25 years. Children's skill learning is separated from the family, directed by day care operators or relegated to peer group education. With greater work identity, community ties and solidarity decline, but the replacement of community and family with corporate life has not led to greater personal satisfaction. By the late 1980s, workers were suffering from more general negative effects of corporate work with increased feelings of depression, irritation, and anxiety. The cause? "Unhealthy work conditions" such as "authoritarian and detailed supervision," "little demand on individuals to contribute knowledge, responsibility, and initiative," and "few or no human contacts during work" (Alvesson, 1987, p. 59). As in the 1920s, forward-thinking corporate leaders have responded with programs intended to head off worker dissatisfaction and production decline.

## Quality of Work Life

To be successful, management needs to let workers *feel* in control without actually increasing their decision-making responsibility or control. Peters and Waterman (1982) call it the "illusion of control"; "if people think they have even the modest personal control over their destinies, they will persist at their tasks. They will do them better." So "provide them with a pretense of participation in decisions that are in fact beyond their influence and control" (quoted in Howard, 1985, p. 129). The corporation accepts the "search for self" to harness personal growth and the desire for meaningful work to corporate needs.

Judged by the reporting of major news magazines of the time, job stress seemed to be the disease of the decade, and it certainly has not subsided in subsequent years. "Quick fixes for motivating employees by changing their attitudes and behavior [were] eagerly sought by some employers" (Eiger, 1989, p. 11). Worker participation programs, termed "quality circles" (QCs), were embraced by companies eager to reduce job stress and maximize productivity. Based on the Japanese model of "corporate culture," employees were brought together in groups to dialogue about workplace design, employee communication, production problems, and other environmental issues. More than 100 major corporations, including Lockheed, GM, Ford, Honeywell, American Airlines, General Electric, and 3M (Grenier, 1988, p. 6) launched up to as many as 1 million QCs (Hoyt, 1984). Guillermo Grenier (1988) explains that in QCs, small-group communication techniques help increase the influence that managers and supervisors have over the attitude and behavior of employees. The QC program allows "management to exert increased control over the selection and socialization of the work force as well as the work relations and leadership patterns . . . as an alternative to unionization" (Grenier, 1988, p. 5).

At first, workers and unions looking for some way to participate in the organization of work were receptive to QCs (Eiger, 1989, p. 4), but the honeymoon was short. In the 1980s, telephone workers saw the Bell System Quality of Work Life program (QWL) as a way to extend the collective power of the Communication Workers of America (CWA). Very quickly, the QWL groups made a difference in the day-to-day workplace relations: instituting flextime work schedules, improving the office physical environment, and no longer having to ask permission to go to the bathroom (Howard, 1985, p. 188). But the closer the committees got to issues involving control of technology or worker performance, the less successful they were. Indeed, most QWL committees at Bell never got beyond "environmental issues." "They get the lounge fixed up, or they get a microwave put into the break room . . . rather than getting into issues about the work process or job redesign" (Howard, 1985, p. 190). Gramsci's hegemony explains why: Technology and work design strike at the "kernel" of capitalist power and are beyond the conversation that management allows QWLs and QCs.

Not all workers participate in QC programs: Companies select employees especially qualified to participate in "team meetings." In Grenier's (1988) study, for example, employees who challenged management prerogatives were identified as "pro-conflict, anti-cooperation, and deviant along moral lines" and were usually excluded from the groups, whereas those favoring management policies were characterized by "cooperation, team spirit and innovation" and considered important to the discussions (p. 19). One QC developer explained the basic mechanisms of control and consent as a three-pronged approach: (a) give workers information the company wants them to have; (b) "pro-actively . . . orchestrate and facilitate the discussion" so company positions get across; and (c) isolate from the group and personally confront workers known to be pro-union (Grenier, 1988, p. 19). Workers were encouraged to criticize others, and QC groups were often pitted against each other by the facilitators (Grenier, 1988, p. 26). Workers who don't "buy into" QCs and similar programs must "opt out" or "exit" as sociologists say. Employers can live with rebellious workers exiting because that too undermines worker collectivity—separating potential leaders (Gramsci's "organic intellectuals") from the ranks. Predictably, during layoffs, downsizing, and mergers, QCs are dismantled by management as quickly as they were established.

The functions of QCs seem remarkably similar to Therborn's (1983) topology of displacement, submission, and isolation. Moreover, these structures provide an excellent forum for consciously constructing attitudes and behaviors according to dominant interests, workplace institutions for constructing capitalist hegemony.

## The Workplace as a Site of Learning

Work is the site of the production or exchange of commodities. At work, workers expend labor power in the production of commodities as designers, engineers, machinists, drivers, and other occupations. At work, managers and owners direct work practices to maximize labor power. In the process of producing, exchanging, and servicing goods for society, workers, managers, and owners also produce, exchange, and service social relations between themselves.

Far too often, the unavoidable necessity of growing up and getting a "good-paying" job forces us to become less than we could be—less free, less creative, less secure, in short, less happy. The intense sameness of factory work, work at the post office, in the computer industry, and in many clerical and secretarial jobs depresses and demoralizes workers unless they develop some means for coping with the drudgery and boredom. Some jobs try to compensate with small pleasantries. Workers sorting mail at the post office, for instance, listen to radios on personal headphones. Other jobs prohibit such diversion for safety or efficiency reasons. At all work, however, workers (and managers) collectively develop a means of social intercourse (Halle, 1991; Willis, 1991). At a factory in New Jersey, for instance, Fantasia (1988) observed a complex process of social interaction that included joking, kidding, football betting pools, water fights in the summer, snowball fights in the winter, and a shared affability that "represented a general social bonding of the factory workforce, and thus essentially a class cohesion within the plant" (p. 79). Communication between workers at most jobs has similar dynamics. Due to the commonality of social class existence, the social interaction between workers rises on the bed of shared, largely homogeneous, experiences within the workplace.

Worker interaction occurs within a structurally constrained system of rules and behaviors. If you punch a time clock to start work and punch it again to leave, symbolically and physically you are giving over your time to the employer to be used as he sees fit. Once employed, you are inserted into an existing set of social relations that are hierarchical; you fit into a specific chain of command, taking orders from your "superiors" and possibly giving directions to those "under you." Everyone who works for the employer knows those power relations and abides by those rules or else faces retribution and punishment. Collective knowledge about incompetent bosses or employees can be expressed through joking, criticizing, and complaining within shared subgroups of workers. Coping with production tasks, interpersonal relations, and the work environment also occurs through shared group communication, occasionally spilling over into conflict with managers and the employer.

Each new worker enters a situation regarded as "normal." Experienced employees, socialized to existing practices and hierarchical relations, serve as educators to each new worker through their own behavior and communication. At each work site, employer and employees create conditions for work and discourse. The symbolic explanation for conditions creates the social knowledge for how to do the job, how to talk about the job and the hierarchy, and what passes as acceptable behavior and conversation. Any refusal to participate in the practices or the conversations according to the recognized "normal" way for that work site either leads to dismissal, ostracism, or if others respond favorably, to the breakdown in consent.

Hegemony becomes the norm in any plant, and throughout capitalist society, whenever past and present *practices* of work and discourse at the work site reinforce existing *relations*. Importantly, the breakdown in consent necessary to establish a new collective culture of solidarity among workers does not occur solely in the world of ideas. Rather, as Gramsci (1947/1971, 1988) argued, Fantasia (1988) and Burawoy (1979) discovered, and thousands of workers have experienced (Dobbs, 1972; Preis, 1964; Yellin, 1974), emergent collective cultures arise through the practical experiences of disruptions to hegemony. Whenever employers violate the established "social contract" with their employees by withdrawing benefits or adjusting working conditions, whenever employees bring in other experiences that challenge existing work relations (e.g., race, gender, or prior labor experiences), or whenever pressures or influences from other cultural practices are imposed on the social relations between workers and employers, the hegemonic equilibrium is upset. If a new relationship cannot be quickly and easily established, conflict develops. In addition, coercion may be imposed on the workers before or after they politically organize to force their demands on the employer. At any rate, the collective culture of worker's solidarity occurs in the midst of hegemonic breakdown—before, after, during, and dialectically—in response to hegemony, even as hegemony adjusts to worker solidarity.

In the workplace, as in society, class in the full sense of creating a counterhegemony comes into existence only when new political and cultural practices emerge that consciously identify the class as a class with its own interests in *opposition* to capitalist interests. Because the language and forms of discourse that people use are grounded in everyday experiences, to be politically effective, a counterhegemonic movement of the working class (or other subordinate group) must begin speaking in a different language than that of the existing hegemony. In keeping with Gramsci's (1947/1971, 1988) claim about knowledge being based on practice, we suggest that different material and social conditions are likely to produce different languages, and concurrently, different languages are likely to produce different responses to those condi-

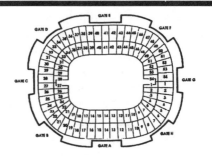

### The Skyboxing of America

Public settings were once celebrated for their democratic mix-ing of people, but in keeping with the increasingly hierarchi-cal economic structure, contemporary society "is being reor-ganized around corporate needs" (Frank, 1996, p. 10). Now, the primary cultural law is that whenever it is even remotely possible, any public place will be segregated by social class. From gated communities with 24-hour surveillance to skyboxes at Kansas City's Arrowhead Stadium and Chicago's United Center, "corporate elites are sequestering themselves in better and better secured sanctums."

> [The skybox] represents a perfect class system, a society in which vast inequality is explained simply and without contro-versy. . . . On a scale of corporate meaning by which nearly ev-ery civic project must now be measured, pro sports franchises rank just below gambling casinos and gigantic convention cen-ters as evidence of a city's willingness to do absolutely any-thing for business. A city without a sports team, a city without skyboxes, is like a city without . . . why, it's like a city without *entrepreneurship!* (pp. 10-12)

Corporate interests, most often represented by advertising logos, increasingly capture cultural practices in sports, fash-ion, recreation, art, and other social activities. Nothing seems beyond the reach of corporate self-promotion in America's flea market culture. Sacramento, California, now has corpo-rate sponsors for everything from its official soft drink to an official city underwear.

tions. When the hegemonic language of the "social contract" between labor and management is discredited by company takebacks, plant closings, or downsizings, the language of shared interest gains wider acceptance. Solidarity leads working-class groups and individuals to find their own political and cultural voice, rely on their own communication, and even establish their own media in the form of newsletters, newspapers, and radio programs.

## The Mass Culture of Class

Social relations that organize work appear outside of work as well, weaving a larger social web of class hegemony. We can discern social and *economic* associations through which dominant classes identify themselves and lead society. We have already mentioned many of the *political* institutions of capitalism. And to complete the hegemonic web, a multitude of *cultural* practices and institutions mark hierarchy in America, including theaters, museums, symphonies, social clubs, music, and sports. In the late 19th century, "polite" upper-class culture determined that Shakespearean plays did not need singers, jugglers, acrobats, orators, or between-play "farces" that characterized popular renditions (Levine, 1984). Audiences were admonished to be quiet, polite, and not to eat or leave early. Once, audiences of all classes sat under one roof and interacted; by the 1900s, audiences, actors, and theatrical styles were segregated. The democratic behavior of audiences bursting with "egalitarian exuberance" gradually led to separate theaters catering to distinct audiences (Levine, 1988, p. 183).

The myth of egalitarianism in the United States is made abundantly clear in the way culture has become spatially segregated by class. As the capitalist class extended its economic and political power, the official structure of legitimate culture was also "governed, patronized, and staffed by the upper class" (DiMaggio, 1982, p. 390). The idea of "high" culture was institutionalized through a "ritual classification and organizational system" controlled by private culture and private funding, creating symphonies and museums (p. 393). Only later were the capitalist classes concerned with establishing hegemony over those they dominated, seeking other ways to "share" appropriate culture with the general populace.

Sport can also serve as a venue for class association. Most select, elite clubs are organized around sporting activities such as yachting, golf, and polo. Working-class associations through sport are more likely to include slow-pitch softball, bowling, or in some cultures, soccer. In an observation that could be extended to all of culture, Bourdieu (1991) notes how the individual practice of certain sports depends not simply on ethical or aesthetic dispositions but on the degree of economic and cultural capital available. Consider, for instance, the disparate costs for equipment and facilities to play basketball compared with golf or yachting and the connection between sport and social class may be clearer.

Historically, the class segregation of culture—whether theater, music, art, or sport—was presented pedagogically as an aesthetic or artistic question, not a class issue, as the keepers of elite culture sought to educate the multitudes into "good" and "bad" art, culture, style, and etiquette. John Kasson (1990) explains that in the late 19th century, "the bourgeois code of manners deflected the pressures and inequities of society back on the individual" (p. 6) in the name of civility and self-discipline. Middle-class advisers helped establish codes of civility that defended emerging class social relations and inequities. Values of these codes radiated out to provide standards by which to assess entire social classes, ethnic groups, and cultures, often justifying subordination. The codes also penetrated deep into the individual personality. In sport, for instance, aesthetics seem to fit the social composition of the fans: Football's need for strength, endurance, violence, hard work, sacrifice, and team discipline are attributes appropriate to a capitalist working class; riding and polo suggest early training, family tradition, obligatory clothing, and techniques of sociability closed to subordinate classes (Bourdieu, 1991, p. 372).

Cultural practices illuminate class distinctions but are generally not a political flash point for social relations in the United States, in large part, because the "outpouring of commodities in the 20th century created a world in which a consumer could possess images of wealth without actually having a large income" (Levine, 1988, p. 223). Consumers eased into a way of life with abundant choices; desirable products (or their cheap imitations) were more afford-able. Here, the hegemonic power of culture intersects with the ma-terial accessibility of cultural goods, reflecting how commodity production nurtures other cultural practices. "An ever widening array of products and pleasures from movies to automobiles, ciga-rettes to household appliances" (Williams, 1991, p. 227) were de-signed as a new economy, and culture conferred greater impor-tance and identity as *consumers* to women, ethnic groups, and the working class in general. Georges D'Avenel (1855-1939) argued that capitalist technology made possible an "equalization of enjoy-ment" without a corresponding "equalization of income" (Wil-liams, 1991, p. 227). Or as Roland Marchand (1994) put it, consum-ers may be convinced that "by buying this toilet seat or that brand of coffee, they can share an experience with the very richest Ameri-cans" (p. 109). In a commodity-driven society, culture for the ma-jority of the working and middle classes has become a culture of consumption—primed by $175 billion in advertising each year. The commodified culture has even tamed contemporary political critiques that focus on equality in consumption styles rather than on political power or the economics of wealth (Marchand, 1994, p. 116).

The American Dream is a dream of consumption. Mass con-sumption encompasses chain department stores, supermarkets, and retail stores with cheap silk, jewelry, and fashion, and mass en-tertainment in movies, music, and sports. Any illusion of wealth today rests on the expansion of credit, which makes possible the enjoyment of wealth (or its imitation) for ordinary citizens. Keeping in mind the material conditions necessary for any cultural practice, we are reminded that all consumer enjoyments are pre-carious: homes, cars, luxuries, and entertainments can be lost at any economic downturn or personal crisis. The myth and its reality are closely tied to the ability of capitalism to deliver the goods, and the myth is defended by an ideology of individual merit that gently obscures collective subordinate conditions and experiences.

## The Consumption of Mass Culture

Mass culture displays an idealized vision of middle-class consumer society. Since World War II, mass culture has become a highly monopolized industry with bureaucratic social relations similar to other industries, including the overriding concern for production of commodities for profit. Consequently, the mass media simply constitute an institutional subsystem of the overarching cultural production system, serving as facilitators for the diffusion of cultural innovations to the mass-consuming audience (Hirsch, 1990). With the exception of the business press, production as a topic has all but disappeared from the mass media where advertising predominates, and depictions of workers and their lives in the news, movies, television, and even music obscure class relations and reinforce the ideologies of a consumer-based democratic pluralism and individual merit.

Communication research suggests that although the media do not *directly* affect public opinion or social knowledge, the media nonetheless do have some power in setting agendas for public discourse and in "controlling opinion visibility" (Parenti, 1986, p. 89). Based on the depictions of workers on television, middle-class audiences see little of working-class conditions and know even less about working-class views. Television characters, in general, live in a professional world of abundance—well dressed, well fed, and for want of nothing. As doctors, lawyers, and cops, television characters generally have their needs met by workers hidden from view. Past studies (International Association of Machinists, 1980; Johnson, 1981; Lieberthal, 1976) have found that television portrays workers as gas station attendants, bartenders, shopkeepers, and the like. In his study of the 20 most popular prime-time TV shows, Ralph Johnson (1981) found that working-class characters were obedient to superiors, often comic and inept, usually dispensable and "mostly silent and nameless" as dominant hegemony desires (p. 203). Today, 20 years after Johnson's study, network television still projects negative working-class images (Butsch, 1997). Labor unions are even more marginal on prime time and have a mostly negative image. Finally, as discussed in the chapter on race, television promotes recognized authority and the status quo and frames the problems of working people as individual deficiencies (such as drugs or crime), not structural or social symptoms (such as unemployment or inequality).

The news media does not provide an objective balance either, providing few opportunities for labor's voice, focusing on strikes and corruption but ignoring union efforts on behalf of their members and the general public. Images more conducive to cultural and political hegemony make the news perspective obvious (Altheide, 1984). Any viewer or reader could do his or her own survey of the nightly network news and daily paper with the Dow Jones and stock market reports and other business news, all of which "accept and promote values of the free market" and disallow class interest (Goldman & Rajagopal, 1991, p. 22). The gross national product is regularly announced, but the quality-of-life index (with ratings of education, health, nutrition, etc.) is reported quarterly, if at all. Every paper has a "Business" section, and business shows are daily fare on television. In contrast, there are no weekly reports on industrial accidents or environmental violations; there is no labor section in the newspaper. The economy is always presented as a business affair, whereas labor tags along as a "troublesome partner" or even a threat to the system (Parenti, 1986, p. 79). Moreover, network news "generally neglects labor-management relations as a news category" (Goldman & Rajagopal, 1991, p. 1) except during strikes.

In the 1980s and 1990s, strikes were the most frequent news of unions; news of strikes emphasized violence, reports never gave reasons for strikes nor benefits to the public if worker proposals were won, and finally, the media used negative language for workers' "demands" but never for management's "offers." According to Parenti (1986), news coverage of strikes subscribes to several rigid criteria: (a) presenting labor as unreasonable, (b) focusing on management's best offer, (c) considering company profits unnewsworthy, (d) avoiding causes of strike and focusing on economic consequences, (e) ignoring worker's interests and solidarity, and (f) presenting the government as a neutral arbiter. Gans (1972) earlier observed that strikes are reported as momentary incidents to be resolved rather than outgrowths of structural conflicts of social class interests.

Reporting to the capitalist class and its management, the business press (*Wall Street Journal, Business Week, Fortune,* etc.) carries in-depth analyses of industrial and political conditions, including union politics, strike prospects, and working conditions. Clearly, information on labor-management relations exists for a meaningful democratic public debate, but network news, daily papers, and weekly news magazines do not find such information newsworthy. Notably, the division between the business press and mass press corresponds to the division between the capitalist class and the working class. Overall, mainstream news reporting of labor obscures class relations because capitalist hegemony prefers working-class audiences that are interested in private consumption and have no political interest in production relations. Because the media monopoly determines how news will be defined, produced, and consumed, issues in strikes can be framed in terms of consumption, not production. Then, to fulfill their hegemonic role as ideological gatekeepers for capitalist social relations, mass media can "balance" strike coverage between two sides: strikers versus the public as consumers.

The complete process of constructing hegemonically acceptable news frames is too complex to outline here (Bennett, 1988; Herman & Chomsky, 1988). Goldman and Rajagopal (1991) provide one example of the detailed and thorough work that would have to be done to evaluate media coverage of specific events. They assessed CBS's coverage of the 1978 coal miners strike by using quantitative analysis, semiotics, ideological critique, and conversational and linguistic analysis of news text. They argue that to offset expected variations in understanding by millions of viewers and readers, journalists "overcoded" their discourse through the selective reporting of union positions, the exclusion of the company's role, and a careful framing of government intervention.

The reputed fairness and neutrality of news media shelters their slant somewhat from public scrutiny, but the effects are felt none-

### Rich Media, Poor Democracy

Doug Henwood's (1989) five-part series on media corporations for *Extra!* provides details of the interlocking media monopoly. Television networks, publishing chains, and other communication enterprises share directors among themselves and with companies such as Morgan Guaranty Trust, Chase Manhattan, Citibank, AT&T, and large insurance companies. These media directors also gather with other corporate leaders in groups such as the Carnegie Institute and the CFR. The consolidation of media has increased even more dramatically since Henwood first wrote. Among other deals, Westinghouse bought CBS, which then took Viacom; Disney took over ABC; AMFM radio merged with Clear Channel; MCI-WorldCom got Sprint; AT&T bought TCI cable; AOL bought Time Warner; and Warner Records (a division of Time Warner) merged with EMI, a U.K. record company. In targeting corporate interaction, Henwood was not arguing conspiracy but simply demonstrating the economic and political connections media giants share.

The shrinking ownership and diversity of the U.S. press prompted former Dean of Journalism at the University of California, Berkeley, Ben Bagdikian (1990) to lament the parallel loss of democracy in public discourse. Bagdikian questioned the future of democracy, as a handful of media businesses serve advertisers by turning news and information into entertainment. Of course, hegemony is bolstered in the short term by such control of information because it limits access and options for communication and organization by subordinate groups.

theless. For example, high school students whose main source of information was the mass media had a positive attitude toward big business but little knowledge of labor unions (Amann & Silverblatt, 1987). If we were to accept the media monopoly's news coverage of workers and unions, we would believe that the capitalist free market is natural and valuable, labor is almost nonexistent, and the working class is unimportant—conclusions that fit nicely with the ideological needs of capitalist hegemony.

## Entertaining the Troops

Many authors (Bennett, 1988; Gitlin, 1980; Goldman & Rajagopal, 1991; Kellner, 1990; Tuchman, 1978) have described the process of securing ideological consent for hegemonic purposes. Goldman and Rajagopal (1991) explain the dual character of hegemonic ideologies as "partially resisted and contested, but at the same time pliable, fluid, and able to encapsulate that which opposes" (p. 5). We have already discussed the corporate channeling of rap music's alternative and oppositional community tendencies into individualistic messages serving cultural hegemony. Top 40 popular music or rap may reflect the tenor and style of youth anxiety, but the lyrics concentrate on personal romance and relationships.

Country music, which might be considered "pro-worker," also stresses themes most acceptable to capitalist hegemony. Occasionally, a Tennessee Ernie Ford may lament labor and debt in "Sixteen Tons," or a Johnny Paycheck will tell his boss to "take this job and shove it!" But mainstream country music favors individual, not collective responses and is laced with strong anti-union sentiments (Juravich, 1988). Although the government is never seen as providing any solutions to the plight of working people, patriotism is prominent, as in Merle Haggard's "Okie From Muskogee" and Lee Greenwood's "I'm Proud to Be an American." In short, what oppositional themes exist in country music are tethered to dominant ideological values. We can observe this same resistance, contestation, inhibition, and confusion in Hollywood movies.

In his capsule analyses of 147 movies with fictional depictions of workers, Zaniello (1996) argues that Hollywood films regularly insult workers and their social role. He believes that Hollywood and network TV exploit and sensationalize labor-related incidents while underplaying or ignoring their radical implications. Labor films are consistently violent in content and filled with gangsters—reinforcing the company line that unions are corrupt. From *Treasure Island* (1934) to *Pretty Woman* (1990), "The entertainment media present working people not only as unlettered and uncouth but also as less desirable and less moral than other people" (Parenti, 1994, p. 283). Denigrating the character and worth of working people while promoting dominant classes as more virtuous and moral inhibits subordinate consciousness and resolve.

Hegemonic cultural institutions adapt emergent and oppositional cultural practices to serve dominant interests. Consent is more than some ideological gloss over dominant interests; it must be negotiated by incorporating subordinate practices into framings acceptable to both subordinate and dominant. In an era of class antagonism, oppositional stances in popular culture are crucial to negotiating hegemony.

Gina Marchetti (1990) illustrates that certain film genres are popular when they "embody and work through those social contradictions the culture needs to come to grips with and may not be able to deal with except in the realm of fantasy" (p. 187). The rash of slasher films in the 1980s could be explained as a backlash to the gains of the women's movement and affirmative action. Action-adventure movies in the 1980s were limited to three plots: the quest for a valuable object, invasion scenarios, and the search for captives. Each story has a male private adventurer who travels to some exotic location and uses military tactics to achieve his goal. Ideological themes include the rights of possession and property, the definition of nation, the right to intervene in other cultures, the value of violence, and the meaning of masculinity (Marchetti, 1990). Noting that the treasure hunt story line rests on a conception of the "proper distribution of wealth," Marchetti suggests that such fantasies had appeal "at a time when American economic 'interests' seem[ed] to be 'threatened' globally . . . the treasure need not be gold or jewels, but could just as easily be South African platinum, Arabian gulf oil, or Central American fruit crops" (p. 189). "Fantasies of Indiana Jones traipsing around the globe looking for treasure seem to have more contemporary significance in supporting capital's power to exploit labor domestically and internationally" (p. 190).

Marchetti (1990) claims that action-adventures "justify the violent suppression of anyone who may interfere with American property rights" (p. 190). Actors such as Chuck Norris in *Invasion USA* rise up as individual heroes defending the interests of the nation and overcoming the lack of government action. Given changing racial and gender roles in America, heroes often have interracial buddies (or female buddies who seem independent and feisty even as they provide some sexual allure, as in *Rambo*, the Indiana Jones films, or Kathleen Turner in *Romancing the Stone*). The hero always acts as an individual torn between his own self-interest and his responsibility to society.

Within the myth of entertainment, action-adventures "are meant to be innocent fun and not serious discussions of political or social issues" (Marchetti, 1990, p. 196). In large part, action-adventures offer spectacle and nonstop violent action rather than narrative, character development, or plot. Furthermore, the ambivalence of Hollywood productions toward race, gender, class, and power seems to allow many different readings. But according to Marchetti, that is the beauty of the genre for constructing ideological hegemony. Within the contradictory configurations of hero, villain, and buddy, Marchetti finds that these movies "also manage to privilege dominant ideology" (p. 197). Heroes are loners, white, male, and at the service of dominant institutions as they champion the values of the American middle class and capitalist hegemony—property rights, individual freedom, and the legitimacy of using coercion against "alien" forces. Tony Bennett (1990) argues that film texts are sifted through other institutional practices and cultural experiences that influence the meanings of images and character representations. This understanding predicts that the political and economic conditions within the United States during the 1980s all but guaranteed that the dominant ideological messages of action-adventure films would not be mistaken.

Most North Americans grew up with cartoons, comics, and children's stories based on these same dominant images and themes. Anyone acquainted with Mickey Mouse and Donald Duck are implicitly familiar with pro-Western, pro-free market themes (Dorfman & Mattelart, 1991). In Disney's Donald Duck comics, "undeveloped" foreign cultures are regularly visited by Scrooge and nephews, who systematically relieve the "savages" of their treasures. Like heroes, buddies, and villains in action adventures,

> Every Disney character stands on either one side or the other of the power demarcation line. All those below are bound to obedience, submission, discipline, humility. Those above are free to employ constant coercion: threats, moral and physical repression, and economic domination. (Dorfman & Mattelart, 1991, p. 25)

Within this fantasy world, property rights and social responsibilities are similarly divided. Like prime-time television and Hollywood movies, Disney displays a world without workers. Workers may be discerned as noble savages or criminals, but in Disney's land, "no one has to work in order to produce. There is a constant round of buying, selling, and consuming, but to all appearances, none of the products involved has required any effort whatsoever to make" (Dorfman & Mattelart, 1991, p. 29). Just as paternity is missing from Disney's family structure, the origin of products is also absent. "They both coincide and reinforce a dominant ideological structure which also seeks to eliminate the working class, the true producer of objects. And with it, the class struggle" (p. 29). The free market system is the supreme arbiter. Thus, according to Dorfman and Mattelart, the magic and adventure of Disney injects into children the same "escapist needs of contemporary society" (p. 30) that can be attained only in their commodity form, now conveniently available as toys, games, and "Happy Meal" prizes.

Whether through the escapism of cartoons or the action of Hollywood adventures, the culture industry promotes ideological messages that coincide with the economic and political needs of hegemony—individualism over collective solidarity, property rights over other social relations, happiness through consumption, and the legitimacy of official coercion. Capitalist hegemony flourishes because such themes are seeded and tended throughout popular culture, and class identities are missing or subsumed by the great professional middle class. Dominant ideology subtly ingratiates itself into music, television, movies, cartoons, and other cultural sites, but capitalist hegemony is also systematically constructed through public and private education.

## Educating the Masses

In their critique, *Schooling in Capitalist America*, Samuel Bowles and Herbert Gintis (1977) write,

> The educational system, perhaps more than any other social institution, has become the laboratory in which competing solutions to the problems of personal liberation and social equality are tested and the arena in which social struggles are fought out. The school system is a monument to the capacity of the advanced corporate economy to accommodate and deflect thrusts away from its foundation. Yet, at the same time, the educational system mirrors the growing contradictions of the larger society, most dramatically in the disappointing results of the reform efforts. (p. 5)

Jonathan Kozol's (1991) moving accounts of the extremes of wealth and poverty in *Savage Inequalities* (1991) confirms Bowles and Gintis's (1977) contentions over two decades later. Schools as hegemonic institutions are central and crucial to producing and reproducing existing social relations, because schools produce workers. Bowles and Gintis argue that "the structure of the educational experience is admirably suited to nurturing attitudes and behavior consonant with participation in the labor force" (p. 9). Their historical investigations suggest that for over 150 years employers have been aware of the function of schools in preparing youth psychologically for work. They cite statistics that demonstrate a congruence between personality traits needed for proper work performance and those rewarded with high grades in the classroom, including, but not limited to punctuality, neatness, thoroughness, consistency, rote learning, respect for authority, acceptance of official explanations, and personal responsibility.

Contradicting popular belief, Bowles and Gintis (1977) argue that

> the educational system does not add to or subtract from the overall degree of inequality . . . it is best understood as an institution which serves to perpetuate the social relationships of economic life . . . facilitating the smooth transition of youth into the labor force. (p. 11)

Despite the continuing expansion of education (along with progressive income tax, Social Security, and welfare programs), inequality in income has not changed. Nor have educational gains by blacks or women enhanced their economic situation relative to whites or men, and there is no evidence that education overcomes family background. In fact, the expansion of education over the last three decades has not increased social mobility in any measurable sense. This condition cannot be excused with claims about the "culture of poverty" or the genetic inferiority of blacks, women, or the working poor because the educational achievements of these groups have improved. As Bowles and Gintis point out, "Access to skill and denial of skill training is an important part of the reproduction of economic and social inequality, yet these skills have little to do with cognitive ability" (p. 94).

The point is simply that educational advances do not and cannot alter the social hierarchy of class. Inequality of income and economic opportunity are inseparable manifestations of the underlying structure of economic life related to the market and property relations and cannot be overcome by more schooling. Public education has deteriorated since Bowles and Gintis wrote, and now it not only fails to impart certain values, it also fails to provide

rudimentary skills. Public high school graduates are poorly qualified in skills and "proper attitude" when (and if) they enter the job
market. A survey of Chicago manufacturers, for example, found
that most companies have an extremely negative perception of the
quality of "workers" being turned out by the Chicago Public
Schools (Ravenswood Industrial Council, 1995). Because employers expect workers to "come to their door qualified to work" (and
to escape union contracts?), they have been leaving the city for the
suburbs in increasing numbers. The situation in Chicago is not unlike that in most major U.S. cities.

In other words, education in the United States does play a role in
creating socioeconomic conditions, especially in the social process
we have described as commodity production for profit. As Bowles
and Gintis (1977) write,

> By imparting technical and social skills and appropriate motiva-
> tions, education increases the productive capacity of workers. On
> the other hand, education helps defuse and depoliticize the poten-
> tially explosive class relations of the productive process by impart-
> ing acceptable ideological constructions of history, inequality, and
> existing social relations. . . . Schools legitimate inequality in the
> manner in which they reward and promote students and create and
> reinforce patterns of social class, racial, and sexual identification
> among students which allow them to "properly" relate to their even-
> tual standing in the hierarchy of authority and status in the produc-
> tion process. (p. 11)

Dominated by the imperatives of profit and domination rather
than by human need, the production process and the education
process interact. Within the production process, educational credentials and a learned demeanor legitimate authority. Within the
educational process, production needs to legitimate certain skills
and knowledge. College advertisements on local radios declare as
much when they tout the value of their diploma for getting a job in
broadcasting, advertising, medicine, business, and even truck
driving.

Although schools provide skills training, they also teach attitude. Schools try to clear the way for the acceptance of the auto-

cratic organization of corporate business that clashes sharply with the democratic ideals of equality and participation. Students become accustomed to acting out subservient behavior, squelching opinions and emotions, and relying on authorities to represent their interests.

The first command of most school systems is discipline. Students who must raise their hands to relieve themselves or are sent to detention for tardiness or laughing out of turn are being prepared to accept the arbitrary actions of a foreman or supervisor. The gross inequities between urban and suburban schools, as well as systems that "track" students according to ability or future prospects, perpetuate a structure of privilege. Successful job performance, ideologically speaking, depends on the proper cognitive, physical, and operational skills, all of which are acquired through the educational system. Moreover, at work, responsibility, privilege, and duties are not determined by preference or collective decision making but by rules that limit worker participation in the job process. Bowles and Gintis (1977) explain that "presentation of self is more important for earnings than grade point average, degree, skill or experience" (p. 97). Clothing, sex, age, race, size, posture, grammar, diction, speech patterns, and facial expression are all socially regulated and channeled because self-presentation has a social class character. In short, class, race, and sex bias in schooling does not simply produce but, more important, reflects the structure of society at large.

Schools promote cognitive growth, the content of which is often cursory and partial, but schools have an equally important social function. Along with gender, age, and race, education is used as a resource of control. By linking technical skills to economic success through the education system, social inequality gains legitimacy. If you don't get the job, the promotion, the salary, it must be due to your own lack of education or lack of skill, which education would provide. According to the American Dream myth, educational and economic success depends on ability, motivation, perseverance, and sacrifice. Failure to achieve in this institutional setting brings student desires and dreams into line with their probable career opportunities. If they are put down enough, they may become convinced of their inability to succeed at the next level. In short, competition, success, and defeat in the classroom reconcile students to their social position. Academic merit thus conforms to the legitimation of economic inequality and unequal work rules at the plant or office. Which merit should be rewarded and through what process depends on how social relationships are organized. In the United States, the production of commodities for profit justifies social privilege and attributes poverty to personal failure.

Bowles and Gintis (1977) make a compelling case for schools as hegemonic institutions that defuse and curtail class conflict. They trace the changing character of social conflict in the United States over the past 100 years through the periodic reorganization of the educational system, which reflected and prepared new hegemonic relationships along the way. The Progressive Era school reform, for example, reflected a strongly upper-class bias. Commitment to social control was its overriding objective. Taylorism in the factory was matched by a school system dedicated to the moral development and domestication of the student body. Educators embraced standardization and testing just as efficiency experts were measuring worker productivity.

Higher education also has a part in reproducing the class structure. Conflicts and reforms in higher education reflect the expanded demand for technical, clerical, and white-collar skills. Since World War II, women and minorities have demanded and won some entrance to universities and colleges. In the 1970s, the Carnegie Commission on Higher Education (a hegemonic policy-making group funded by leading capitalist forces) proposed fragmenting higher education into elite universities, state universities, community colleges, and vocational institutions as a means of restricting white-collar professional workers. Community colleges—"high schools with ashtrays" as one critic said—create a kind of class stratification in college education (Bowles & Gintis, 1977, p. 211). Future workers attend community colleges. In community colleges, education becomes skill directed and fragmented, creating workers who are more knowledgeable about a particular task but thereby less autonomous and more consensual. Significantly, less than half finish with a 2-year degree. Middle-class managers tend to enroll at state universities and private colleges. The children of the elite, of course, attend Ivy League schools and elite universities such as Stanford. Education, like any other commodity, goes to the highest bidder. This segregation of students continues the process of bringing student hopes into line with the realities of the job market. In other words, the exchange value of the student as a commodity becomes more important than the use value of the student as a human being. The imperative of class relations thus appears in and through educational institutions.

## Conclusion

Class is important to the maintenance of contemporary culture. More exactly, the diffusion and dispersal of class consciousness by individual consumerism drives contemporary culture. Thus, unlike the incorporation of images, interests, and themes important to African Americans and women, dominant cultural hegemony has incorporated much less that can be clearly identified with subordinate class practice. Contemporary capitalist hegemony has negotiated more by way of avoidance, diversion, and cover-up. A continued stable class hegemony in the United States depends, of course, on sufficient material resources, an adequate political leadership, and effective cultural practices.

From inexpensive watches to mass-produced fashion clothing, from prefab housing to affordable college education, the material conditions of life in the United States have been adequate for the bulk of the working class. Lacking appealing alternatives, subordinate classes of workers, farmers, and small-business people have consequently identified with the ideology and practices of consumer society. The political and cultural leadership of major hegemonic institutions in government, politics, education, art, and the media have been legitimated in the process.

This chapter has by no means exhausted the topic of class in contemporary culture, as numerous references to other works indicated. Here, we have simply introduced some conceptual terms (social class, commodity production, solidarity, collectivity, hegemony) and presented a few living examples. Many of the works mentioned give more thorough investigations and offer other references of specific instances of class and hegemony in the United States.

We have tried to demonstrate that hegemony is always unstable, always being rearranged, as material conditions change, political leaderships reposition, and new cultural practices emerge. Will dominant-subordinate class relations change in the United States? What impact will changing race and gender relations have on other hegemonic relationships? In the closing chapter, we look at the future of cultural hegemony in the United States.

# 5

## Prospects for Challenge and Change

Observing popular culture through the lens of hegemony often seems like peering through the end of a kaleidoscope. Each image rests against others as colors and shapes overlap. Just when one thing comes into focus, the entire panoply of images shifts, and the pattern changes. How do we make sense of the connections? In many ways, this book has been a kaleidoscopic introduction to a complex concept. All the examples given in this book do not suffice; they only add up to lots of examples. Indeed, any one example, paragraph, or even chapter tells only part of the complexity of the hegemonic relationships between race, gender, class, and a multitude of other social variables in popular culture. A deeper appreciation of hegemony and its analytical and practical usefulness can be attained only with further study, reading, discussion, and application. It is hoped that this writing has indicated the significance of the concept and illustrated that popular culture is always negotiated between competing and cooperating social groups. In this presentation of hegemony and culture, we sought to provide a glimpse of how capitalist hegemony transforms itself, meeting some of the interests of subordinate groups but short-circuiting their full realization.

Patterns of social life are not so haphazard as patterns in a kaleidoscope; they are more dependent on and subject to human action.

Yet even politically conscious cultural practices cannot escape interconnection with other social and cultural activities. Especially in a mass market consumer society like the United States, popular culture can never clearly and unequivocally reflect the self-awareness of subordinate groups because the power to produce and distribute mass culture belongs to corporate rulers. On the other hand, dominant leadership or even control does not mean that cultural practices are simply a reflection of dominant interests; heroes and villains in popular culture do not simply don white and black hats and mouth morals according to a scripted program. The contemporary culture of consumption neither simply advertises an omnipotent capitalist ideology nor manipulates the public as if it were the offspring of the Stepford wives.

Accordingly, the critique of race, gender, and class in American culture given in the previous three chapters recognizes that capitalist hegemony has not and does not obliterate black, feminist, or working-class social and cultural practices. Hegemony in the United States works because emergent oppositional cultural practices have been tolerated—even encouraged—while being altered in their political affiliations. Contemporary popular culture is thus a shifting, colorful amalgam of subordinate demands filtered through ideologies and cultural artifacts trademarked by American corporations. And as these currents of contemporary cultural hegemony shift, lurking within are strands of counterhegemonic impulses.

In those social spaces crucial to corporate power, such as the decision-making institutions of government, finance, and production, alternative practices and relations have been quite limited and subdued. Meanwhile, dominant interests are protected by the invisible hand of the marketplace, where emergent oppositional cultural practices never seem to find an audience on network TV or readers in the mass press.

Other social spaces removed from political decision making have been more open to subordinate group contributions. Contemporary music, movies, television, fashion, sports, language, and other popular cultural practices thus reflect creative responses to various subordinate interests and practices. After the radical impulses of subordinate groups are disconnected, emergent cultural practices are marketed by dominant institutions as the latest trend. Like the mother bunny in *Runaway Bunny* (Brown, 1972), hegemonic leaders have used the imaginations of race, gender, and class subordinates to bolster values suitable to hegemonic relations. In particular, hegemonic institutions attempt to popularize the morals of individualism, consumerism, law and order, and the Protestant work ethic.

## Fractures, Shifts, and Openings

Poststructuralist and cultural studies scholars have been impressed and fascinated by the continuously changing social patterns that appear when they gaze through the hegemonic lens. However, the outcome of conflicting social tensions cannot be determined by simply tilting some analytical kaleidoscope to create a different view or different social identity. The postmodern impulse to obscure the monopolized production of culture by reference to shifting meanings avoids the important issue of social inequality. To say any reading is possible, including an oppositional reading, of any and all mass-produced texts ignores the undeniable impact of corporate control, a control that all but guarantees that certain readings have more prominence than others. Undoubtedly, each individual has multiple, disjointed, and contingent social identities in his or her gender, race, religion, occupation, neighborhood, pastime, and so forth. But to conclude that *any* social identity is possible denies the actual connections that predominate in *every* particular social crisis. Whatever identities are possible are necessarily based on the actual social connections that exist and influence groups and individuals. Changing hegemonic relations and practices ultimately depend on the organization and mobilization of competing social groups into historic blocs capable of winning widespread consent. In short, overcoming capitalist hegemony requires more than resistive readings or even resistant practices.

Throughout this century, significant political and social changes in the United States have been won by the struggles of labor, African Americans, women, and other subordinate groups. These often separate struggles have expanded democracy and improved the quality of life for the general population, from unemployment insurance and Social Security to free public education and a national public culture and media. Jim Crow, the systematic legal segregation of blacks, is no more. Women have secured important political rights and economic opportunities. And the working class has repeatedly, if sporadically, won economic and political concessions from corporations and the government. Black middle-class progress is evident; women have made advances in education, government, and business; and American workers have some of the best benefits and working conditions of any working class in the world.

Nonetheless, recurring battles over wages, job security, working conditions, and political rights have not settled the underlying structural tension between dominant capitalist forces and the subordinate social and political majority. Major social tensions over race, gender, and class in American society have usually been refracted and frequently initiated in corresponding battles over cultural practices. Cultural change has thus always accompanied the modest improvements in subordinate living conditions. Black cultural images and concerns have been featured in film and television, along with more positive female roles and narratives. Even the antiauthoritarian resistance of the working class has appeared in mass-produced culture, from action-adventure movies to fashion and the occasional political campaign. These social and cultural changes are largely the result of subordinate groups gaining strength through significant structural change (e.g., the industrial revolution, migration, immigration, world war, etc.), recognizing their interests, and forming political alliances to wrench concessions from dominant institutions and renegotiate the terms of hegemony.

At least since World War II, moments of rupture in U.S. capitalist hegemony have been met with quick, tactical attacks against protesting subordinates followed by significant doses of concession to subordinate demands. Each nascent crisis of hegemony (e.g., the call for women's suffrage, the Great Depression, the rise of mass industrial unions, civil rights demands, and the anti-Vietnam War movement) prompted orchestrated "passive revolutions" on the part of hegemonic capitalist leaders. Each time, hegemonic leaders pushed through major structural adjustments to better protect capitalist relations. And as noted, reforms to capitalist hegemony have generally improved social conditions for blacks, women, labor, and other subordinate groups. However, to conclude that subordinate groups thus prosper under hegemonic relations overstates the case. No matter how significant the social change, simply *re-forming* hegemony still leaves subordinate groups subordinate and their needs and interests shortchanged.

Subordinate interests cannot fully be secured without replacing the existing hegemony. To fundamentally change dominant-subordinate capitalist relations and end social inequality, hegemonic relations cannot simply be reformed or renegotiated. Rather, existing hegemony needs to be *trans*formed into something that hasn't existed and cannot exist without disrupting, dismantling, and reconfiguring social relations *and* social structures.

It should be evident from the examples and references included in this text that there have always been fissures in American hegemony. Some of those fissures have become more like cracks, providing openings for the expression of subordinate demands and the renegotiation of the social contract. Until now, however, the fissures, fractures, and cracks have been successfully repaired. Hegemonic institutions have been able to make adjustments and recemented subordinate interests into dominant frames.

No hegemony dissolves until its material, political, and cultural options have been exhausted or until a new historic bloc attracts social forces capable of reorganizing society. Of course, hegemonic leaderships easily forgo the niceties of negotiation and compromise if structures and relations fundamental to their dominance are under attack, as we have seen in previous examples. Even the emergence of a new subordinate culture may rouse the organized wrath of hegemonic political leaders. In less "democratic" hegemonies, consent depends more readily on coercion. In Indonesia, Nigeria, Guatemala, and other repressive states, for instance, force appears in uniform and as paramilitary death squads. In the United States, and other more benevolent hegemonies, the legal system of police, courts, and prisons metes out coercion on a daily basis.

The ability to use more organized physical coercion against specific subordinate groups, such as desegregation coalitions, labor unions, or even black and Latino youth, depends on the rest of the subordinate population consenting to the selective use of force. Consequently, attacks on emerging counterhegemonic movements must be preceded by and cloaked in a defensive rhetoric appealing to other subordinate interests (or fears): safety, property values, neighborhood traditions, individual rights, cultural preferences, and the so-called due process of law and order. Such themes are creatively expressed in television dramas, such as *NYPD Blue*, *Homicide*, and *Law and Order*.

## The Crisis in Economics, Politics, and Culture

Contemporary capitalist hegemony needs all the ideological help it can muster, and morally loaded television fare may not be sufficient. American hegemony is about to be seriously tested. Increasingly, material conditions are frustrating working people and the great American middle class. Combined with internationally shrinking markets, corporate cost cutting, downsizing, and other profit-driven measures, government policies are threatening the future of the American Dream (see "Census," 1994; Longworth & Stein, 1995). Median real income continues to decline while the income gap between rich and poor increases (by 12.4% in the 1990s; Chomsky, 1996, p. 25). If Americans can't afford the Dream, its appeal diminishes. If income and credit fail to match the wants, needs, and expectations of U.S. workers, consent for capitalist social relations might even be reconsidered. According to *Business Week*, 70% of Americans feel that "business has gained too much power over too many aspects of American life," and 80% feel that the economic system is "inherently unfair" (Chomsky, 1996, p. 26). This makes fertile ground for counterhegemonic seeds of resistance.

The unabashed drive for corporate profits so eloquently related in *Barron's*, *Business Week*, and the *Wall Street Journal* severely limits the political options available for maintaining hegemony. So-called liberal measures, such as welfare, affirmative action, and job security, which helped win consent from women, blacks, workers, and other subordinate groups, have been discarded by hegemonic institutions as they impose a new "Contract With America" that limits social benefits and lets free enterprise (the presumed ultimate force of nature) determine social conditions.

It is significant that the two-party political system (historically the most important hegemonic political practice in the United States) is crumbling. Long true and now more evident, Democratic politicians are joining Republicans in showering favors on corporate America as the quality of life for the middle class, working class, and poor worsens. In the late 1990s, President Bill Clinton, like Democrats before him, repeatedly came down on the same side as the Republicans on issues such as health care, welfare, environmental deregulation, and corporate tax reform.

Although the populist rhetoric of Pat Buchanan generated some interest in early 1996, in general, voters have paid little attention to the two-party charade, despite the abundance of media enthusiasm and coverage. The widespread public distrust in corporate America and the massive disaffection with the two major parties leaves ample room for counterhegemonic invitations. Whereas the media has focused on the antics of Ross Perot or Jesse Ventura, others, including Ron Daniels, Labor Party Advocates, and the Independent Progressive Politics Network, have found favorable responses to their call for political institutions independent of the two major parties (e.g., Hawkins, 1996, p. 17). Given the racial and social divide in the United States, another possible response could be some nastier appeals to hate, anxiety, and fear fomented by right-wing militias, Christian fundamentalists, white power groups, Rush Limbaugh's "ditto-heads," Pat Buchanan, David Duke, and other social conservatives.

In the context of increasing economic disruption and political realignments, conflicts within and over culture have also increased. In Congress, the courts, the media, and community meetings, debates have broken out over the National Endowment for the Arts and public television and radio, music lyrics, graphic sex and violence on television and in film, Internet communication, advertising, children's television programming, and new telecommunications technologies.

Just as various social classes of the late 19th century identified themselves through distinct cultural practices, such as their dining habits, etiquette norms, entertainment forms, architectural designs, and other markers of lifestyle, so too in the late 20th century, different social classes and subordinate cultural groups create and practice identifiable forms of entertainment, language, fashion, and lifestyle. Different cultural practices have always sustained different cultural and class relations, but the opportunity to establish and influence cultural practice is much more limited now, given the monopolization of cultural production by a handful of corporations (Westinghouse-CBS-Infinity-Viacom; GE-NBC; Disney-ABC; Time Warner-Turner-AOL-EMI; AMFM-Clear Channel; ATT-TCI-Liberty, etc.). Hence, subordinate cultural practices, such as rap music, "working-class" fashion, or feminist narratives, appear in highly contradictory form. Access to economic and material resources and control over political decision making depends on the presence of a counterhegemonic historic bloc. Likewise, the creation of consciously active oppositional cultural images, themes, and practices depends on the creation of an independent social (and cultural) movement.

This is not to say that no oppositional images or practices appear in current hegemonic productions. At least since the 1960s, actions and activities by individuals and subordinate groups have been featured in our mass-produced consumer culture. Women's participation in sports, media, and education has increased dramatically;

multicultural influences regularly appear in popular music, movies, and television. Counterhegemonic themes have appeared in mainstream media: Characters on *Murphy Brown* and *Ellen* have challenged dominant gender stereotypes; *Frank's Place* disrupted accepted beliefs and expectations about race stereotypes; with wit and offbeat humor, Michael Moore's *TV Nation* and *The Awful Truth* demonstrated that television programming can be entertaining, enlightening, and meaningful; Public Enemy has done politically biting rap without insulting women or advocating gangster violence. In each case, however, the counterhegemonic thrust has bumped up against the realities of commercialized culture: *TV Nation*, *Frank's Place*, and *Ellen* were canceled as networks made peace with the status quo. Under the guise of tolerance, new characters and situations on *Will & Grace*, *Frasier*, *Drew Carey*, and other sitcoms actually reinforced gender stereotypes.

An important shift is occurring in the midst of corporate downsizing and monopolization: the construction of a veritable propaganda network of cultural production in music, movies, magazines, radio, television, cable, telecommunications, and corporate, government, and organization direct marketing. These hegemonic institutions spend billions—advertising alone exceeds $175 billion each year—inundating the public with subtle, blatant, alluring, tasteful, and tasteless messages about the wonders of free market consumption. Blanketing public discourse and public awareness with the charms of consumerism dulls the critical senses and weakens the political resolve of subordinate resistance.

Capitalist hegemony can be nicely buffered if the "objective" vagaries of the so-called free market can be blamed for social ills. Indeed, the coercion of censorship is not usually necessary because the market easily directs social and cultural practice. As John Cassidy (quoted in Chomsky, 1996) concluded in a *New Yorker* report on the socioeconomic crisis of the middle class, "This is nobody's fault; it is just how capitalism has developed. . . . it is what the free market has decided, in its infinite but mysterious wisdom" (p. 31). Accordingly, *TV Nation*, *The Kwitney Report*, and other potentially disruptive television shows are simply canceled for lack of corporate sponsorship. Pantheon Press and other outlets for artistic, critical, and experimental writings are absorbed and then dismantled as media giants monopolize and streamline their operations to maximize profits. Moreover, as long as companies can persuade the public that high costs or low profits legitimize low wages, layoffs, unsafe working conditions, and environmentally destructive productive practices, hegemony will be maintained, and oppositional movements will be severely hampered.

With major cultural production being regulated by corporate giants, it has fallen to a handful of independent media (with limited resources) to circulate critical analyses of consumer society. In radio, Pacifica Radio, David Barsamian, Norman Solomon's "Making Contact," and a few others (such as the National Federation of Community Broadcasters) struggle to challenge mainstream hype. Likewise, in print, a small number of respected journals and magazines, such as *The Nation, Z Magazine, Labor Notes,* and *Extra!,* provide alternative views on politics and culture. With some success, independent publishers, such as South End, Common Courage, and New Press, have been distributing books and pamphlets with alternative political visions. These media are important. However, any successful counterhegemonic movement must also directly challenge the seductive grip that commodification has on mass popular culture.

## Redefining the Possibilities

One of the key tasks confronting any counterhegemonic movement is to redefine social issues in terms that advance the interests of subordinate groups and their historic bloc. Building from the so-called common sense of existing hegemonic relations and ideologies, counterhegemonic definitions must emphasize the shared experiences, current social positions, and future capacities of collective, democratic leadership. In some ways, the rearticulation of social truth is easier because capitalist hegemony has adopted many subordinate cultural practices legitimizing independent political interests of the working classes. Having attained a certain respectability, subordinate "common sense" is then better able to question dominant reasonings, especially ones justifying social inequality and corporate and government irresponsibility. A more difficult but much more important shift in definition concerns the seductive power of commodity production that reduces most political and social issues to questions of cost and profit.

Hegemonic ideology and propaganda, including the lived experience of consumerism, cannot by themselves overcome major social contradictions, however. When subordinate experiences of inequality become too acute, opposition to hegemony emerges. Despite the wealth of a society, if large parts of the population do not have the income or ability to float credit, the goods and services are unattainable. Living poor in a land of plenty often leads to political dissatisfaction. A fair reading of current material, political, and cultural trends must conclude that capitalist hegemony will face serious challenges in the not-too-distant future. Whether a counterhegemonic historic bloc will be assembled remains to be seen. Mostly, it depends on how well the "organic intellectuals"— the leaders of the working class, including its African American, female, and other socially subordinate members and allies—respond to the awakenings, desires, interests, and needs of the subordinate majority.

Hegemony, according to Gramsci (1947/1971, 1988), builds consent for the social order based on the shared experiences of subordinate groups and individuals. These experiences arise from shared social positions, social privileges, and social responsibilities. In the context of satisfied needs and unappealing alternatives, hegemony can construct reasonable explanations for predominate social and cultural relations and practices. A counterhegemony does not develop without regard for the conditions confronting interconnected subordinate groups and individuals. In other words, a counterhegemony cannot even be conceived in a society where subordinate needs and interests are adequately met. Conversely, an existing hegemony will likely be challenged to the degree that material, political, and cultural conditions fail to meet subordinate interests and demands. In most instances, neither extreme exists. Rather, social conditions are full of contradictions: Some needs are met or exceeded; other needs go wanting. Of course, different cultural experiences, including appeals by organized political groups, may awaken dormant desires and articulate them as immediate needs that hegemony must then meet. In short, as we have argued throughout this text, all aspects of culture—our whole way of life—constitute an arena of struggle for hegemony and counter-hegemony.

To overcome the propaganda and withstand the coercion of any hegemony, an alternative historic bloc needs to construct its own counterhegemony of political, social, ideological, and cultural practices, independent of existing dominant classes, their hegemony, their institutions, their leaderships, their ideologies, and their culture. This counterhegemonic historic bloc can coalesce around a multitude of issues, depending on the severity of existing social contradictions. It may first emerge from conflicts over education, race relations, foreign policy, or unexpected economic crises. Above all, as Gramsci (1947/1971, 1988), Trotsky (1973, 1938/1974), and Therborn (1983), among others have noted, a counterhegemony must develop an alternative leadership and a political program based on the *solidarity* and *collectivity* of subordinate popular classes and groups, breaking with the culture of commodity production.

Counterhegemony cannot be imposed; it must win the hearts and minds of masses of individuals to a new vision of culture, society, and humanity. The political and intellectual leadership must meet people where they are, responding to concerns and awakenings created by the failures and contradictions of capitalist hegemony, whether material, political, or cultural. If the observations recorded in this book are any guide, the solidarity and shared collective interests of an oppositional hegemonic alliance in the contemporary United States must clearly champion the interests of African Americans, women, the working class, and their potential allies (e.g., Chicanos, Mexican Americans, small farmers, the working middle class, etc.). A counterhegemony of such social character would have significant social power and pose real problems for hegemonic institutions. The likelihood of physical confrontation between contending social forces would be great.

## The Usefulness of Hegemony and the Expectation of Counterhegemony

Hegemony has many uses. This book has been primarily concerned with how hegemony aids our understanding of many cultural practices, from the popularity of art forms, sports, or housing trends to why policies change in law, education, and recreational pastimes. Others (Adamson, 1980; Buci-Glucksmann, 1980) have argued that seeing society as a conglomerate of hegemonic power relations helps explain social consent and social unrest. Understanding hegemony also allows us to anticipate the character and themes of contending social forces.

Hegemony encourages us to look more closely at the significance of many controversies in culture and society. Indeed, because hegemony centers conscious human action in the makeup of all social structures, relations, and practices, we must look at culture as *politics*—our whole way of life is a bundle of practices that have been contested and negotiated (consciously or not) among social groups, especially those of race, gender, and class.

The so-called culture wars, which have erupted in communities, schools, government, and the media, are an example of how culture is politics (Delpit, 1995; Pollitt, 1995). The culture wars are conflicts over values, norms, and practices important for organizing our world. Whether representatives of hegemonic institutions understand hegemony or not, they spend time, energy, and money in their cultural crusades because they recognize that being dominant does not mean being omnipotent.

Capitalist hegemony in the United States is actually quite fragile and dearly needs subordinate participation for its survival. The culture wars are part of the battle over what kind of participation subordinate groups and individuals will be allowed, what kind of hegemony will be negotiated, and what kind of society we will live in, now and in the future. Given the handicaps of capitalist hegemony and the rush of material, political, and cultural changes, real prospects for a counterhegemonic movement exist.

We should expect increasing opportunities for counterhegemonic movements. Their success will depend on whether the leadership of a new historic block can maintain its political independence from hegemonic institutions and ideologies. The success of any counterhegemony depends on the ability of subordinate groups and their organizations to push not for reform of hegemony but for transformation of social relations on new terms. Any successful counterhegemonic historic bloc in the United States will need to challenge the consumer culture, break with the two-party electoral system of Democrats and Republicans, organize independent oppositional political institutions, and create an ideological and cultural movement based on the values of participatory democracy, solidarity, and community.

Of course, history has shown that in the struggle for a new hegemony, dominant forces from the status quo will adjust, adapt, concede, and failing to win consent, will scratch, claw, and kill to maintain power. To ease the confrontation, a counterhegemony needs to maximize the consent and desire for socioeconomic, political, and cultural change. To build a historic bloc capable of creating a more humane culture and society, a counterhegemonic leadership must represent, communicate, and champion the needs of the overwhelming majority of society: working people and their allies.

# References

Adamson, W. L. (1980). *Hegemony and revolution: A study of Antonio Gramsci's political and cultural theory.* Berkeley: University of California Press.

Adorno, T. W. (1945/1977). A social critique of radio music. *Kenyon Review, 6,* 208-217.

Altheide, D. L. (1984). Media hegemony: A failure of perspective. *Public Opinion Quarterly, 48,* 476-490.

Althusser, L. (1969). *For Marx.* New York: Pantheon.

Althusser, L. (1972). *Lenin and philosophy, and other essays.* London: New Left.

Alvesson, M. (1987). *Organization theory and technocratic consciousness: Rationality, ideology, and the quality of work.* New York: De Gruyter.

Amann, R. J., & Silverblatt, R. (1987). High school students' views on unionism. *Labor Studies Journal, 12*(3), 44-61.

Amariglio, J. (1991). Review of descent into discourse: The reification of language and the writing of social history, by Bryan D. Palmer. *Journal of Economic History, 51,* 532-535.

Anderson, E. (1990). *Streetwise: Race, class, and change in an urban community.* Chicago: University of Chicago Press.

Anderson, P. (1977). The antinomies of Antonio Gramsci. *New Left Review, 100,* 5-78.

Another legend of the rails, the Broadway Limited, fades. (1995, September 10). *New York Times,* p. 14.

Aronowitz, S. (1974). *False promises: The shaping of American working class consciousness.* New York: McGraw-Hill.

Aronowitz, S. (1983). *Working class hero: A new strategy for labor.* New York: Pilgrim.

Artz, B. L. (1998). Hegemony in black and white. In Y. R. Kamalipour & T. Carilli (Eds.), *Cultural Diversity and the U.S. Media,* (pp. 67-78). Albany, NY: SUNY Press.

Asante, M. K. (1988). *Afrocentricity.* Trenton, NJ: Africa World Press.

305

Atallah, P. (1984). The unworthy discourse: Situation comedy in television. In W. D. Rowland, Jr., & B. Watkins (Eds.), *Interpreting television: Current research perspectives* (pp. 222-249). Beverly Hills, CA: Sage.

Bagdikian, B. H. (1990). *The media monopoly* (3rd ed.). Boston: Beacon Press.

Bales, F. (1986). Television use and confidence in television by blacks and whites in four selected years. *Journal of Black Studies, 16,* 283-291.

Banta, M. (1987). *Imaging American women: Idea and ideals in cultural history.* New York: Columbia University Press.

Barthes, R. (1972). *Mythologies* (A. Lavers, Trans.). New York: Hill & Wang.

Barthes, R. (1977). *Image, music, text* (S. Heath, Trans.). New York: Hill & Wang.

Becker, L. B., Kosicki, G. M., & Jones, F. (1992). Racial differences in evaluations of the mass media. *Journalism Quarterly, 69,* 124-134.

Bennett, T. (1986). Introduction: Popular culture and the "turn to Gramsci." In T. Bennett, C. Mercer, & J. Woollacott (Eds.), *Popular culture and social relations* (xi-xix). Philadelphia: Open University Press.

Bennett, T. (1990). *Popular fiction: Technology, ideology, production, reading.* New York: Routledge.

Bennett, T. (1992). Useful culture. *Cultural Studies, 6,* 395-408.

Bennett, W. L. (1988). *News: The politics of illusion* (2nd ed.). White Plains, NY: Longman.

Berger, M. (1991, Summer). On black power/white fear. *Artforum,* 16-17.

Berryman, P. (1987). *Liberation theology: Essential facts about the revolutionary movement in Latin America—and beyond.* New York: Pantheon.

Boggs, C. (1984). *The two revolutions: Antonio Gramsci and the dilemmas of Western Marxism.* Boston: South End.

Bogle, D. (1994). *Toms, coons, mulattoes, mammies, & bucks: An interpretive history of blacks in American films.* New York: Continuum.

Bosmajian, H. A. (1983). *The language of oppression.* Lanham: Maryland University Press.

Boston, T. D. (1990). Segmented labor markets: New evidence from a study of four race-gender groups. *Industrial and Labor Relations Review, 44,* 99-115.

Bourdieu, P. (1977). *Outline of a theory of practice* (R. Nice, Trans.). New York: Cambridge University Press.

Bourdieu, P. (1978). Sport and social class. *Social Science Information, 17,* 819-840.

Bourdieu, P. (1984). *Distinction: A social critique of the judgement of taste* (R. Nice, Trans.). Cambridge, MA: Harvard University Press.

Bourdieu, P. (1987). What makes a social class? On the theoretical and practical existence of groups (L. J. D. Wacquant & D. Young, Trans.). *Berkeley Journal of Sociology, 32,* 1-16.

Bourdieu, P. (1991). *Language and symbolic power* (G. Raymond & M. Adamson, Trans.). Cambridge, MA: Harvard University Press.

Bowles, S., & Gintis, H. (1977). *Schooling in capitalist America: Educational reform and the contradictions of economic life.* New York: Basic Books.

Braverman, H. (1974). *Labor and monopoly capital: The degradation of work in the twentieth century.* New York: Monthly Review Press.

Broderick, D. M. (1973). *Image of the black in children's fiction.* New York: Bowker.

Brow, J. (1990). Notes on community, hegemony, and the uses of the past. *Anthropological Quarterly, 63,* 1-6.

Brown, H. G. (1962). *Sex and the single girl.* New York: Geis.

Brown, M. W. (1972). *The runaway bunny.* New York: HarperCollins.

Brown, S. (1968). *The negro in American fiction.* Port Washington, NY: Kennikat.

Buci-Glucksmann, C. (1980). *Gramsci and the state.* London: Lawrence & Wishart.

Budd, M., Craig, S., & Steinman, C. (1999). *Consuming environments: Television and commercial culture.* New Brunswick, NJ: Rutgers University Press.

Budd, M., Entmann, R. M., & Steinman, C. (1990). The affirmative character of U.S. cultural studies. *Critical Studies in Mass Communication, 7,* 169-184.

Buechler, S. M. (1990). *Women's movements in the United States: Woman suffrage, equal rights, and beyond.* New Brunswick, NJ: Rutgers University Press.

Burawoy, M. (1979). *Manufacturing consent: Changes in the labor process under monopoly capitalism.* Chicago: University of Chicago Press.

Burns, I. F. (1957). Charities. In J. Hastings (Ed.), *Encyclopedia of religion and ethics* (Vol. 3, pp. 372-373). New York: Scribner's.

Butsch, R. (1997). Ralph, Archie and Homer: Why television keeps recreating the white male working-class buffoon. In L. Artz (Ed.), *Communication practices and democratic society* (pp. 213-220). Dubuque, IA: Kendall Hunt.

Carey, J. (1989). *Communication as culture: Essays on media and society.* Boston: Unwin Hyman.

Carmichael, S., & Hamilton, C. V. (1967). *Black power: The politics of liberation in America.* New York: Vintage.

Census sees falling income and more poor. (1994, October 7). *New York Times,* p. 1ff.

Chomsky, N. (1987). *On power and ideology: The Managua lectures.* Boston: South End.

Chomsky, N. (1989). *Necessary illusions: Thought control in democratic societies.* Boston, MA: South End.

Chomsky, N. (1996, June). From containment to rollback. *Z Magazine,* 22-31.

Cloud, D. L. (1996). Hegemony or concordance? The rhetoric of tokenism in "Oprah" Winfrey's rag-to-riches biography. *Critical Studies in Mass Communication, 13,* 115-137.

Cohen, J., & Solomon, N. (1993). *Adventures in medialand: Behind the news, beyond the pundits.* Monroe, ME: Common Courage.

Cohen, L. (1990). *Making a new deal: Industrial workers in Chicago.* New York: Cambridge University Press.

Condit, C. M. (1989). The rhetorical limits of polysemy. *Critical Studies in Mass Communication, 6,* 103-122.

Condit, C. M. (1994). Hegemony in a mass-mediated society: Concordance about reproductive technologies. *Critical Studies in Mass Communication, 11,* 205-230.

Cooper, M. (1996, April 8). Harley-riding, picket-walking socialism haunts Decatur. *The Nation,* 21-25.

Crane, D. (1992). *The production of culture: Media and the urban arts.* Newbury Park, CA: Sage.

Cripps, T. (1993). Oscar Micheaux: The story continues. In M. Diawara (Ed.), *Black American cinema* (pp. 71-79). New York: Routledge.

Cronen, V., & Pearce, W. B. (1982). The coordinated management of meaning: A theory of communication. In F. E. X. Dance (Ed.), *Human communication theory* (pp. 61-89). New York: Harper & Row.

Dahl, R. A. (1967). *Pluralist democracy in the United States: Conflict and consent.* Chicago: Rand McNally.

Dahrendorf, R. (1959). *Class and class conflict in industrial society.* Stanford, CA: Stanford University Press.

Davis, F. (1981). *Moving the mountain: The women's movement in America since 1960.* New York: Simon & Schuster.

Davis, M. (1992, June 1). In L. A., burning all illusions. *The Nation,* 743-746.

Deetz, S. A. (1992). *Democracy in an age of corporate colonization.* Albany, NY: State University of New York Press.

Delpit, L. (1995). *Other people's children: Cultural conflicts in the classroom.* New York: New Press.

Derrida, J. (1976). *Of grammatology* (G. Spivak, Trans.). Baltimore: Johns Hopkins University Press.

de Ste. Croix, G. E. M. (1981). *Class struggle in the ancient Greek world: From the archaic age to the Arab conquest.* Ithaca, NY: Cornell University Press.

Diawara, M. (1993). Black American cinema: The new realism. In M. Diawara (Ed.), *Black American cinema* (pp. 3-25). New York: Routledge.

Did you know? (1992, September-October). *Counselor,* 7.

DiMaggio, P. (1982). Cultural entrepreneurship in nineteenth-century Boston: The creation of an organization base for high culture in America. *Media, Culture and Society, 4,* 383-397.

Dobbs, F. (1972). *Teamster rebellion.* New York: Pathfinder.

Domhoff, G. W. (1967). *Who rules America?* Englewood Cliffs, NJ: Prentice Hall.

Domhoff, G. W. (1979). *The powers that be: Processes of ruling class domination in America.* New York: Vintage.

Domhoff, G. W. (1986). *Who rules America now? A view for the '80s.* New York: Touchstone.

Dorfman, A., & Mattelart, A. (1991). *How to read Donald Duck: Imperialist ideology in the Disney comic.* New York: International General.

Douglas, M. (1991). Jokes. In C. Mukerji & M. Schudson (Eds.), *Rethinking popular culture: Contemporary perspectives in cultural studies* (pp. 291-310). Berkeley: University of California Press.

Douglas, S. (1994). *Where the boys are: Growing up female in the mass media.* New York: Random House.

Douglas, S. (1995, November/December). Sitcom women: We've come a long way. Maybe. *Ms.,* 76-80.

Dow, B. (1995). Feminism: Entertainment television and women's progress. In C. M. Lont (Ed.), *Women and media: Content, careers, and criticism* (pp. 199-216). San Francisco: Wadsworth.

Drummond, W. J. (1990, July-August). About face from alliance to alienation: Blacks and the news media. *American Enterprise,* 23-29.

DuBois, W. E. B. (1969). *The souls of black folks.* New York: New American Library. (Original work published in 1903)

Durkheim, E. (1964). *The division of labor in society.* New York: Free Press.

Durkheim, E. (1995). *The elementary forms of religious life* (K. E. Fields, Trans.). New York: Free Press. (Original work published in 1916)

Dye, T. R. (1979). *Who's running America?* Englewood Cliffs, NJ: Prentice Hall.

Dyer, R. (1993). Is "Car Wash" a black musical? In M. Diawara (Ed.), *Black American cinema* (pp. 93-106). New York: Routledge.

Eagleton, T. (1991). *Ideology: An introduction.* New York: Verso.

Egger-Bovet, H., & Smith-Baranzini, M. (1994). *US kids history: Book of the American revolution.* Boston: Little, Brown.

Ehrenreich, B. (1999, November 28). Doing it for ourselves: Can feminism survive class polarization? *In These Times,* 10-12.

Eiger, N. (1989). Organizing for quality of working life. *Labor Studies Journal, 14*(3), 3-22.

Esping-Anderson, G. (1978). *Social class, social democracy and state policy.* Unpublished doctoral dissertation, University of Michigan, Ann Arbor.

Essed, P. (1991). *Understanding everyday racism: An interdisciplinary theory.* Newbury Park, CA: Sage.

Evans, S. M. (1989). *Born for liberty: A history of women in America.* New York: Free Press.

Ewen, S. (1989). *All consuming images: The politics of style in contemporary culture.* New York: Basic Books.

Ewen, S., & Ewen, E. (1982). *Channels of desire: Mass images and the shaping of American consciouness.* New York: Basic Books.

Faludi, S. (1991). *Backlash: The undeclared war against American women.* New York: Crown Books.

Fantasia, R. (1988). *Cultures of solidarity.* Berkeley: University of California Press.

Feagin, J. R. (1991a, February 27). Blacks still face the malevolent reality of white racism. *Chronicle of Higher Education,* A44.

Feagin, J. R. (1991b). The continuing significance of race: Antiblack discrimination in public places. *American Sociological Review, 56,* 101-116.

Feagin, J. R. (1994). *Living with racism: The black middle-class experience.* Boston: Beacon.

Feagin, J. R., & Feagin, C. B. (1978). *Discrimination American style: Institutional racism and sexism.* Englewood Cliffs, NJ: Prentice Hall.

Feenberg, A. (1981). *Lukács, Marx and the sources of critical theory.* New York: Oxford University Press.

Feminist Majority Foundation, Task Force on Women and Girls in Sports. (1995). *Empowering women in sports (women still on the sidelines).* New York: Author and New Media Publishing.

Fink, L. (1988). New labor history and the powers of historical pessimism: Consensus, hegemony, and the case of the Knights of Labor. *Journal of American History, 75,* 115-161.

Fiske, J. (1987). *Television culture: Popular pleasures and politics.* London: Methuen.

Fiske, J. (1989). *Reading the popular.* Boston: Unwin Hyman.

Fiske, J. (1991). *Understanding popular culture.* New York: Routledge.

Fiske, J. (1995). Gendered television. In G. Dines & J. M. Hunez (Eds.), *Gender, race, and class in the media: A text-reader* (pp. 340-347). Thousand Oaks, CA: Sage.

Foner, E. (1970). *America's black past: A reader in Afro-American history.* New York: Harper & Row.

Frank, T. (1996, January 12). Seats of power. *Chicago Reader,* 10-12.

Friedan, B. (1963). *The feminine mystique.* New York: Norton.

Fuller, L. K. (1992). *The Cosby show: Audiences, impact, and implications*. Westport, CT: Greenwood.

Gans, H. (1972). *Deciding what's news*. New York: Pantheon.

Gaston, J. C. (1986). The destruction of the young black male: The impact of popular culture and organized sports. *Journal of Black Studies, 16*, 369-384.

Gates, H. L., Jr. (1989, November 12). TV's black world turns—but stays unreal. *New York Times*, p. H1ff.

Genovese, E. D. (1979). *From rebellion to revolution: Afro-American slave revolts in the making of the new world*. New York: Vintage.

Gettye, I. (1993, April). Public enemy number one. *Afrique*, 4.

Gilroy, P. (1987). *There ain't no black in the Union Jack: The cultural politics of race and nation*. London: Hutchinson.

Gingrich, N. (1995). *To renew America*. New York: HarperCollins.

Giroux, H. A. (1994). *Disturbing pleasures: Learning popular culture*. New York: Routledge.

Gitlin, T. (1980). *The whole world is watching: Mass media in the making and unmaking of the new left*. Berkeley: University of California Press.

Gitlin, T. (1987). Prime time ideology: The hegemonic process in television entertainment. In H. Newcomb (Ed.), *TV: The critical view* (pp. 426-454). New York: Oxford.

Glasheen, L. K., & Crowley, S. L. (1999, November). More women in driver's seat. *AARP Bulletin, 3*, 24-26.

Goffman, E. (1959). *The presentation of self in everyday life*. New York: Anchor.

Goldman, R., & Rajagopal, A. (1991). *Mapping hegemony*. Norwood, NJ: Ablex.

Good, L. T. (1990). Power, hegemony, and communication theory. In I. Angus & S. Jhally (Eds.), *Cultural politics in contemporary America* (pp. 51-64). New York: Routledge.

Gordon, D. M. (1996, June 17). Values that work. *The Nation*, 16-22.

Gottdiener, M. (1985). Hegemony and mass culture: A semiotic approach. *American Journal of Sociology, 90*, 979-999.

Gould, S. J. (1981). *The mismeasure of man*. New York: Norton.

Gramsci, A. (1967). *The modern prince* (L. Marks, Trans.). New York: International Publishers.

Gramsci, A. (1971). *Selections from the prison notebooks* (Q. Hoare & G. N. Smith, Trans.). New York: International Publishers. (Original work published in 1947)

Gramsci, A. (1988). *Selected writings: 1918-1935* (David Forgacs, Ed.). New York: Shocken.

Gray, H. (1986). Television and the new black man: Black male images in prime time situation comedy. *Media, Culture & Society, 8*(2), 223-242.

Grenier, G. J. (1988). Quality circles in a corporate antiunion strategy: A case study. *Labor Studies Journal, 13*(2), 5-27.

Gronbeck, B. E. (1984). Functional and dramaturgical theories of presidential campaigning. *Presidential Studies Quarterly, 14*, 486-499.

Guerrero, E. (1993). The black image in protective custody: Hollywood's biracial buddy films of the eighties. In M. Diawara (Ed.), *Black American cinema* (pp. 237-246). New York: Routledge.

Gutman, H. (1977). *Work, culture, and society in industrializing America.* New York: Vintage.

Hall, S. (1980). Cultural studies: Two paradigms. *Media, Culture & Society, 2,* 57-72.

Hall, S. (1982). The rediscovery of "ideology": Return of the repressed in media studies. In M. Gurevitch, T. Bennett, J. Curran, & S. Woollacott (Eds.), *Culture, society, and the media* (pp. 56-90). London: Methuen.

Hall, S. (1984). Signification, representation, ideology: Althusser and the post-structuralist debates. *Critical Studies in Mass Communication, 2,* 91-114.

Hall, S. (1986). Gramsci's relevance for the study of race and ethnicity. *Journal of Communication Inquiry, 10,* 5-27.

Hall, S., Critcher, C., Jefferson, T., Clarke, J., & Roberts, B. (1978). *Policing the crisis: Mugging, the state, and law and order.* New York: Holmes & Meier.

Halle, D. (1991). Bringing materialism back in: Art in the houses of the working and middle classes. In S. G. McNall, R. F. Levine, & R. Fantasia (Eds.), *Bringing class back in: Contemporary and historical perspectives* (pp. 241-260). Boulder, CO: Westview.

Hampton, H., & Fayer, S. (Eds.). (1990). *Voices of freedom: An oral history of the civil rights movement from the 1950s through the 1980s.* New York: Bantam.

Haskell, M. (1974). *From reverence to rape: The treatment of women in the movies.* New York: Holt, Rinehart and Winston.

Hawkins, H. (1996, June). Independent progressive politics network. *Z Magazine,* 17-21.

Henwood, D. (1989, March-December). [Series on media]. *Extra!, 2*(5) through *Extra!, 3*(3).

Herbert, B. (1995, February 11). Lawrence must go. *New York Times,* p. A19.

Herman, E., & Chomsky, N. (1988). *Manufacturing consent: The political economy of the mass media.* New York: Pantheon.

Hernnstein, R. J., & Murray, C. (1994). *The bell curve: Intelligence and class structure in American life.* New York: Free Press.

Hertsgaard, M. (1992). The five o'clock follies: Then and now. In D. Barsamian (Ed.), *Stenographers to power: Media and propaganda* (pp. 115-138). Monroe, ME: Common Courage.

Hildreth, G. (with Felton, A., Henderson, M., & Meighen, A.) (1940). *Faraway ports.* Philadelphia: John C. Winston.

Hill, C. (1972). *The world turned upside down: Radical ideas during the English revolution.* New York: Viking.

Hine, T. (1986). *Populuxe.* New York: Knopf.

Hirsch, E. L. (1990). *Urban revolt: Ethnic politics in the nineteenth-century Chicago labor movement.* Berkeley: University of California Press.

Hoare, Q. (1983). Introduction. In A. Gramsci, *Selections from the prison notebooks* (pp. i-xcvi; Q. Hoare & G. N. Smith, Trans.). New York: International Publishers.

Honey, M. (1983). The working-class woman and recruitment propaganda during World War II: Class differences in the portrayal of war work. *Signs, 8,* 672-687.

hooks, b. (1995, October 11). *Representing whiteness in the black imagination.* Lecture at Loyola University, Chicago.

Horkheimer, M. (1972). *Critical theory.* New York: Seabury.

Horkheimer, M., & Adorno, T. W. (1975). *Dialectic of enlightenment*. New York: Seabury.

Howard, R. (1985). *Brave new workplace*. New York: Viking.

Hoyt, D. (1984). *Quality circles: Short-term fad or long-term trend?* Paper presented to South Belt Labor Conference, University of Texas-Arlington.

Huggins, N. I. (1971). *Harlem renaissance*. New York: Oxford University Press.

Huizinga, J. (1938/1950). *Homo ludens: A study of the play element in culture*. Boston: Beacon.

Ibalema, M. (1994). Identity crisis: The African connection in African American sitcom characters. In S. Maasik & J. Solomon (Eds.), *Signs of life in the USA: Readings on popular culture for writers* (pp. 198-208). Boston: Bedford.

International Association of Machinists. (1980, June 12). IAM television entertainment report, Part II: Conclusions and national summary of occupational frequency in network primetime entertainment for February 1980. *The Machinist*, 11-12.

Jackson, J. (1993, September 10). In CPB's public hearings conclusions seem foregone. *Extra!*, 22.

Jalée, P. (1977). *How capitalism works*. New York: Monthly Review Press.

Jaynes, G. D., & Williams, R. M., Jr. (Eds.). (1989). *A common destiny: Blacks and American society: Committee on the status of black Americans, commission on behavioral and social sciences and education, National Research Council*. Washington, DC: National Academy Press.

Jeansonne, J. (1996, July 31). Female athletes grab spotlight at biggest show. *Newsday*, A70.

Jennings, P. (1989, January). On media celebrity. *Extra!*, 9.

Jensen, A. R. (1972). *Genetics and education*. New York: Harper& Row.

Jhally, S., & Lewis, J. (1992). *Enlightened racism: The Cosby show, audiences, and the myth of the American dream*. Boulder, CO: Westview.

Johnson, D. (1995, February 28). In Chicago, a gang tries to show political muscle. *New York Times*, p. A8ff.

Johnson, R. A. (1981). World without workers: Prime time's presentation of labor. *Labor Studies Journal*, 5(3), 199-206.

Johnston, C. (1992). *Sexual power: Feminism and the family in America*. Tuscaloosa: University of Alabama Press.

Jones, C. (1994, April 10). Years on integration road: New views of an old goal. *New York Times*, p. A1ff.

Jordan, W. D. (1974). *The white man's burden: Historical origins of racism in the United States*. New York: Oxford University Press.

Joreen, B. (1970). The 51 percent minority group: A statistical essay. In R. Morgan (Ed.), *Sisterhood is powerful* (pp. 39-43). New York: Vintage.

Josephson, M. (1934). *The robber barons: The great American capitalists, 1861-1901*. New York: Harcourt, Brace.

Jowett, G., & O'Donnell, V. (1992). *Propaganda and persuasion* (2nd ed.). Newbury Park, CA: Sage.

Juravich, T. (1988). Workers and unions in country music: A look at some recent releases. *Labor Studies Journal*, 13(2), 51-60.

Kasson, J. (1990). *Rudeness & civility: Manners in nineteenth century urban America*. New York: Hill & Wang.

Kellner, D. (1990). *Television and the crisis of democracy*. Boulder, CO: Westview.

Kerbo, H. R. (1983). *Social stratification and inequality: Class conflict in the United States*. New York: McGraw-Hill.

Kerner Commission on Civil Disorder. (1968). *Report of National Advisory Commission on Civil Disorder*. New York: Bantam.

King, A. (1987). *Power & communication*. Prospect Heights, IL: Waveland.

Kozol, J. (1991). *Savage inequalities: Children in America's schools*. New York: Crown.

Kron, J. (1994). The semiotics of home decor. In S. Maasik & J. Solomon (Eds.), *Signs of life in the USA: Readings on popular culture for writers* (pp. 66-77). Boston: Bedford.

Laclau, E., & Mouffe, C. (1985). *Hegemony and socialist strategy: Towards a radical democratic politics*. London: Verso.

Lakoff, R. (1975). *Language and woman's place*. New York: Harper & Row.

Le Goff, J. (1980). *Time, work & culture in the middle ages* (A. Goldhammer, Trans.). Chicago: University of Chicago Press.

Lears, T. J. (1985). The concept of cultural hegemony: Problems and possibilities. *American Historical Review, 90*, 567-593.

Lee, M. A., & Solomon, N. (1990). *Unreliable sources: A guide to detecting bias in news media*. New York: Lyle Stuart.

Leland, J. (1992, June 29). Rap race. *Newsweek*, 46-52.

Lembcke, J. (1991). Class analysis and studies of the U.S. working class: Theoretical, conceptual, and methodological. In S. G. McNall, R. F. Levine, & R. Fantasia (Eds.), *Bringing class back in: Contemporary and historical perspectives* (pp. 83-97). Boulder, CO: Westview.

Lerner, G. (1979). *The majority finds its past: Placing women in history*. New York: Oxford University Press.

Lerner, G. (1986). *The creation of patriarchy*. New York: Oxford University Press.

Levine, L. W. (1984). William Shakespeare and the American people: A study in cultural transformation. *American Historical Review, 89*, 34-66.

Levine, R. (1988). *Class struggle and the new deal*. Lawrence: University of Kansas Press.

Levi-Strauss, C. (1963). *Structural anthropology* (C. Jacobson, B. G. Schoepf, & M. Layton, Trans.). New York: Basic Books. (Original work published in 1958)

Levitt, M. J. (1993). *Confessions of a union buster*. New York: Crown.

Lewin, T. (1992, January 8). Study points to increase in tolerance of ethnicity. *New York Times*, p. A10.

Licata, J. W., & Biswas, A. (1993). Representation, roles, and occupational status of black models in television advertisements. *Journalism Quarterly, 70*, 868-882.

Lieberthal, M. (1976). TV images of workers—reinforcing stereotypes. *Labor Studies Journal, 1*(2), 165-180.

Lind, M. (1991, June). To have and have not: Notes on the progress of the American class war. *Harper's Magazine*, 35-47.

Lindsey, A. (1942). *The Pullman strike: The story of a unique experiment and of a great labor upheaval*. Chicago: University of Chicago Press.

Lippmann, W. (1922). *Public opinion*. New York: Harcourt, Brace.

Longworth, R. C., & Stein, S. (1995, August 22). Middle class finds odd jobs may be only way to stay afloat. *Chicago Tribune*, p. 6.

Lukács, G. (1971). *History and class consciousness: Studies in Marxist dialectics.* Cambridge: MIT Press. (Original work published in 1923)

Luke, T. W. (1989). *Screens of power: Ideology, domination, and resistance in informational society.* Urbana: University of Illinois Press.

Lull, J. (1995). *Media, communication, culture: A global approach.* New York: Columbia University Press.

Lundberg, F. (1937). *America's 60 families.* New York: Vanguard.

Lyotard, J. F. (1984). *The postmodern condition: A report on knowledge* (G. Bennington & B. Massumi, Trans.). Minneapolis: University of Minnesota Press.

MacDonald, J. F. (1992). *Blacks and white TV: African Americans in television since 1948* (2nd ed.). Chicago: Nelson-Hall.

Majors, R. (1994). Cool pose: The proud signature of black survival. In S. Maasik & J. Solomon (Eds.), *Signs of life in the USA: Readings on popular culture for writers* (pp. 471-476). Boston: Bedford.

Mannegold, C. S. (1994, January 18). Fewer men earn doctorates, particularly among blacks. *New York*, p. 10.

Manoff, R. K., & Schudson, M. (Eds.). (1986). *Reading the news: A Pantheon guide to popular culture.* New York: Pantheon.

Mansbridge, J. (1986). *Why we lost the E.R.A.* Chicago: University of Chicago Press.

Marchand, R. (1994). The parable of the democracy of goods. In S. Maasik & J. Solomon (Eds.), *Signs of life in the USA: Readings on popular culture for writers* (pp. 109-116). Boston: Bedford.

Marchetti, G. (1990). Action-adventure as ideology. In I. Angus & S. Jhally (Eds.), *Cultural politics in contemporary America* (pp. 182-197). New York: Routledge.

Marcus, S. (1996, June 22). Title IX needs NCAA's push. *Newsday*, p. A34.

Marcuse, H. (1964). *One-dimensional man.* Boston: Beacon.

Marilyn Defends Mothers, Chides "Boomer Opponents." (1992, August 20). *Washington Times*, Sec. B, col. 1, p. 1.

Marsden, M. T. (1980). Television watching as ritual. In R. B. Browne (Ed.), *Rituals and ceremonies in popular culture* (pp. 120-124). Bowling Green, KY: Bowling Green University Popular Press.

Martin, B. A., & Martin, J. H. (1996). Comparing perceived sex role orientations of the ideal male and female athlete to the ideal male. *Journal of Sport Behavior, 18,* 286-300.

Martin-Barbero, J. (1993). *Communication, culture and hegemony: From the media to mediations* (E. Fox & R. A. White, Trans.). Newbury Park, CA: Sage.

Martindale, C. (1988). *The white press and black America.* New York: Greenwood.

Marx, K. (1970). *Contribution to the critique of political economy* (S. W. Ryansanskaya, Trans.). New York: International Publishers. (Original work published in 1859)

Marx, K., & Engels, F. (1970). *The German ideology, Part 1* (C. J. Arthur, Ed.). New York: International Publishers. (Original work published in 1932)

Masterman, L. (Ed.). (1984). *Television mythologies: Stars, shows & signs.* London: Comedia.

Mattelart, A. (1979). For a class analysis of communication. In A. Mattelart & S. Siegelaub (Eds.), *Communication and class struggle: 1. Capitalism, imperialism* (pp. 23-72). New York: International General.

Mattelart, A. (1980). *Mass media, ideologies and the revolutionary movement.* Atlantic Highlands, NJ: Humanities.

Mattelart, A. (Ed.). (1986). *Communicating in popular Nicaragua.* New York: International General.

McCombs, M. E., & Shaw, D. L. (1972). The agenda-setting function of mass media. *Public Opinion Quarterly, 36,* 176-187.

McNall, S. G. (1988). *The road to rebellion: Class formation and Kansas populism, 1865-1900.* Chicago: University of Chicago Press.

McNall, S. G., Levine, R. F., & Fantasia, R. (Eds.). (1991). *Bringing class back in: Contemporary and historical perspectives.* Boulder, CO: Westview.

Medhurst, A. (1990). Laughing matters: Situation comedies. In T. Daniels & J. Gerson (Eds.), *The colour black: Black images in British television* (pp. 15-60). London: British Film Institute.

Media Foundation & FAIR. (1994). *The date rape backlash: The media and the denial of rape* [video]. Author.

Meltzer, M. (1967). *Bread and roses: The struggle of American labor, 1865-1915.* New York: Knopf.

Merelman, R. M. (1992). Cultural imagery and racial conflict in the United States: The case of African-Americans. *British Journal of Political Science, 22,* 315-342.

*Merriam-Webster's collegiate dictionary* (10th ed.). (1993). Springfield, MA: Merriam-Webster.

Miller, M. C. (1986). Deride and conquer. In T. Gitlin (Ed.), *Watching television* (pp. 182-228). New York: Pantheon.

Mills, C. W. (1956). *The power elite.* New York: Oxford University Press.

Mintz, B. (1975). The president's cabinet, 1897-1972: A contribution to the power structure debate. *Insurgent Sociologist, 5,* 131-148.

Morgan, R. (1992). *The word of a woman: Feminist dispatches, 1968-1992.* New York: Norton.

Morrow, L. (1978, March 27). Blacks on TV: A disturbing image. *Time,* 100-102.

Mosco, V. (1998). *The political economy of communication.* Thousands Oaks, CA: Sage.

Moses, W. J. (1978). *The golden age of black nationalism, 1850-1925.* New York: Oxford University Press.

Murphy, B. A. O. (1994a, Spring). Greeting cards and gender messages. *Women and Language, 27,* 25-29.

Murphy, B. A. O. (1994b). Women's magazines: Confusing differences. In L. Turner & H. Sterk (Eds.), *Differences that make a difference: Examining the assumptions in gender research* (pp. 119-128). Westport, CT: Bergin & Garvey.

Murphy, B. A. O. (1995). Gendered interaction in professional relationships. In J. T. Wood (Ed.), *Gendered relationships* (pp. 213-232). Mountain View, CA: Mayfield.

Muwakkil, S. (1999, October 11). Pervasive influence of race in wealth gap. *Chicago Tribune,* p. 17.

Myrdal, G. (1944). *An American dilemma: The negro problem and modern democracy.* New York: Harper & Brothers.

Nelson, C., & Grossberg, L. (Eds.). (1988). *Marxism and the interpretation of culture.* Urbana: University of Illinois Press.

Nelson, J. (1995, June 5). Talk is cheap. *The Nation,* 800-802.

Novack, G. (1978). *Polemics in Marxist philosophy.* New York: Monad.

Oliver, R. T., & White, E. E. (Eds.). (1966). *Selected speeches from American history.* Boston: Allyn & Bacon.

Omi, M., & Winant, H. (1986). *Racial formation in the United States from the 1960s to the 1980s.* New York: Routledge & Kegan Paul.

Orr, J. R., & McNall, S. G. (1991). Fraternal orders and working-class formation in nineteenth-century Kansas. In S. G. McNall, R. F. Levine, & R. Fantasia (Eds.), *Bringing class back in: Contemporary and historical perspectives* (pp. 101-118). Boulder, CO: Westview.

Parenti, M. (1986). *Inventing reality: The politics of the mass media.* New York: St. Martin's.

Parenti, M. (1994). Class and virtue. In S. Maasik & J. Solomon (Eds.), *Signs of life in the USA: Readings on popular culture for writers* (pp. 283-286). Boston: Bedford.

Partington, A. (1993). Popular fashion and working-class affluence. In J. Ash & E. Wilson (Eds.), *Chic thrills: A fashion reader* (pp. 145-161). Berkeley: University of California Press.

Perkins, K. P. (1994, April 20). Skimming the surface. *Chicago Tribune,* Sec. 5, p. 2.

Peters, T. J., & Waterman, R. H., Jr. (1982). *In search of excellence: Lessons from America's best-run companies.* New York: Harper & Row.

Petras, J. (1993). Cultural imperialism in the late 20th century. *Journal of Contemporary Asia, 23*(2), 139-148.

Pines, J. (1990). I fought the law: Drama series and serials. In T. Daniels & J. Gerson (Eds.), *The colour black: Black images in British television* (pp. 63-70). London: British Film Institute.

Pipher, M. (1994). *Reviving Ophelia: Saving the selves of adolescent girls.* New York: Ballantine.

Pollitt, K. (1995). *Reasonable creatures: Essays on women and feminism.* New York: Knopf.

Polsby, N. W., & Wildavsky, A. (1967). *Presidential elections* (2nd ed.). New York: Scribner's.

Population Reference Bureau. (1991). *African-Americans in the 1990s.* Washington, DC: Author.

Poulanzas, N. (1978). *Class in contemporary capitalism.* London: Verso.

Poulson-Bryant, S. (1994). B-Boys. In S. Maasik & J. Solomon (Eds.), *Signs of life in the USA: Readings on popular culture for writers* (pp. 56-59). Boston: Bedford.

Pozzolini, A. (1990). *Antonio Gramsci: An introduction to his thought* (A. S. Sassoon, Trans.). London: Pluto.

Preis, A. (1964). *Labor's giant step: Twenty years of the CIO.* New York: Pioneer.

Quin, M. (1979). *The big strike.* New York: International Publishers.

Quindlen, A. (1993). *Thinking out loud: On the personal, the political, the public, and the private.* New York: Fawcett Columbine.

Rachlin, A. (1988). *News as hegemonic reality: American political culture and the framing of news accounts.* New York: Praeger.

Radway, J. (1984). *Reading the romance: Feminism and the representation of women in popular culture.* Chapel Hill: University of North Carolina Press.

Radway, J. (1993). The institutional matrix of romance. In S. During (Ed.), *The cultural studies reader* (pp. 438-454). New York: Routledge.

Rapping, E. (1995). Daytime inquiries. In G. Dines & J. M. Hunez (Eds.), *Gender, race, and class in the media: A text-reader* (pp. 377-382). Thousand Oaks, CA: Sage.

Ravenswood Industrial Council. (1995). *Strategic development plan for industrial retention and expansion Ravenswood industrial corridor.* Chicago: City of Chicago.

Ravitch, D. (Ed.). (1990). *The American reader: Words that moved a nation.* New York: HarperCollins.

Remnick, D. (1996, August 5). Inside-out olympics. *New Yorker, 72*(22).

Riggs, M. (Prod.). (1987). *Ethnic notions* [Video]. San Francisco: California Newsreel.

Riggs, M. (Prod.). (1991). *Color adjustment* [Video]. San Francisco: California Newsreel.

Riley, G. (1987). *Inventing the American woman: A perspective on women's history.* Arlington Heights, IL: Harlan Davidson.

Ritzer, G. (2000). *The McDonaldization of society: An investigation into the changing character of contemporary social life* (3rd ed.). Thousand Oaks, CA: Pine Forge.

Roediger, D. R. (1991). *The wages of whiteness: Race and the making of the American working class.* London: Verso.

Rogers. D. (1995). Daze of our lives: The soap opera as feminist text. In G. Dines & J. M. Hunez (Eds.), *Gender, race, and class in the media: A text-reader* (pp. 325-331). Thousand Oaks, CA: Sage.

Rohwer, R. (1994). "Prep voices; an even field? Are boys' and girls' athletic programs treated equally at the high school level?" (1994, November 1). *Los Angeles Times,* Part V, Col. 1, p. 1.

Rothman, S. M. (1978). *Woman's proper place: A history of changing ideals and practices, 1870 to the present.* New York: Basic Books.

Rothschuh, G. V. (1986). Notes on the history of revolutionary journalism in Nicaragua. In A. Mattelart (Ed.), *Communicating in popular Nicaragua* (pp. 28-36). New York: International General.

Roy, W. G. (1991). The organization of the corporate class segment and the U.S. capitalist class at the turn of this century. In S. G. McNall, R. F. Levine, & R. Fantasia (Eds.), *Bringing class back in: Contemporary and historical perspectives* (pp. 139-163). Boulder, CO: Westview.

Sassoon, A. S. (1987). *Gramsci's politics* (2nd ed.). Minneapolis: University of Minnesota Press.

Saussure, F. (1986). *Course in general linguistics.* (R. Harris, Trans.). Lasalle, IL: Open Court.

Schiller, H. I. (1989). *Culture, Inc.: The corporate takeover of public expression.* New York: Oxford University Press.

Schiller, H. I. (1990). The privatization of culture. In I. Angus & S. Jhally (Eds.), *Cultural politics in contemporary America* (pp. 333-342). New York: Routledge.

Schwartz, F. (1993). *Breaking with tradition: Women and work, the new facts of life.* New York: Time Warner.

Scott, J. C. (1990). *Domination and the arts of resistance: Hidden transcripts.* New Haven, CT: Yale University Press.

Shames, L. (1994). The more factor. In S. Maasik & J. Solomon (Eds.), *Signs of life in the USA: Readings on popular culture for writers* (pp. 25-31). Boston: Bedford.

Shoup, L. (1975). Shaping the postwar world: The Council of Foreign Relations and U.S. war aims during WW II. *Insurgent Sociologist, 5,* 9-52.

Shuster, D. (1994, August 26). NFL broadcast crews need diversification. *USA Today,* p. C2.

Sigal, L. V. (1986). Who? Sources make the news. In R. K. Manoff & M. Schudson (Eds.), *Reading the news: A Pantheon guide to popular culture* (pp. 9-37). New York: Pantheon.

Silk, C., & Silk, J. (1990). *Racism and anti-racism in American popular culture: Portrayals of African-Americans in fiction and film.* Manchester, UK: Manchester University Press.

Simon, R. J., & Danziger, G. (1991). *Women's movements in America: Their successes, disappointments, and aspirations.* New York: Praeger.

Smitherman-Donaldson, G., & van Dijk, T. A. (Eds.). (1988). *Discourse and discrimination.* Detroit, MI: Wayne State University Press.

Sommers, C. H. (1994). *Who stole feminism: How women have betrayed women.* New York: Simon & Schuster.

Sowell, T. (1975). *Affirmative action reconsidered: Was it necessary in academia?* Washington, DC: American Enterprise Institute.

Spencer, N. (1993). Menswear in the 1980s: Revolt into conformity. In J. Ash & E. Wilson (Eds.), *Chic thrills: A fashion reader* (pp. 40-48). Berkeley: University of California Press.

Stangenes, S. (1993, October 13). Fair-lending group says bias continues. *Chicago Tribune,* Sec. 3, p. 1.

Steele, R. (1985). *Propaganda in an open society: The Roosevelt administration and the Media, 1933-1941.* Westport, CT: Greenwood.

Steele, S. (1990). *The content of our character: A new vision of race in America.* New York: St. Martin's.

Stein, S. (1995, May 18). Making a life or a living? *Chicago Tribune,* p. 1ff.

Stephens, J. (1979). *The transition from capitalism to socialism.* New York: Macmillan.

Study finds wider gap for black, white elderly. (1993, May 10). *Chicago Tribune,* Sec. 4, p. 3.

Survey. (1992, December 10). *Loyola World,* p. 1.

Taxel, J. (1991). The American revolution in children's books: Issues of race and class. In B. Bacon (Ed.), *How much truth do we tell the children: The politics of children's literature* (pp. 157-172). Minneapolis, MN: MEP.

Taylor, H., & Dozier, C. (1983). Television violence, African-Americans, and social control, 1950-1976. *Journal of Black Studies, 14,* 107-136.

Teachout, T. (1986, July 18). Black, brown and beige. *National Review,* 59.

Therborn, G. (1983). Why some classes are more successful than others. *New Left Review, 138,* 37-55.

Thomas, S. (1990). Myths in and about television. In J. Downing, A. Mohammadi, & A. Sreberny-Mohammadi (Eds.), *Questioning the media: A critical introduction* (pp. 330-344). Newbury Park, CA: Sage.

Thompson, J. B. (1990). *Ideology and modern culture.* Cambridge, UK: Polity.

Trotsky, L. (1973). *Problems of everyday life and other writings on culture and science.* New York: Monad.

Trotsky, L. (1974). *The death agony of capitalism and the task of the Fourth International: The transitional program for socialist revolution* (2nd ed.). New York: Pathfinder. (Original work published in 1938)

Trouillot, M. (1990). *Haiti: State against nation, the origins and legacy of Duvalierism.* New York: Monthly Review Press.

Tuchman, G. (1978). *Making news: A study in the construction of reality.* New York: Free Press.

Tulloch, C. (1993). Rebel without a pause: Black street style and black designers. In J. Ash & E. Wilson (Eds.), *Chic thrills: A fashion reader* (pp. 84-100). Berkeley: University of California Press.

Turner, P. A. (1994). *Ceramic uncles & celluloid mammies: Black images and their influence on culture.* New York: Anchor.

Usdansky, M. L. (1991, September 11). Laws fail to conquer segregation. *Des Moines Register,* p. 1ff.

Valocchi, S. (1991). The class basis of the state and the origins of welfare policy in Britain, Sweden, and Germany. In S. G. McNall, R. F. Levine, & R. Fantasia (Eds.), *Bringing class back in: Contemporary and historical perspectives* (pp. 167-184). Boulder, CO: Westview.

van Dijk, T. A. (1991). *Racism and the press: Critical studies in racism and migration.* New York: Routledge.

Vilas, C. (1986). *The Sandinista revolution: National liberation and social transformation in Central America* (J. Butler, Trans.). New York: Monthly Review Press.

Vincent, T. G. (Ed.). (1973). *Voices of a black nation: Political journalism in the Harlem renaissance.* San Francisco: Ramparts.

Vincent, T. G. (1980). *Black power and the Garvey movement.* San Francisco: Ramparts.

Wacquant, L. J. D. (1991). Making class: The middle class(es) in social theory and social structure. In S. G. McNall, R. F. Levine, & R. Fantasia (Eds.), *Bringing class back in: Contemporary and historical perspectives* (pp. 39-64). Boulder, CO: Westview.

Walbank, F. W. (1982). *The Hellenistic world.* Cambridge, MA: Harvard University Press.

Walker, C. R. (1971). *American city: A rank-and-file history.* New York: Arno.

Watrous, P. (1993, July 4). Laying claim to the mantle of Motown. *New York Times,* p. B1.

Weber, M. (1946). *From Max Weber: Essays in sociology* (H. Gerth & C. W. Mills, Eds. & Trans.). New York: Oxford University Press.

Weisbrot, R. (1990). *Freedom bound: A history of America's civil rights movement.* New York: Plume.

West, C. (1988). Marxist theory and the specificity of Afro-American oppression. In C. Nelson & L. Grossberg (Eds.), *Marxism and the interpretation of culture* (pp. 17-29). Urbana: University of Illinois Press.

West, C. (1991). *The ethical dimensions of Marxist thought.* New York: Monthly Review Press.

West, C. (1993). *Race matters.* Boston: Beacon.

Wicker, T. (1996, June 17). Deserting the democrats: Why African Americans and the poor should make common cause in their own party. *The Nation,* 11-16.

Widick, B. J. (1972). *Detroit: City of race and class violence.* Chicago: Quadrangle.

Williams, R. (1976). *Keywords: A vocabulary of culture and society.* New York: Oxford University Press.

Williams, R. (1977). *Marxism and literature.* London: Oxford University Press.

Williams, R. (1991). The dream world of mass consumption. In C. Mukerji & M. Schudson (Eds.), *Rethinking popular culture: Contemporary perspectives in cultural studies* (pp. 198-235). Berkeley: University of California Press.

Willis, S. (1991). *A primer for daily life.* New York: Routledge.

Wilson, C. C., II, & Gutierrez, F. (1985). *Minorities and the media: Diversity and the end of mass communication.* Beverly Hills, CA: Sage.

Winkler, K. J. (1991, September 1). While concern over race relations has lessened among whites, sociologists say racism is taking new forms, not disappearing. *Chronicle of Higher Education,* A8-A11.

Wolf, N. (1991). *The beauty myth: How images of beauty are used against women.* New York: Morrow.

Wonsek, P. L. (1992). College basketball on television: A study of racism in the media. *Media, Culture & Society, 14,* 449-461.

Wood, E. M., & Wood, N. (1984). *Class ideology and ancient political theory: Socrates, Plato, and Aristotle in social context.* Minneapolis: University of Minnesota Press.

Woolcock, J. A. (1985). Politics, ideology and hegemony in Gramsci's theory. *Social and Economic Studies, 34,* 199-210.

Woollacott, J. (1986). Fictions and ideologies: The case of situation comedy. In T. Bennett, C. Mercer, & J. Woollacott (Eds.), *Popular culture and social relations* (pp. 196-218). Philadelphia: Open University Press.

Wright, E. O. (1985). *Classes.* London: Verso.

Wright, E. O. (1991). The conceptual status of class structure in class. In S. G. McNall, R. F. Levine, & R. Fantasia (Eds.), *Bringing class back in: Contemporary and historical perspectives* (pp. 17-38). Boulder, CO: Westview.

X, M. (1965). *The autobiography of Malcolm X.* New York: Grove.

Yellin, S. (1974). *American labor struggles, 1877-1934.* New York: Monad.

Zaniello, T. (1996). *Working stiffs, union maids, rebs, and riffraff: An organized guide to films about labor.* Ithaca, NY: ILR/Cornell.

# Index

# About the Authors

**Lee Artz** is Associate Professor and Director of the Social Justice Curriculum in the Department of Communication at Loyola University, Chicago. He received his PhD from the University of Iowa, where he was Research Assistant at the Center for Labor Studies. Previously, he was the director for the Peninsula Peace Center in Palo Alto, California, and taught at Stanford University. A former machinist and steelworker, he has served on union negotiating committees and twice was affirmative action director for his local. He has published numerous articles and chapters on communication and social change, hegemony and power, and media images of race and the book *Communication Practices and Democratic Society* (1997). From 1996 to 1998, he was the editor of the *Democratic Communique*, the journal of the Union for Democratic Communication. He was honored with the 1998 Sujack Award for Teaching Excellence at Loyola University.

**Bren Ortega Murphy** is Associate Professor of Communication and Chairperson of the Department of Communication at Loyola University, Chicago, where she also has served as an assistant dean in the College of Arts and Sciences. She received her PhD from Northwestern University and has published articles and chapters on communication issues, primarily in areas of gender socialization and relationships, cinematic treatment of history, and service learning as an approach to communication education. Her most recent book is *Voices of a Strong Democracy: Concepts and Models for Service Learning in Communication*. She is producer of the documentary video, *A College of Her Own: A History of Women's Education in the United States*. Recipient of several scholastic and teaching honors, she received the 1996 Sujack Award for Teaching Excellence at Loyola University. She has also served as consultant to several corporations and nonprofit organizations throughout North America and Western Europe.